DATE DUE

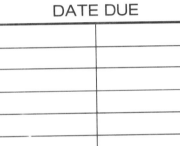

BRODART   Cat. No. 23-221

« TEJANO JOURNEY »

TEXAS

Río Colorado

Río Pecos

Dept. of
Béxar

Río Bravo del Norte

Río Brazos de Dios (Brazos)

Río Trinidad (Trinity)

Dept. of
Brazos

Washington
on the Brazos

Río Guadalupe

Río San Antonio

San Fernando
de Béxar

San Felipe

San Felipe

Gonzales

Victoria

Río Nueces

La Bahía

Presidio del
Río Grande

Refugio

Río Sabinas (Sabine)

Río Rojo (Red River)

Nacogdoches

Natchitoches

Los Adaes

Dept. of
Nacogdoches

Liberty

Houston

LOUISIANA

Mississippi

New Orleans

COAHUILA

Monclova

Río Salado

Río (Grande)

Río San Fernando

Matamoros

Saltillo

Monterrey

Río Nazas

Río

Soto la Marina

Gulf
of
Mexico

MEXICO

Tampico

Río Pánuco

Río Grande de Santiago

Dolores

Guanajuato

Lago de Chapala

Río Lerma

Ciudad de México

Veracruz

Río Balsas

Río Sto. Domingo

Coatzacoalcos

Merida

Campeche

N

MEXICO and
TEXAS
c. 1740-1840

• Towns and Settlements

A.C.Castillo Crimm-1995

TEJANO JOURNEY, 1770–1850

EDITED BY GERALD E. POYO

ILLUSTRATED BY JACK JACKSON
MAPS BY ANA CAROLINA CASTILLO CRIMM

University of Texas Press
AUSTIN

The chapter "Community and Autonomy" by Gerald E. Poyo originally appeared as "Roots of Tejano Dissatisfaction with Mexican Rule" in *Recent Research* 2 (Jan., 1992); reprinted courtesy of the Institute of Texan Cultures. The chapter "The Córdova Revolt" by Paul D. Lack originally appeared as "Los tejanos leales a México del este de Texas, 1838–1839" in *Historia Mexicana* 168 (Apr.–June, 1993); reprinted with permission of *Historia Mexicana*.

Requests for permission to reproduce material from this work should be sent to Permissions, University of Texas Press, P.O. Box 7819, Austin, TX 78713-7819.

Library of Congress Cataloging-in-Publication Data
Tejano journey, 1770–1850 / edited by Gerald E. Poyo ; illustrated by Jack Jackson ; maps by Ana Carolina Castillo Crimm. — 1st ed.
p.   cm.
Includes bibliographical references and index.
ISBN 0-292-76570-3 (alk. paper)
1. Mexican Americans — Texas — History — 18th century. 2. Mexican Americans — Texas — History — 19th century. 3. Texas — History — To 1846. I. Poyo, Gerald Eugene, 1950–
F395.M5T45   1996
976.4'00468372 — dc20   95-41290

Dedicated to Henry Guerra and Mary Ann Noonan Guerra for their years of promoting community awareness of Texas's Spanish and Mexican heritage.

CONTENTS

ACKNOWLEDGMENTS

In March, 1993, a conference at St. Mary's University entitled "Tejano Identity, Resistance and Accommodation, 1770–1860" explored the Tejano journey across sovereignties, from being Spanish subjects to Mexican citizens to independent Texans to citizens of the United States. In looking at Tejano communities and learning about their path toward integration into the United States, a better understanding emerges about continuities in Mexican American history. At the same time, in discovering the linkages across time, we learn that changing conditions affected the very nature of the communities themselves. This dialectical process of continuity and change created shifting identities as people struggled to survive and adapt. Conference participants hoped that a close look at the regional example of Tejanos could help us uncover the complex historical themes that stretch across the political boundaries of Spanish colonial, Mexican, and Mexican American history.

My appointment as O'Connor Chair at St. Mary's University in the fall of 1992 gave me the time and opportunity to organize a forum in which these ideas could be explored. Since 1982 the O'Connor Chair has provided support for scholars to research, write, and speak about the Spanish colonial era in Texas and the U.S. Southwest.

A first step was to raise the necessary resources to undertake the project. The Texas Committee for the Humanities (TCH) graciously funded our grant proposal, as it has all our endeavors to promote the study of Tejano and Latino history. Matching grants from the Kathryn O'Connor Foundation (Victoria) and the Summerlee Foundation (Dallas) completed the financial package and an idea became a reality.

After a successful conference, I turned to editing the collection of papers. As a group we agreed to give the volume a certain unity of purpose, which meant that several of the authors reworked their chapters in light of the proposed thematic goals. Though the editor of a collection of diverse essays can never hope to achieve full thematic integration, the authors' cooperative spirit and flexibility made it possible to move a long way toward that goal. All of the authors offered thoughts and suggestions about individual papers and the collection as a whole. Frank de la Teja was particularly involved in reading and commenting on the various drafts of the collection and he also played a critical role in helping identify the historians who could make this project a reality and a success. In thinking about illustrations, Jack Jackson's well-known artwork came to mind and his artistic interpretations set the tone for each chapter. One of our authors, Ana Carolina Castillo Crimm, is an experienced cartographer and her maps are found in this volume. We worked very well as a group, and I appreciate the contributions and commitment of everyone involved.

Gilberto M. Hinojosa, Oakah L. Jones, and David J. Weber, who participated in the conference, encouraged us to publish the essays. Alida Metcalf served as the TCH adviser for the project. These friends have shown interest and encouraged my scholarly pursuits over the years. I want to thank them.

As is usually the case in San Antonio, people highly conscious of Texas's Hispanic heritage enthusiastically stepped forward and backed the project. Leaders of San Antonio's historical societies and community, including Henry Guerra, Mary Ann Noonan Guerra, Gloria Cadena, Robert Benavides, and Mary Vaughn, recommended our project to TCH and promoted the program in San Antonio and across Texas. The turnout at the conference is evidence of their good work and continuing dedication to Tejano history. I applaud our local community for its contributions and commitment.

The St. Mary's University community also contributed to making the conference and book possible. Susan Galloway helped develop a successful grant proposal and Dean Charles Miller and Vice-President Charles Cotrell lent university resources. Dan Bjork, head of the History Department, has supported all of my activities at St. Mary's, and student assistants Laura López and Laura Márquez did a variety of things, from handling conference logistics to tracking down bibliographic entries and checking footnotes. All their help is greatly appreciated.

I also want to thank Miryam Bujanda, Gilberto Hinojosa, Brent Fisher, Tom Shelton, Mariano Díaz-Miranda, Dan Bjork, and Chip Hughes for the conversations, advice, support, and friendship they have offered me during the last few years. My parents' constant support must also be acknowledged and appreciated. But my deepest appreciation is reserved for Noel, my son, who during a very difficult period in our lives not only managed to keep heart and soul together but learned from adversity and kept on his chosen path. His strength and sensitivity are an inherent element of this book.

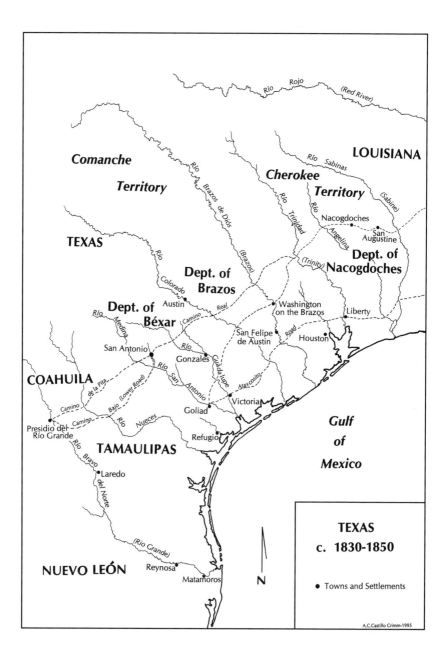

Comanche
Territory

Comanche
Territory

Cherokee
Territory

LOUISIANA

Río Sabinas

(Sabine)

Nacogdoches

San
Augustine

Dept. of
Nacogdoches

Río Rojo
(Red River)

Río Trinidad

Río Angelina

(Trinity)

TEXAS

Río Brazos de Diós

Río

(Brazos)

Dept. of
Brazos

Río Colorado

Austin

Real

Washington
on the Brazos

Liberty

Dept. of
Béxar

Camino

San Felipe
de Austin

Road

Houston

Río Medina

Río

San Antonio

Río San Antonio

Gonzales

Guadalupe

Atascosito

COAHUILA

Camino de la Pita

Bajo (Lower Road)

Río

Nueces

Goliad

Victoria

Camino

Camino

Presidio del
Río Grande

Río

Refugio

TAMAULIPAS

Río Bravo del Norte

Laredo

Gulf
of
Mexico

(Río Grande)

NUEVO LEÓN

Reynosa

Matamoros

N

TEXAS
c. 1830-1850

● Towns and Settlements

A.C.Castillo Crimm-1995

INTRODUCTION
Gerald E. Poyo

This book emerges from a recent boom in research on early Tejano (Texas Mexican) communities and their evolution. During the last decade Texas's Mexican American, or Chicano, history has emerged forcefully and in the last five years a number of studies of pre-1860 Texas Mexican communities have begun to give Tejanos the centrality they deserve in early Texas history.[1] These recent studies reveal that Tejano communities were small, deeply rooted, stable communities that were at the very heart of life in Texas through the 1850s. At the same time, they were changing communities that had to contend with historical forces that directed them on a path toward integration into the United States.

The story of Tejano integration into the United States has traditionally been told from the perspective of Euro-American immigration to Texas and conflicts with Mexico; Tejanos themselves have been mostly absent from the story. Through their silence about local Tejano communities, most sources imply that Tejanos were irrelevant to the region's destiny. The truth, however, is that Tejanos influenced events significantly and acted out of their own traditions in diverse and complex ways to defend and promote their perceived interests.

Indeed, how could it be otherwise? Tejanos settled the land and established communities in the early eighteenth century. They established an economic foundation, practiced politics in defense of their interests, and evolved a culture that expressed their identity by at least the 1770s. From the 1770s through the 1840s, Tejanos faced considerable turbulence and change as active and involved citizens of Spain, Mexico, the Republic of Texas, and, finally, the United States. While these journeys across sovereignties redefined the context within which their political, economic, social, and cultural community life evolved, Tejanos embarked on change with a clear understanding of and connectedness to their traditions and interests.

Tejano history began in the territorial triangle encompassed by the Spanish colonial communities of San Antonio de Béxar, La Bahía (Goliad), and Los Adaes. Established between 1716 and 1718 as military and missionary outposts, these gathering points for soldiers, priests, Indians, and civilian settlers from New Spain grew into settlements that gave birth to a Tejano identity.

Their story began to be told in some detail beginning in the first half of this century by historians like Herbert E. Bolton and Carlos E. Castañeda. Building on Fray Juan Agustín Morff's history of Texas (written in 1777), these historians and others constructed the chronologies and related the stories of explorations, foundings, institution building, and international power struggles and intrigues, but they also created the narrative framework within which histories of communities and a people could emerge. Even as this traditional framework was being built, other historians began the complex task of looking at the inner workings of Texas's early Hispanic communities and telling their story.² Much of this research is presented in Donald Chipman's narrative synthesis of Spanish Texas history, *Spanish Texas, 1519–1821*, which draws on the traditional research as well as the socioeconomic historiography that has emerged since the 1970s.

If Chipman's book provides a broad view of the Spanish-era history, a number of other studies published in recent years point to the intricacies of Tejano community life from the 1770s through the 1850s. A collection edited by me and Gilberto M. Hinojosa, *Tejano Origins in Eighteenth-Century San Antonio*, reinforces the notion that the inhabitants of San Antonio had by the end of the eighteenth century established an integrated, socially stratified community deeply connected with this region that was called Texas. Tejano identity had begun to emerge. The full complexity of that San Antonio community is revealed in Jesús F. de la Teja's *San Antonio de Béxar: A Community on New Spain's Northern Frontier*. De la Teja's detailed study shows that while the community was materially poor, San Antonio had a sophisticated legal, economic, political, and social system that has not been very well recognized in the historiography.

Andrés Tijerina's revision of his pioneering 1977 doctoral dissertation not only shows us the continuity from Spanish to Mexican rule but provides us with a detailed vision of Tejano community life in the 1820s and the 1830s. In *Tejanos and Texas under the Mexican Flag, 1821–1836*, Tijerina reveals that Texas history in this period included more than just the Anglo American immigration and colonization story. Tejano communities had their own political ideals, economic visions, and social structure and customs, inherited from their eighteenth-century ancestors. This fills an enormous void in the published historiography on Tejanos.

New studies have also increased our understanding of how Tejanos fit into the Texas rebellion. Paul Lack dedicates an entire chapter of *The Texas Revolutionary Experience: A Political and Social History, 1835–1836* to Tejanos in his reinterpretation of the rebellion, and Jesús F. de la Teja gives us an excellent introductory biography of Juan Seguín in *A Revolution Remembered: The Memoirs and Selected Correspondence of Juan N. Seguín*. Timothy M. Matovina presents Tejano accounts of the Alamo in *The Alamo Remembered: Tejano Accounts and Perspectives*. He and David McDonald have also published *Defending Mexican Valor in Texas: José Antonio Navarro's Historical Writings, 1853–1857*, with an introductory reinterpretation of the traditional view of Navarro as an Anglophile not much interested in Tejano interests.

How Tejanos fared during the Mexican period and after the region's separation from Mexico is the subject of yet another study by Matovina. In *Tejano Religion and Ethnicity: San Antonio, 1821–1860* he describes Tejano traditions and shows that Tejanos maintained a strong allegiance to their religion and culture in the face of Euro-American and Protestant cultural penetration of the region. This study, along with work by Hinojosa and Robert Wright, has contributed to reinterpreting the role of Catholicism in the life of Tejanos during these years. These historians are successfully challenging the general view that Tejanos were not much influenced by religious matters.[3] They are also rounding out the story of the frontier church, which for many years was thought to be exclusively mission history. Parish churches and secular priests are emerging to take their place in Tejano history.

This important body of published historical research will force a revision of early Texas history on many fronts. It is no longer possible to exclude detailed references to early Tejano communities and their development (whether speaking of Spanish Texas, Texas under Mexico, the Texas rebellion, or Euro-American dominated Texas) by citing lack of research. This literature is giving life and form to Tejano history.

Drawing on the research of many of these same authors, the essays in this volume demonstrate how the continuities of tradition and cultural struggle interact with the turbulence inherent in change across time. The essays show, for example, how political thinking, economic interests, and religious and cultural traditions linked the Spanish, Mexican, and post-1836 eras. When, during the 1770s to the 1840s, Tejanos struggled for political autonomy, for the right to freely pursue their economic advantage, for the defense of their social traditions, or for the maintenance of Catholicism, they demonstrated a consistency of tradition that emerged logically from their local origins and interest. This consistency was expressed by the fact that, even though the legitimacy of Tejano interests was challenged by outside forces over and over again, and their way of life was dismissed as inconsequential, they strove fiercely to define their destiny and defend their ways. That struggle is clearly revealed by the essays in this volume.

Indeed, in describing Tejano traditions and strategies for survival, the historical literature also reveals that Tejanos were contributors to their own destiny. Arnoldo De León commented over a decade ago that the history of Tejanos "is not solely a story of people victimized by oppression. It is much more the history of actors who have sought to take measures in their own behalf for the sake of a decent living."[4] De León writes of people seeking not only to survive, but also to adapt, grow, and better themselves. He speaks of the identity that emerges from the process of living and the commonalities of lifestyle. If the story of this living is not told, in history books, songs, oral tradition, or other forms, the sense of identity is lost or, at least, not conveyed. In guiding the reader on the Tejanos' journey across sovereignties, the contributions in this volume tell about Tejano culture and life, Tejanos' struggles to defend their ways, and their strategies for adapting to the inevitable changes required by the onset of turbulent times.

« TEJANO JOURNEY »

ONE

COMMUNITY AND AUTONOMY

Gerald E. Poyo

I n 1789, two prominent residents of San Antonio de Béxar, don Juan Flores and don Macario Sambrano, presented the interim governor, don Rafael Martínez Pacheco, with an official *memoria* signed by the *cabildo* (town council). The document's goal was to continue an ongoing debate and express unreserved opposition to the Spanish Crown's usurpation of the province's cattle resources in a decision published some ten years earlier. The decree had created considerable conflict in the province, and the *cabildo* sought to reestablish its position. Speaking in the name of "our town and the citizenry of the jurisdiction," the writers of the document announced the *cabildo*'s intention and obligation to "defend [the community's] rights and possessions, as we have defended and protected them up to now."[1]

The *memoria* presented to governor Martínez Pacheco by councilmen Flores and Sambrano recounted a specific grievance, but the document also expressed community solidarity in the face of expanding Crown influence over local affairs. Indeed, since its founding in 1731, the town council had guarded local interests with considerable effectiveness, but by the 1780s it seemed clear that local authorities faced a challenge from an increasing Crown presence. During the reign of Carlos III (1759–1788), political and economic developments in the Spanish empire initiated a process of greater Crown authority that increasingly whittled away at Tejano autonomy.

While it is true that this competition between Spanish officials and local communities was an ever-present reality in colonial Latin America, it is also the case that this competition reflected the growth of local and regional identities and fueled discontentment. Feelings of dissatisfaction regarding outside political interference in local affairs emerged as an important theme in the late eighteenth century and would continue as a prominent feature in Tejano communities for the next half century.

SAN ANTONIO DE BÉXAR: FROM BUFFER TO COMMUNITY

Residents' sense of belonging to and owning Texas and its resources had its origins in the second decade of the century, when Spanish authorities created the province's first settlements—Los Adaes, La Bahía, and San Antonio de Béxar—in response to French encroachment in the northeastern regions of New Spain. Interested in defending its prosperous Mexican heartland from European rivals, Spain founded the presidios of Los Adaes and La Bahía, along with several missions, to ensure a barrier on the frontier facing French Louisiana. To link these communities with Mexico, officials also ordered the establishment of a settlement along the San Antonio River.

The settlement of San Antonio de Béxar, founded in 1718, began as a mission and presidio outpost. Within fifteen years, four additional missions and a civil settlement, San Fernando de Béxar, were built along the banks of the river, converting the region into Texas's most populous. The settlement grew rapidly during the next fifty years.[2] In 1777, 1,351 persons lived in the civilian and presidio communities and another 709 resided in the five missions.[3]

Although the Crown founded Béxar as a buffer settlement, the town naturally took on a life of its own, with its particular traditions and identity. During the five decades after Béxar's founding, the inhabitants developed a sense of belonging to the region and increasingly shared aspirations and goals that did not always conform to the Crown's strategic objectives.

The settlers along the San Antonio River did not initially form a cohesive community. The missions, administered by Franciscan priests, constituted independent social units designed as pueblos for Texas Indians. Mexican frontiersmen from Saltillo, Monterrey, and other northern territories of New Spain garrisoned the presidio, while immigrants from the Canary Islands founded the town of San Fernando de Béxar. Despite their physical proximity and shared allegiance to Crown objectives, as a practical matter, in 1731 the three principal population groups competed more than they cooperated. In fact, each group initially sought exclusivity rather than interdependence and a vision of a common future.

In time, however, cultural integration, social accommodation, similar economic interests, and political convergence contributed to the emergence of a sense of community. The strict divisions that initially separated the ethnic groups slowly diminished. Intermarriage and other kinship ties linked the Canary Islanders and the members of the presidio community to create a mestizo elite by the final third of the eighteenth century. Furthermore, cultural traditions based on the local agricultural and ranching economy gave local residents a sense of unity that overcame the sharp differences in heritage that existed when various groups first arrived.[4] The ranching economy particularly tied the local residents to a shared economic vision and destiny. By the 1770s, Béxar had developed a relatively lucrative ranching industry that relied on markets in Coahuila and Louisiana.[5]

The development of Béxar's culturally distinct and self-sufficient frontier lifestyle led to relative political autonomy. Béxar's residents (Bexareños)—living deep in New Spain's northeastern frontier, where they daily faced the realities of a hard and isolated life—grew used to self-government. Although members of the *cabildo* and the presidio captain naturally identified with the Spanish empire and its political structures, they also developed a certain independence of action aimed at maximizing community interests. These officials, often completely autonomous of the governors, who usually resided in Los Adaes and concerned themselves with monitoring the French presence on the Texas-Louisiana border, oversaw affairs in Béxar. This resulted in a population imbued with an independent spirit that eventually came into conflict with a rapidly changing Spanish empire intent on centralizing power and reforming its economic system.[6]

WINDS OF CHANGE IN NEW SPAIN

By the time reformist monarch Carlos III assumed the Spanish throne in 1759, the people of Béxar had developed their own way of life and grown used to conducting their affairs with minimal interference from the Crown. Their original commitment to advancing Crown objectives by acting as a buffer to French expansionism into the heart of New Spain had been complemented by a desire to promote their community. At the same time, developments in Spain initiated a political process that impinged on the autonomy of the local populations in the American colonies.

With the passing of the last Spanish Hapsburg at the end of the seventeenth century, Spain embarked on a period of imperial reevaluation under the French Bourbon dynasty. Spain suffered from declining commerce, inefficient bureaucracies, and regional conflict that undermined its status as a European power. Reformers responded by attempting to solidify the Crown's authority and seeking solutions to the persistent and dangerous problems on the Iberian peninsula. The Bourbon monarchs sought more efficient and effective government, a prosperous economic system, and a society rooted in secular ideas. Reforms had swept through Spain by the 1740s, and they were extended to the American colonies in a systematic fashion after Carlos III's ascension.

Reforms received a special boost in New Spain when the Spanish monarch charged José de Gálvez with traveling to Mexico in 1765 to report on conditions in the colony. Gálvez arrived with the authority to implement reforms and quickly launched an all-out attack on what he considered a sluggish system controlled by entrenched Creole interests dedicated to their own prosperity, often at the expense of the Crown. Experimentation and change thus characterized the final half of the eighteenth century, during which, for better or for worse, crown authority asserted itself.[7]

The Crown's interest in reform inevitably affected Texas and the rest of the northern provinces. At first, policy changes relating to the North were primarily defense-related and were influenced by dramatic changes in international conditions. The end of the Seven Years' War altered borders considerably in North America. Under the terms of the Treaty of Paris signed in early 1763, Spain ceded Florida to England in return for Havana and Manila, which had been occupied during the war. Spain received Louisiana from France, and English sovereignty extended to the Mississippi. Moreover, the Russians had become active in the Aleutian Islands and posed a threat to Spain's control over California. Finally, increased hostilities with the Indians affected Spain's defense capabilities and threatened to destroy the Spanish presence in these northern regions.

In response to these developments, Gálvez ordered an inspection of the northern provinces and reorganized the frontier defense system in 1772. This led, four years later, to the establishment of the northern provinces as an independent administrative unit, the Provincias Internas, governed by a commandant general responsible directly to the Council of the Indies in Spain.[8]

The impact on Texas was significant. The 1772 reorganization eliminated the East Texas presidio of Los Adaes and its associated mission. With Louisiana safely under Spain's control, the community of Los Adaes no longer seemed necessary to Crown officials. Most of the area's residents relocated in Béxar, as did the governor, making the Central Texas community the provincial capital.[9]

IN DEFENSE OF AUTONOMY

While the residents of Béxar welcomed their town's designation as the provincial capital, the administrative changes brought unexpected complications. Within a short time the town council in San Antonio realized that for the first time it would have to contend with a resident governor whose very presence, and Bourbon-inspired authority, challenged the community's independent traditions.[10] The governor's transfer to Béxar might not have caused significant problems in earlier years, when officials routinely winked at the lack of enforcement of Crown regulations and prohibitions, but the reform mentality of the 1760s and 1770s brought a new breed of Spanish bureaucrat to Texas. Governors dedicated to Crown goals and trained in the autocratic and reform philosophy of the Bourbons appeared in Texas, where they asserted the power and prerogatives of office.[11] The governors immediately came into conflict with the local town council.

Since 1731 Béxar's Canary Islander founders had used their town council offices to attain a privileged social and economic position within the community. On arriving in Béxar, ten Islanders, or Isleños, had received life appointments to govern the villa. Six *regidores* (councilmen), an *alguacil* (constable), an *escribano* (notary), a *mayordomo* (overseer of lands), and a *procurador* (legal officer) annually selected the two *alcaldes ordinarios* (municipal magistrates) who ruled on the legalities of community life.[12] Initially, the only non-Isleño in a position of authority in the town council was the presidio captain, who served as *justicia mayor* (senior magistrate). The precise powers of that office are not clear, since daily administrative and legal activities seem to have been handled by the city magistrates, but the office did moderate Isleño power to some degree.[13]

While technically subservient to the governor in Los Adaes, in fact the town council ruled in Béxar through the 1760s. One way or another, the council usually had its way.[14] Despite the wishes of some governors to the contrary, Isleños used the town council, for example, to ensure control over economic resources. The council, decreeing that land and water be distributed for use among all the town's residents, successfully sidestepped viceregal rulings in 1734 and again in 1745.[15] In later years, others in the community became part of the ruling elite and also used their influence in the town council to promote their status in Béxar. Those governors who did aspire to some influence in Béxar cooperated with the town council. Too far away to manage the town's affairs on a daily basis and preoccupied with the French presence on the Texas border, governors through the 1750s did not often contradict Béxar's leading citizens.

Beginning with Governor Ángel Martos y Navarrete's inspection tour of Texas in 1762, however, governors began to abandon their passive posture. During his stay in Béxar the governor received numerous petitions from settlers demanding access to agricultural lands. Discovering the town council's obvious disregard for long-standing viceregal decrees relating to land distributions, the governor ordered that residential land grants be allotted to needy citizens from the town's communal holdings north of the town plaza. The governor also reaffirmed the right of settlers to construct a new dam on the San Antonio River, to dig another irrigation system, and to expand the settlement's agricultural lands. This was a direct assault on the town council's de facto authority to regulate the expansion of irrigable agricultural lands in Béxar. Several prominent members of the town council openly objected to the action, causing the governor to threaten them with removal from office if they did not cease their "civil disturbances."[16]

Thus, gubernatorial authority had already partially asserted itself when Colonel Juan María Vicencio de Ripperdá arrived in Béxar in 1770 to take up the task of ruling Texas. A native of Madrid steeped in Bourbon traditions of reform and regal authority, Ripperdá set out to "improve" government, economy, and society in Texas. On inspecting the province, the new governor quickly discovered that local practices did not always conform to Crown military and civilian regulations. Presumably interested in impressing his superiors so as to reduce his time in the purgatory that was Texas, Ripperdá and his successor, Domingo Cabello, exhibited an uncompromising attitude toward the population's less-than-orthodox interpretations of royal law.

Furthermore, these Crown officials often expressed open disdain for what they considered to be crude Texas society. Such attitudes were not uncommon among Spanish state and church officials who visited the northern frontiers. In writing about Béxar, for example, Franciscan priest Juan Agustín Morfí, who accompanied one official inspection tour, characterized the people as "indolent and given to vice" and thus "not deserving of the blessings of the land."[17] Morfí expressed a basic aversion to frontier life and criticized a previous governor mightily for living "among the Indians at Los Adaes with so little pride that in his dress and manners he resembled one of them more than the commander and governor."[18]

Ripperdá reacted similarly when he observed what he considered to be an unindustrious populace consumed by vice. Believing he needed to be firm to establish acceptable standards, Ripperdá challenged the local elites to serve as examples for the rest of the population. Shortly after arriving, the new governor took steps to promote agricultural production. He also attempted to reduce what he perceived to be the residents' indolence. To this end, he enforced regulations against local production of alcoholic beverages by ordering all stills destroyed. Further, he initiated the practice of inspecting local reserves of *aguardiente*, an alcoholic beverage. In a particularly humiliating affair for constable Vicente Álvarez Travieso and several other prominent residents, Governor Ripperdá ordered their *aguardiente* tested for purity. An investigation revealed that the constable and several other citizens, who apparently sold *aguardiente* out of their homes, not only overcharged their customers but also adulterated the drink. The governor warned the offending residents to heed the established standards and fined them for their excesses.[19]

Much to the governor's dismay, however, the residents of Béxar jealously guarded their way of life and demonstrated refined skills in utilizing the Spanish bureaucracy to derail or at least to delay the implementation of measures they deemed detrimental to their interests. The governor received a taste of local defiance when he attempted to extend his authority in the political arena during 1771. He confronted the town council on an issue that, for the local population, took on an importance far beyond its immediate practical significance. Indeed, the disagreement symbolized the clash of interests between Crown and local objectives, a contest that became a central dimension of politics in Texas during the reign of Carlos III and beyond.

One of Governor Ripperdá's first acts on arriving in Texas was to prepare a report to the viceroy describing conditions in the province. Among other things, he pointed out that the barracks and guardhouse were in an advanced state of deterioration and he asked for ten thousand pesos to rebuild the structures. The viceroy refused to provide the money "because it is the obligation of the . . . population of the villa and presidio . . . to build the said palisade or fortification."[20] The governor informed Béxar's residents of their obligation and ordered them to lend their services to the task.

The town council immediately objected and reacted in time-honored fashion to an order it did not intend to obey: it petitioned the viceroy for relief. The petition informed the authorities in Mexico City that the residents had always cooperated with all reasonable requests from Crown representatives. In this case, however, the governor's requirements created excessive hardship. "He has forced them [the residents] to personally transport in their own wagons, pulled by their own oxen, beams and rocks, in order to build the barracks . . . and the jail now in construction."[21] The problem, the town council argued, was that "this new imposition . . . is not allowing them any time for the cultivation of their lands."[22] The petition also complained of the poor timing of the decree, issued just as the residents were preparing to sow their fields. Moreover, they claimed, the lack of compensation for their work was unjust.

The town council succeeded in stalling implementation. To its delight, officials in Mexico City accepted their protestations and advised the viceroy to instruct Governor Ripperdá to negotiate terms with the town council for building the barracks and jail.[23]

Despite viceregal officials' efforts to encourage a compromise, the town council refused to cooperate on the grounds that any such work had to be compensated financially. Finally, losing all patience, Ripperdá suspended the town council members from office, only to be reprimanded by Viceroy Antonio Bucareli for overstepping his authority. Bucareli ordered the governor to restore the town council and encouraged him to find a "peaceful" and satisfactory solution to the problem.[24] No doubt frustrated by the town council's ability to maintain its position through constant appeals and litigation, Ripperdá finally tired. The barracks and jail remained in disrepair.

Ripperdá's successor, Governor Cabello, launched a second effort to build the barracks and jail in 1785. Dusting off the viceregal order of 1771 to reconstruct the barracks and jail, the governor ordered the town council to select individuals to transport boards and beams on carts and to choose others to assist in the construction, "to which the troops will contribute as much as is necessary."[25] Again the town council refused. This time the governor arrested the council members. Despite the governor's actions, the town leaders continued to insist that they were under no obligation to work for the governor without compensation. Apparently, Cabello never succeeded in having the barracks constructed before he departed for a new position in Havana in 1786.

While Governors Ripperdá and Cabello never managed to intimidate the town council and force it to accept their authority beyond the rhetorical level, they did initiate a process that led eventually to the town council's subjugation to gubernatorial authority. Despite the council's constant resistance, governors after Cabello expanded their authority throughout the 1790s, and another series of disputes after 1800 finally led to the town council's demise. In May, 1807, Governor Antonio Cordero received a ruling from his superiors indicating that, in fact, the town council of San

Antonio de Béxar had no legal standing. According to the ruling, Béxar had been given the right to establish a town council, but the institution had never actually been confirmed. The citizens had no recourse, and the governor received the authority to function with or without a council, as he saw fit. After over seventy years, Béxar's local governing body had been stripped of all authority. Cordero proceeded to reduce the number of town council officers from ten to five, and in December, 1808, he eliminated elections altogether in favor of an appointed body.[26]

ECONOMIC REFORM AND COMMERCIAL RESTRICTION

This political struggle in Béxar evolved from the governors' insistence on exercising their authority, an attitude that was consistent with their understanding of the entire thrust of royal policy. On the other hand, economic reforms enacted during the same period were less a result of direct gubernatorial initiatives than of the political reorganization of the northern frontier areas. The creation of the Provincias Internas in the 1770s was in part calculated to place the burden of economic accountability on regional officials. Charged with establishing security on the frontier without increasing Crown expenditures, regional officials looked to the local communities for solutions.

Until about the 1760s, Béxar had little to offer the Crown economically, and local residents went about their business with a minimum of interference from governors or other outside officials. Initially, Béxar's settlers concentrated on agricultural pursuits, and an intricate *acequia* (irrigation) system provided the basis for farming in the civilian and mission communities. Later, however, ranching became the most important economic activity. The missions first exploited the cattle resources in Texas on their extensive lands between Béxar and the settlement of La Bahía to the south. Franciscan friars and Indian vaqueros pursued what became a relatively lucrative enterprise of rounding up cattle that roamed freely on mission and surrounding lands. Civilian settlers also requested and received ranchlands during the 1740s and 1750s. By the 1770s, they were full partners in a thriving ranching economy.

Predictably, however, competition between the missions and civilian ranchers for control of cattle became the province's most difficult political problem. Settlers struggled to restrain the physical growth of missions by opposing their requests for additional lands. Moreover, they often took the liberty of rounding up cattle on mission ranches.[27] Perhaps exasperated at his inability to subdue the town council on the barracks construction issue, Ripperdá prosecuted several prominent ranchers and leading citizens for trespassing on mission lands and appropriating cattle illegally. A bitter trial that lasted for some seven months resulted in their convictions and set the stage for stronger actions than even Ripperdá himself had contemplated.[28]

During late 1777, Teodoro de Croix, commandant general of the Provincias Internas, arrived in Béxar on an inspection tour. Preoccupied primarily with developing an effective Indian policy in Texas, he met in Béxar with Ripperdá, Captain Luis Cazorla of Presidio La Bahía, and Captain Rafael Martínez Pacheco of the Presidio La Babia (Coahuila). Much to his distress, however, Croix found himself having to lend his attention to an angry populace seeking clarification on the land and ranching issues. Petition after petition from missionaries and local ranchers crossed Croix's desk.[29]

The central and recurring theme was lack of definition regarding the ownership of the province's stray cattle herds. Croix listened to the concerns of the inhabitants, studied the problem, and concluded that a regulatory action in the spirit of the Bourbon reforms could solve a number of the issues in question. In January, 1778, Croix stunned the community with a decree declaring all stray cattle and horses the property of the king. In addition, the decree ordered officials to regulate and tax the cattle industry and apply the funds to local Indian affairs. Furthermore, regulation protected the wild herds from destruction through the local ranchers' unrestrained exploitation and presumably removed the main source of controversy between the missionaries and the civilian ranchers.[30]

The ranchers and missionaries, however, viewed the action as an unprecedented Crown imposition on their long-standing rights and traditions. They insisted that "we, the inhabitants of the villa of San Fernando and the presidios of Béxar and Bahía, plus the Indians of these missions, are, have been, and always shall be the recognized owners of the cattle and horses found on the pastures between here and the Guadalupe River, which we have possessed in good faith for the past sixty or seventy years." Historically in competition and conflict over local resources, missionaries, soldiers, and civilians pooled their energies for the first time to try to overturn the ruling. Decision after decision, however, confirmed and extended the Crown's authority over Texas's ranching industry.[31]

Despite the Crown's firm intention, local residents violated the new ranching regulations with some frequency. Left with the task of enforcement, Governors Ripperdá and Cabello incurred the wrath of Béxar residents. The governors brought numerous indictments against the local ranchers who refused to obey the new cattle regulations. One prominent family, the Menchacas, particularly suffered the consequences of attempting to maintain their traditional way of life. Among the oldest of Béxar's families, the Menchacas participated in the founding of the presidio in 1718. Luis Antonio Menchaca launched his family into ranching in the 1750s and served as captain of the presidio in the 1760s. By the late 1770s, Menchaca was probably the most successful rancher in the province. According to the 1777 census, he owned about three thousand head of cattle, horses, goats, sheep, and mules. Furthermore, he and other family members regularly served in the town council. When Governor Cabello arrested several of the Menchaca family for illegally rounding up and exporting cattle, he challenged one of the region's most influential families. In time, the Menchacas and others suffered economically for their defiant attitude, which accounts for their active opposition to Spain during the turbulent times after 1810.[32]

The resentment in Béxar over the ranching regulations became even more intense as a result of the Crown's inconsistent policy with regard to commerce. For generations the Spanish Crown had embraced mercantilist economic philosophy and prohibited free trade. Only designated American ports traded with Spain and commercial interactions between the colonies and foreign powers was absolutely forbidden. Despite Spain's inflexible commercial policies, settlers on Texas's eastern frontier engaged in illegal trade with French Louisiana from the moment the communities formed. Initially, trade was modest but necessary for Los Adaes's very survival, since supplies did not usually arrive in a timely fashion from Mexico. This trade grew with the development of Béxar's ranching economy. Béxar's ranchers marketed their cattle and horses in Louisiana and in return received tobacco and goods manufactured in Europe.[33] While this trade proved lucrative, it was also troublesome for Texas's residents, since they always risked arrest. Fortunately, many Texas governors understood the importance of this trade to the province's survival. Some ignored the illegal trade while others participated. Before the 1750s, an understanding existed between the people and their governors.

Although the international developments that made Louisiana part of the Spanish empire in 1762 offered the possibility of regularizing Texas-Louisiana trade, commercial reforms were not forthcoming. Texas's inhabitants could understand and accept, though not obey, Spanish trade prohibitions when Louisiana belonged to the French, but after the mid-1760s Tejanos increasingly resented such restrictions. Not only was Louisiana now a part of the Spanish empire, but during that decade the Crown had embarked on an ambitious policy of liberalizing commercial arrangements throughout the Americas. In 1765, Spain allowed trade between Cuba, other Caribbean ports, and several Spanish cities. This trend continued until 1789, when Spain allowed free trade across the entire American colonial empire. Even New Orleans received the privilege of trading directly with Spain, a commercial reform that proved to be an economic boon for Louisiana.

On the margins of the empire, however, Texas did not exercise sufficient influence to change the situation, despite efforts of some Crown officials. In 1783, for example, Teodoro de Croix urged officials in Mexico City to allow trade between Texas and Louisiana. Furthermore, he recommended that a seaport be licensed on the Texas coast. He received support from José de Gálvez, now minister of the Indies in Spain. Gálvez pointed out that the only way to ensure Spanish control of the borderlands provinces in the face of an expanding and aggressive Euro-American frontier was by encouraging Texas's economic development. Officials who formulated New Spain's commercial policies did not agree. They argued that New Spain depended heavily on the pastoral and agricultural products of the northern provinces, which Louisiana trade would siphon off. Probably interested in winning friends in Mexico City, Governor Cabello agreed and, perhaps more to the point, added that trade with Louisiana would create competition for Central Mexico's merchants. The entrenched merchant class of Mexico City and Veracruz feared that free trade with Louisiana and the establishment of a Texas port might undermine their long-standing commercial monopoly in northern New Spain. No doubt they made their views known to the king, who maintained the status quo.[34]

During the last thirty years of the century, Crown officials in Texas had little choice but to enforce the trade prohibition. The lax attitude with regard to trade regulations that existed before the 1750s gave way to a more inflexible position by the 1770s. In fact, during the 1750s and 1760s, at least two Texas governors fell victim to prosecution for their involvement in illegal commerce. Probably cognizant of the fate of their predecessors, Governors Ripperdá and Cabello spent considerable energy keeping contraband under control.[35] In response to a royal decree, during the 1770s and 1780s the two governors named agents to watch for *contrabandistas*.[36] All concerned received direct rewards for apprehensions. In one case, an auction netted 491 pesos and 4 reales from contraband items, which was partially distributed among the governor, the contraband official, the apprehenders, and the informer. The remainder was deposited with the presidio paymaster to purchase playing cards.[37]

Smuggling between Texas and Louisiana never ceased; instead, it grew throughout the period of Spanish rule. The trade prohibitions restricted the province's economic growth and served as a constant source of friction between the local residents and their governors.

CONCLUSION

During the late eighteenth century, Béxar's relationship with the Spanish Crown suffered considerable stress. Béxar's socioeconomic development, cultural affinities, and political autonomy combined to create an awareness among its inhabitants that, although they composed part of the Spanish empire, their local and regional traits and interests often conflicted with the broader objectives of the Crown and other power centers in New Spain.

This contradiction between local and outside interests and objectives became a major theme in Béxar's development in coming years. Crosscurrents of loyalty and disaffection characterized the Tejano community as it promoted its interests in spite of opposition from the south. Spanish and, later, Mexican officials in Mexico City and in Coahuila constantly struggled to keep Tejano interests within the bounds of their political and economic definitions. And after 1836, this same struggle shifted to the east, as Tejanos, now living in a radically new political reality, had to defend themselves from Euro Americans interested in stripping them of political and economic power. Tejanos faced their first great challenge for control of their own destiny with the outbreak of the Mexican War of Independence led by Father Miguel Hidalgo in 1810.

TWO

REBELLION ON THE FRONTIER

Jesús F. de la Teja

Ln January, 1811, at the height of Mexico's insurrection against Spanish colonial rule, a retired military officer from Nuevo Santander living in San Antonio organized the overthrow of provincial authorities. The insurrection quickly removed the governor and other Spanish officials in the province. Dissension and unclear goals among rebel leaders, however, resulted in a counterrevolt in early March. Eighteen months later, between August, 1812, and April, 1813, the province succumbed again, this time to an invading force of Mexican rebels and Anglo-American filibusters. A royal army, more successful in controlling Texas than the earlier rebels had been, defeated the insurrectionists that summer in a pitched battle.

These events were significant politically and economically, yet the reasons why Béxar residents (Bexareños) teetered between loyalty and disloyalty remain unclear. Some historians have suggested that Tejanos opposed Spanish authority because they believed in the Enlightenment ideals of the day, especially as represented by the United States. Others have viewed rebelliousness in Texas as a result of Spain's inability to promote growth in the province.[1] Recent research on the Mexican independence movement suggests that such explanations are too limited and that clues to Béxar's role should be sought in the complex political, economic, and socioeconomic realities affecting the province as a result of changing circumstances at the beginning of the nineteenth century.[2]

FROM AUTONOMY TO A
CROSSROADS PROVINCE

Early nineteenth-century San Antonio de Béxar was a quite different place from what it had been throughout the eighteenth century. From its founding as a military buffer in 1718 to Louisiana's retrocession to France in 1800, Béxar had developed according to the vagaries of Spanish imperial policy. At San Antonio military settlers mixed with a small group of Canary Island immigrants to produce a population that by the end of the century had clearly established a regional identity.[3] As residents of the only chartered civilian settlement in Texas, and enjoying numerical predominance over La Bahía and Nacogdoches, Bexareños came to see their community as representing Texas itself.

Béxar's eighteenth-century economy was simple and limited. Local agriculture was sufficient to provide subsistence to the population and meet the demands of Béxar's and nearby La Bahía's (Goliad's) garrisons. Livestock, mostly wild cattle in the late 1700s and equine stock after the turn of the century, provided the only real, if limited, export earnings. San Antonio's most important economic institution was the presidio, which provided a market for local produce and services and was the settlement's largest employer. All Bexareños were poor by the standards of outsiders looking in, and by their own standards even the wealthiest were men of very limited means.[4]

Béxar was secure, if not entirely content, in its relative poverty and isolation. At least three native sons had successfully studied for the priesthood; another had attained the rank of presidial commander at Agua Verde, Coahuila; one other was a successful lawyer practicing before the Audiencia of Guadalajara. Most Bexareños of some means had small business dealings with neighboring provinces, and there were particularly close ties with the presidial settlement of Río Grande as well as with Monclova and Saltillo. Some citizens made regular trips to Saltillo to attend the annual autumnal fair, where they sold or traded their cattle and a few other items in return for goods from the interior; others conducted commerce — illegally — with Louisiana. An occasional business trip to Mexico City and a steady stream of litigation over any number of issues were the most notable linkages to Central New Spain.[5]

The nineteenth century opened on an ominous note with Spain's transfer of Louisiana back to France followed by Napoleon's sale of the immense and vaguely defined region to the United States. Spanish concerns over American encroachments into New Spain, exemplified by Philip Nolan's mustanging expeditions, now turned into fear of an American invasion.[6] What had been the undefended border between two Spanish provinces began to produce refugees who claimed a desire to remain subjects of his Catholic Majesty. As a result, royal policymakers ordered hundreds of troops—from fewer than 200 presidial troops in 1801 to a high of 1,368 in mid 1806—into Texas to protect what was now New Spain's border with the land-hungry United States.[7]

The largest long-term military reinforcement took place at Béxar, where the presence of such a large body of soldiers and their dependents not only swelled the town's population but strained its productive capacity. The troops stationed at San Antonio were for the most part outsiders brought to Texas after 1805 in response to U.S. occupation of Louisiana. In addition to the garrison company of 104, composed chiefly of Bexareños, there were the 69 men of the Parras Company, who had been transferred to San Antonio permanently in 1803—a total of 173 troops who may be considered locals. There were, moreover, 50 soldiers from the Punta de Lampazos garrison, 254 militiamen from Nuevo León, and an equal number from Nuevo Santander, for a total of 558 temporarily stationed troops.[8]

THE MEXICAN WAR OF INDEPENDENCE

As if the border difficulties were not trouble enough, Texas was also affected by the increasing political turmoil in both Spain and New Spain.[9] Having participated in the French revolutionary and Napoleonic wars, as both an enemy and an ally of France, Spain faced a deepening economic crisis, which its rulers attempted to remedy by increasing colonial revenues. In 1804, a royal decree confiscated the assets of church charitable funds and placed them at the disposal of the Crown. The action, coming on top of the economic downturn caused by disruptions in overseas trade and bad harvests, created a financial crisis as the church was forced to call in mortgages and loans. As disaffection grew, royal authority suffered its most severe blow when, in 1808, Napoleon invaded Spain, forced Carlos IV to abdicate, and arrested the heir, Fernando. He placed his own brother, Joseph, on the Spanish throne.

Unwilling to accept a French-imposed king, the colonials also could not decide on a clear course of action. Majority sentiment among the *criollo* (white Spanish American) elites seems to have favored some sort of provisional government acting in the name of the legitimate king, Fernando VII. Not only peninsular Spaniards but most white elites in the Americas feared the consequences of involving the Indian and mixed-blood masses, which made up over 80 percent of the population, in any struggle for power. The peninsulars favored rule by the viceroy and Audiencia, the traditional royal authorities, while Mexico City's *criollo* leadership advocated a provisional council, or junta, to manage affairs until Fernando's restoration. When Viceroy José de Iturrigaray sided with the American elites, a force of peninsulars packed him off to Spain, arrested a number of local leaders, and named an aged Spanish field marshal, Pedro Garibay, viceroy.

While Mexico City entered into a period of uneasy calm in 1809, other parts of the viceroyalty became increasingly agitated. Continued disruptions in trade and poor crops in that year led to an economic slowdown and famine in 1810, particularly in the Bajío, the viceroyalty's leading mining center. It was in the area of Guanajuato, capital of the region, that a number of disgruntled *criollos*, hoping to wrest power from the peninsulars, determined to employ the Indian and mixed-blood peasantry in the effort. Among the conspirators was the parish priest of Dolores, a small agricultural town east of Guanajuato. Father Miguel Hidalgo y Costilla formally began the rebellion against "bad government" and Spaniards on the morning of September 16, 1810, from the steps of the parish church, after receiving news that the conspiracy had been exposed.

The early progress of the revolt, particularly the looting of Guanajuato, which was accompanied by the killing of large numbers of peninsulars and *criollos*, led these groups to close ranks behind the viceregal government. The able leadership of Viceroy Francisco Javier Venegas and General Félix María Calleja (who succeeded Venegas as viceroy), soon had Hidalgo's Indian army on the run. In January, 1811, Calleja defeated Hidalgo outside Guadalajara, forcing the rebel leadership to flee northward, where they were eventually captured in March. Leadership of the rebellion devolved on José María Morelos, a mestizo priest whose organizational and political skills far surpassed Hidalgo's. Still, Morelos was unable to convince *criollos* to support the insurrection, which now became a mestizo movement for independence. By November, 1815, Morelos, too, had been captured, leaving only a handful of ill-equipped and undermanned guerrilla groups in the field.

THE TEXAS INSURRECTIONS, 1811–1813

From 1811 to 1813, the tensions and conflicts associated with the United States' westward movement and the Mexican War of Independence met in Texas and erupted in warfare. Aside from Anglo-American expansionist threats, foreign intrigue was in the air. As Spain succumbed to Napoleonic France, Spanish colonial officials were severely tested in trying to hold the empire together. French agents working to destabilize the colonies were soon joined by disgruntled colonials who began to conspire against Spain. Despite or because of its remote location, Texas did have something to offer the agents of change, a channel through which propaganda, money, arms, and, eventually, men could be introduced into New Spain from the United States. Correspondence between Commandant General Nemesio Salcedo and the governors of Texas during this time shows mutual concern over the problem.[10]

As New Spain destabilized following Father Hidalgo's declaration of war on "bad government," Crown officials in the northern provinces prepared for the rebel onslaught. At the end of 1810, the royalist forces rebelled against the governor of Nuevo Santander after orders arrived that they were to be sent to San Luis Potosí to fight the insurgents. In early January, 1811, as Governor Antonio Cordero of Coahuila arranged his seven hundred troops to meet an insurgent force of between seven thousand and eight thousand, his entire command mutinied and went over to the rebels. As insurgent forces were sent to Nuevo León, local officials there declared for Hidalgo.[11]

The news arriving in Béxar from the surrounding provinces in mid-January indicated the complete overthrow of royalist rule in the region. Governor Manuel Salcedo, who had previously received instructions to prepare a force to march against insurgents in the interior, called for calm and loyalty even as he ordered his troops to prepare for an expedition. Salcedo went so far as to call a meeting of Béxar's ecclesiastical, military, and civilian officials on January 18, 1811, to discuss the situation. The meeting did little to settle the situation, however, for on January 22, Juan Bautista de las Casas, a retired officer living in San Antonio, led a bloodless coup in which royalist officials were removed and all Spaniards arrested.[12]

Rebel fortunes collapsed about as quickly as they emerged, however. Dissatisfaction with Casas as governor combined with the continued loyalist leanings of many among Béxar's elite to produce a counterrevolutionary movement in February. The conspirators were led by Juan Manuel Zambrano, an ordained priest and native of Béxar whose family was among the wealthiest of the town. Working first among the most prominent citizens and then among disaffected military officers, he represented his movement to revolutionary leaders who had arrived in Béxar as wishing only the replacement of the incompetent Casas. Having gained the support of the troops, the counterrevolutionaries took an oath of loyalty to Ferdinand VII and appointed a governing junta of twelve in the early morning hours of March 2, 1811.[13]

The restoration in Texas succeeded because the insurgency was coming apart in the interior as well. General Joaquín Arredondo successfully invaded Nuevo Santander and began its restoration. At Saltillo Ignacio Allende removed Father Hidalgo from the rebellion's leadership and made plans for a retreat through Texas to the United States. Farther north, Governor Manuel Salcedo was liberated by a counterrevolutionary junta, which also convinced a retired lieutenant colonel and hacienda owner, Ignacio Elizondo, to lead loyalist forces. Taking control of Monclova, Elizondo learned of Allende's plans for the retreat to the United States and, on March 21, 1811, captured Allende, Hidalgo, and their insurgent chiefs. With the exception of pockets of resistance in Nuevo Santander, the northeastern provinces again came under the commandant general's orders.[14]

Not all insurrectionaries were disposed of, although Hidalgo, Allende, Casas, and numerous others lost their heads. One who managed to escape was Bernardo Gutiérrez de Lara. A native of Revilla, Nuevo Santander, who had early adopted Hidalgo's cause, he held a commission as revolutionary ambassador to the United States, where he met with Secretary of State James Monroe and President James Madison as well as French agents and other Spanish American revolutionaries in late 1811 and early 1812. With limited support from the U.S. government, Gutiérrez de Lara made his way back to the Texas border by way of New Orleans and Natchitoches, where he met Anglo Americans desirous of assisting Mexico in its struggle for liberty and others whose eyes may have looked no farther than liberating Texas for the United States. He had determined to recruit an army capable of taking Texas and revitalizing the rebellion.[15]

It was at Natchitoches, Louisiana, that Gutiérrez de Lara met Augustus Magee, a lieutenant in the U.S. army who had acquired an interest in Mexican affairs. In June 1812 Magee resigned his army commission and went to work for Gutiérrez de Lara as recruiter for the Republican Army of the North. Samuel Davenport, erstwhile Indian agent of the Spanish Crown in Nacogdoches, became quartermaster. Preparations continued through the early summer and, in August, 1812, Magee ordered the advance. One of the first victims of the invading force was Manuel Zambrano, who lost a shipment of wool he was taking to Louisiana. Confusion, rumors of an irrepressible force, and Davenport's assurances of good treatment resulted in the flight of those royalist troops who chose to remain loyal and the quick submission of Nacogdoches to the Republican Army of the North.

Magee and Gutiérrez reinforced their troops and sent propaganda to the other Texas settlements before taking their next step. At first they planned to head straight for Béxar, but reports of Salcedo's continued control of the town and the presence of only a small garrison at La Bahía led the Republican Army to redirect itself to the old presidio, which it occupied on November 7, 1812. When Salcedo and his military commander, Simón Herrera, marched their forces to La Bahía, the republicans found themselves under siege. When the governor refused to accept the invaders' requested terms for surrender — safety and pardons for all Texans who had embraced the republican cause and the withdrawal of the Republican Army from the province — the siege continued.

In spite of the early despair of the republicans, it was the royalists who were sapped of strength during the siege. After the pessimistic Magee died in early February, his place was taken by Samuel Kemper, who may have had a more optimistic outlook. Skirmishes between the two forces routinely favored the invaders, whose equipment and munitions were in superior shape and of better quality than that of the royalists. Disheartened, suffering increasing desertions, and unable to prevent resupply of the presidio, Governor Salcedo lifted the siege in mid-February and retired with what remained of his army to Béxar. There, about thirteen miles southeast of Béxar, he dug in at Salado Creek to await the republican advance, which came on March 29, 1813. The Battle of Salado left a hundred royalists dead, their baggage and cannon captured, and the road to Béxar open. On April 2, 1813, the royalist government of Texas surrendered unconditionally to the Republican Army of the North.

Success proved illusory for the republicans as they fell out among themselves. They were also dissatisfied with the form of government established in a constitution written by Gutiérrez de Lara and Tejanos without input from the Anglo Americans. Furloughs granted to Kemper and other officers led to deteriorating morale and discipline, as did the arrival of new recruits whose loyalty was questionable. By the beginning of August, Tejanos and Anglo Americans had determined that the blame for the new republic's ills lay with Gutiérrez de Lara, who was forced to resign and leave Texas. His place was taken by José Álvarez de Toledo, a native of Cuba who had met Gutiérrez de Lara in the United States and shared an interest in liberating Mexico from Spain.

Toledo had little time to regroup. General Arredondo, who had successfully campaigned against insurgents in Nuevo Santander, mustered an army on the Río Grande and marched on Béxar in early August. Toledo decided to meet the royalist army outside the town and marched his two divisions, one composed of Anglo Americans and the other of Mexicans and Indians, on the road to Laredo. On August 18, 1813, the two armies met southwest of the Medina River, and Arredondo, having outflanked Toledo, led the royalists to a decisive victory. The rout was such that Colonel Elizondo chased the remnants of the Republican Army beyond the Sabine, killed numerous rebels, and captured hundreds of men, women, and children.[16]

The royalist victory in Texas was complete. Despite the almost complete ruin of the province — Nacogdoches was virtually abandoned; Béxar and La Bahía were subject to constant Indian depredations; ranches were deserted and herds either destroyed or taken to safety in the interior — the royalist governors managed to retain control of the province and repulse or dissipate incursions by filibusters, revolutionaries, and French exiles. Independence came to Texas when it arrived for the rest of Mexico, with Iturbide's triumph under the Plan of Iguala in 1821.[17]

SOURCES OF DISAFFECTION

Events in Texas from 1811 through 1813 clearly indicate that disaffection with Spanish rule had existed in Texas at the time of Hidalgo's revolt in 1810. Crown authority, which had begun to increase some thirty years earlier, often conflicted with local interests and irritated some elements in Béxar. A few years prior to the Casas revolt, Governors Antonio Cordero and Manuel Salcedo had introduced local measures to regulate town life and reduce contraband.[18] While the governors attempted to keep Tejanos from trading illegally with Louisiana, however, Spanish officers remained deeply involved in contraband. In 1808, an anonymous informant told the viceroy that Commandant Herrera was involved in a profitable trade of Texas horses and mules for finished goods. The strength of Herrera's ties with the French were such, according to the informant, "that anyone wishing portraits of Napoleon and his field marshals should visit Herrera's own quarters where an assortment would be found."[19] Such contradictory behavior could not but have helped create resentment toward provincial officials.

Another and perhaps more irritating measure of the town's elite was Cordero's *ayuntamiento* (town council) reform. The six governors who held office between 1772 and 1808 all viewed the council as a strong-willed, uncooperative group of ill-qualified yokels. Needless to say, more than one governor called for the council's abolition or its reduction to manageable size from the six *regidores*, two *alcaldes*, and a *procurador* it had had since its founding. It was not until Cordero's administration, however, that a legal opinion was obtained allowing the governor to modify the council as he saw fit, and Cordero lost no time in reducing membership to two *alcaldes*, two *regidores*, and a *procurador*. Disturbed by the abridgment of local prerogatives, a group of town leaders sent a secret complaint against the action to the Audiencia.[20]

Some in Béxar resented the governor's increasing authority. While there is no evidence that Béxar was divided into distinct political factions, some members of the community's oldest elite families were perhaps the most hostile. Some Canary Islander descendants, particularly from the Travieso and Arocha families, who had traditionally exerted undue influence in local affairs, resented the governors and their activities. But it is also true that they were rebuffed by members of their own families who had established cordial relations with the governors. Another prominent family, the Menchacas, also included controversial members who played roles on both sides of the two uprisings that affected the town. The Zambranos also had their share of troublesome family members, particularly Manuel, who had been banished from the province after complaints by the citizenry. Nevertheless, he later served as a counterrevolutionary leader.[21] In general, the close-knit and isolated nature of Béxar society meant that most families were related and that rivalries often took place among kinfolk, albeit sometimes distant ones.

So while it is difficult to identify the branches of the specific families who were unhappy with Spanish rule, it seems they did exist, both at the political and the personal levels. Governor Salcedo, for example, found it necessary to warn the townspeople not to pay attention to the anti-Spanish rhetoric being spread by some.[22] And it is clear that at least some of those who acted against Spanish rule did so with great personal bitterness and a desire for vengeance. Indeed, one of the most cold-blooded acts of the period was the murder of Governor Salcedo, auxiliary-troop Commander Simón Herrera, and a dozen other Spaniards taken prisoner in Béxar. According to Father Feliciano Francisco Vela and Guadalupe Caso, who escaped to the royalists with news:

> On the fourth of this month, Governor Manuel de Salcedo, Captain Arrambide, and all the other leaders and officers . . . were executed. They had their throats cut, their anguished requests for spiritual comfort denied. And, in order to perform this sacrifice, they were all stripped and Mr. Salcedo had his tongue taken out. They were all scalped and not permitted burial. That

they might not be interred, Indians were left to guard that unfortunate place.[23]

According to one version, Salcedo and Herrera were condemned to death for having participated in Hidalgo's capture and for luring a local rebel, Captain José Menchaca, to his death, but as the above account suggests, the execution was unduly violent. Another account argues that the Spaniards were executed by Béxar militia commander Antonio Delgado in revenge for the murders of his father and brother.[24] While the specific motivations cannot be confirmed, it is probable that the killings resulted from the combination of a private act of revenge and a general antagonism toward Spanish rule among a small group.

THE CAUTIOUS MAJORITY

It seems that considerable friction existed in Béxar between Spanish officials and local residents, but evidence does not support the idea that the town was a seething revolutionary center waiting to rise against Spain's rule. The thoughts and actions of the local population were cautious, complex, and aimed at preserving their interests.

While many actions of the governor and his officials had no doubt irritated and offended the residents of Béxar, most probably would not have sanctioned the actions against Salcedo and his officials. The reduction of the *cabildo*'s size, for example, was unprecedented and outraged many, but by itself it probably did not foster revolutionary and separatist feelings.[25] Indeed, the citizens of Béxar had a long history of opposition to governors' actions and they usually sought relief by appealing to the courts. In most cases, they sought compromises that preserved local prerogatives.[26]

The contraband and corruption issues were also long-standing in the province. Tejanos had traded illegally with Louisiana since early in the eighteenth century, and Crown officials paid only lip service to fighting contraband. Some governors battled more efficiently than did others, and those who acted effectively usually alienated the local population; but most Bexareños found ways to sidestep Spanish officials.

A significant group in Béxar was unhappy with Spanish rule, but most Tejanos remained cautious and seemed reluctant to unconditionally throw in their lot with ill-defined revolutionary movements led by outsiders like Casas, Gutiérrez, and Toledo. These leaders, being unfamiliar to the local population, failed to inspire confidence in the residents and many, perhaps most, Bexareños watched developments closely and changed sides whenever necessary to protect themselves and their community.

The Casas revolt is illustrative. When Casas seconded Hidalgo's revolutionary call in Béxar, he rallied a small group of sympathizers, but they turned against him and deposed him when events suggested that the revolution was not likely to triumph.[27] Casas was not from Béxar, nor was he a long-standing (or influential) member of Béxar's social elite; thus, some may have suspected his interest in the matter. Indeed, the junta that removed Casas took great pains to regain favor with the Spanish authorities. In a communication dated April 28, 1811, the junta expressed its concern that the official government report on the capture of Hidalgo and the crushing of the revolt in Coahuila had not acknowledged the five hundred troops sent by Béxar in support of that goal. The same soldiers who had initially supported Casas willingly collaborated in putting down the Hidalgo revolt. The junta explained its about-face by saying that the military uprising had resulted from the hysteria occasioned by the continual arrival of distressing news from other provinces. Bexareños did not want to support lost causes but, rather, hoped to preserve and protect the town's interests.[28]

Even Gavino Delgado and Francisco Travieso, Casas's two primary civilian supporters named in testimony concerning the insurrection in Béxar, switched sides when the counterrevolt came along. Delgado not only became a member of the junta that deposed Casas, but also was praised for playing an important role in removing the rebel leader. Although Travieso remained under suspicion and was removed from the province after Governor Salcedo's return, he had been selected by the junta as senior *alcalde* immediately after Casas's overthrow.[29] Both men supported the insurrection when it seemed that victory against the Spanish might be possible, but quickly backed away when success seemed doubtful.

Events at La Bahía substantiate the view that Tejanos acted primarily to protect local interests in these increasingly difficult times. Lieutenant Luciano García remained loyal to the Crown and was forced to flee when Casas's emissaries arrived to take over the town. José Agabo de Ayala, who replaced García, cooperated with the insurgents but could not muster support from the settlement's prominent citizens. Father Miguel Martínez, presidial chaplain, Postmaster Bernardo Amado, and Manuel de la Concha, royal monopoly administrator, led a resistance against Casas that was coming to a head when the counterrevolt in San Antonio restored loyalists to power.[30]

Similar strategic considerations also influenced the actions of those who supported the Gutiérrez de Lara–led invasion of Texas in 1812–1813. Two Bexareños caught bringing seditious material into San Antonio in the fall of 1812, for example, believed they were saving the town from destruction by preparing the citizenry for the filibusters' arrival.[31] An Anglo-American traveler at the time found "everything in confusion, every person alarmed for the security of his person and property. Officers spoke publicly against the Captain General [Don Nemecio]. The Indians had at that time killed fifty-four persons, had stolen 5,000 sheep and 10,000 head of horses and mules."[32] Such conditions created considerable fear that the Spanish forces in Béxar could not hope to protect the citizenry. Bexareños perhaps accepted the invaders out of fear rather than sympathy for their cause.

Military participation during the Gutiérrez-Magee episode rested on equally pragmatic grounds. At first, Governor Salcedo managed to maintain the loyalty of the local population. While there were numerous individual desertions, Salcedo's forces did not go over to the rebels en masse. In fact, Salcedo marched his army to La Bahía, where the Gutiérrez-Magee forces were encamped, and lay siege to the town for four months. The governor eventually retreated to Béxar and surrendered to the filibusters after the battle at Salado Creek.

The soldiery, with families to maintain, was confronted with the choice of becoming prisoners of war or joining the ranks of the Republican Army of the North.[33] It is not surprising, then, that the Republican Army found a contradictory ambiance upon entering San Antonio in April, 1813. Though local citizens accepted their presence and often cooperated with them, they did not seem enthusiastic or particularly anxious to embrace the republicans.[34] It is quite possible that residents of Béxar saw the large presence of Anglo Americans as an indication of imminent U.S. occupation, as had happened in Louisiana, and that preservation of property depended on cooperation with the new regime.

Similar attitudes played a role in the acceptance of the filibusters at Nacogdoches and La Bahía. When Captain Bernardino Montero and Juan Manuel Zambrano attempted to retreat from Nacogdoches with the local militia, they were challenged by a militia captain who declared that they would not abandon their homes and families in the face of an invading force whose intentions were not known. At La Bahía the presidial company and citizenry spent the day before the Republican Army's arrival in chapel, hoping for some miracle. When the filibusters continued their approach, the soldiery abandoned the fort while the residents looked on.[35] Magee did not mince words after taking La Bahía: "we are differently received in this country to what we expected and the treachery of the people is beyond belief."[36]

Testimony from individuals escaping Béxar in the days following the surrender to the American force suggests that many, perhaps most, people acted to preserve themselves rather than to support one cause or the other. Guillermo Saldaña, a servant in the employ of one of the Spanish officers taken prisoner, declared that, while the royal troops from outside the province had been disarmed, the local military units remained under arms. "The day before their entry into Béxar, said troops and militiamen . . . and many women went to Mission Concepción to incorporate themselves to the said Americans."[37] A priest and two civilians who escaped soon thereafter reported on the lukewarm nature of the military companies' support for the invaders. In particular, an expeditionary force of five hundred that had intended to march south on Presidio del Río Grande had been reduced to three hundred men, half of them Anglo Americans, because of the neutrality of the Texas companies.[38]

Ignacio Elizondo, who led the vanguard of the royalist army that reconquered Béxar, reported that more than three hundred soldiers, residents, women, and children had escaped to his camp shortly after his arrival. Elizondo continued, describing a phenomenon similar to that exhibited by the population earlier in favor of the filibusters: "the rest of the citizenry has not come out because of the guards maintained by the rebels. Yet, in spite of the guards, I believe that the whole town will leave today, for now they are all disabused and have recognized their error."[39]

AFTERMATH: PARDONS AND RECONCILIATION

With the defeat of the insurgent forces, the authorities set about reestablishing local confidence in Spanish rule. They treated unrepentant insurgents harshly, but left the door open to those who wanted to make peace with Spanish authority. Elizondo, for example, reported sparing the lives of more than one hundred men, including soldiers and civilians, and an equal number of women. Arredondo, however, executed hundreds of men in the aftermath of the battle and chased many into Louisiana. He then turned his attention to restoring confidence in the government and containing only clearly dangerous individuals. A general pardon excepted only four local men — Francisco Arocha, Francisco Ruiz, Juan Veramendi, and Vicente Travieso. The pardon, a tool widely used in other parts of New Spain to pacify rebels, proved effective in quieting the province. Bexareños also moved to lessen tensions by requesting that families and individuals still considered dangerous or suspicious be removed from Texas.[40] The authorities recognized and distinguished between those who accepted Spanish rule and those who remained firmly rebellious. In the fall of 1813 one individual asked that property confiscated from his father, who had joined the insurgents, be given to him, since he had joined the royalist army and had seen action in Texas twice. The petition was granted. Fernando Veramendi, the town council's choice for teacher in a new primary school, not only had collaborated with the insurgents but had acted as a member of the insurgent junta. Arrested for having provided letters of recommendation for the insurgent José Álvarez de Toledo, Erasmo Seguín refused to accept a pardon, claiming he had provided the letters under duress and wished to be exonerated. The authorities found him to be honest and released him on his own recognizance. Ultimately cleared of all charges, Seguín retook his place as one of Béxar's most prominent citizens.[41] He later represented Texas at the Mexican Constitutional Congress in 1823–1824 and remained postmaster and quartermaster until 1835.

Bexareños quickly regained a measure of control over their affairs, most important, in the institution that represented local prerogatives, the *ayuntamiento*. In December, 1813, the appointed *alcaldes* and *procurador* elected their successors, and the following year a council of four *regidores* ruled in Béxar. The council itself selected commissioners for the town's four wards. In the restored elections, old patterns reemerged, with governors having to reject some elected officials on the grounds that they were often out of town on business or were illiterate, among other reasons.[42] Perhaps the most important indicator of returning stability was the governor's declaration in September, 1815, that "the *ayuntamiento*, as is my understanding from what my predecessor told me and the acceptance of various of its actions by the Commandant General, should be considered a legal body entitled to all rights and privileges."[43]

Other local initiatives show that the community reasserted itself beginning in the mid-1810s. During 1815, the town council once again organized the town's official religious feasts, celebrated since the mid-eighteenth century.[44] On February 1, 1816, the municipal council addressed a grievance to the interim governor, Mariano Varela, concerning the townspeople's provisioning of meat and firewood to the troops without payment. The corporation pleaded that Indian hostilities and scarcity of livestock made life impossible for many and that the government therefore should assume the burden of supplying the garrison. A year and a half later the council protested charges made against their honor and their loyalty to the government of Spain.[45] "Since 1813," the council declared, "the only people inhabiting this province were those who, after undergoing a strict examination, were shown to be free from the ugly crime of revolution, together with some former insurgents who had been forgiven because they had not done much damage."[46]

In spite of desperate and almost chaotic conditions in Texas, and Béxar in particular, the province remained squarely in royalist hands. On numerous occasions, troops had to be sent to the abandoned eastern part of the province and to the coast, where filibusters and French exiles were attempting to establish themselves. Troops also had to be sent out frequently in pursuit of Indians who committed depredations at both Béxar and La Bahía. Surprisingly, especially in light of the fact that the troops' pay remained in arrears throughout the entire period and that they received almost no supplies, they executed their orders with remarkable efficiency. In 1817, near La Bahía, Governor Antonio Martínez defeated a band of filibusters under Henry Perry, a participant in the Gutiérrez-Magee Expedition and, in 1819, he sent a force of 550 men under Colonel Ignacio Pérez to drive James Long's men out of Nacogdoches.[47]

When independence came to Texas in the summer of 1821, it arrived clothed in reserve and respectability. Béxar supported it only after news arrived in San Antonio of Commandant General Arredondo's acceptance of the Plan of Iguala at Monterrey on June 3, 1821. In mid-July the royalist governor, Antonio Martínez, led the military and civilian establishment in the oath to the new Mexican nation with all the decorum and ceremony that might have attended the celebration of a victory by the king's arms.[48]

CONCLUSION

The events of 1811–1813 reveal that Tejanos faced a dilemma that would remain a central theme over the next forty years. On the one hand, they had to contend with the turbulence associated with anti-government sentiment in New Spain; on the other, they had to weigh that dissatisfaction with the potential problems connected to the United States' westward movement toward their land. During the years in question, Spanish troops and Anglo-American filibusters occupied Texas. Both posed a threat to local interests and freedom of action, and Tejanos dealt with these difficult times in highly pragmatic and self-interested ways. Though Tejanos certainly had views about whether Mexico should be independent of Spain, and those views naturally varied, their actions in relation to such discussions reflected local imperatives. The same can be said of their reactions to the filibuster invasion. Most residents of Béxar probably had legitimate complaints about Spanish rule, but that certainly did not translate into support for a U.S. takeover of the region. Throughout 1811–1813, long-standing loyalties, fears, and grave uncertainties created caution and an interest in self-preservation as guiding principles for many. Buffeted by forces largely outside their control, Bexareños learned to place a priority on their local needs. Not surprisingly, they later became strong supporters of Mexican federalism until their loyalties were once again tested by the Anglo American–led rebellion against Mexican sovereignty in Texas.

THREE

UNDER THE MEXICAN FLAG
Andrés Tijerina

I
n 1821, Tejanos became citizens of
an independent Mexican nation. During the next fifteen years, they struggled to protect and advance their political and socioeconomic interests
within a continually shifting environment. Mexico had to redefine itself,
and Tejanos had to find their place within the new definition without
abandoning their traditions. At the same time, Mexico's and Texas's relations with the United States became increasingly troubled, and this had
to be sorted out. All of these realities affected Tejano communities, which
devised active strategies for protecting their interests in these complicated
and sometimes treacherous times.[1]

Texas had been established initially by the Spanish colonial administrators of New Spain as a buffer against encroachment from the northeast.
Its colonizers, the Tejanos, thus entered the region to defend this northern
boundary. On this fringe of the Mexican provinces, Tejanos developed a
distinctive culture and economic imperatives that differed from those of
their countrymen to the south. Texas had vast herds of mustangs and
longhorn cattle that defined Tejano interests, and Tejanos traded directly
overland with the United States. Texas's political and legislative perspectives often conflicted greatly with those of other provinces in the interior
of Mexico. Thus, Tejano traditions and interests not only set them apart
culturally and politically, but also caused continuing tensions with the
more conservative forces in Mexico City.

SETTLERS ON THE *FRONTERA*

The Tejano experience made their full integration into the new Mexican nation a difficult proposition from the very outset. Texas's frontier life and its border with the United States gave the region a special character that was not easily understood in the provinces to the south. During the Spanish era, Tejanos established and protected the northern regions against foreign intrusion. They acted in the tradition of their Spanish ancestors, who had used buffer zones, or *fronteras*, for defensive purposes in their reconquest of the Iberian peninsula from the Moors. In the northern borderlands, Spanish authorities had been suspicious of potential French, English, Russian, and, later, U.S. encroachment on their vast possessions, and they founded communities to consolidate their claims. In fact, French incursions into the region during the late seventeenth and the eighteenth centuries instigated Spanish expeditions of exploration into Texas. By the close of the 1700s, Texas had emerged as a vital defensive frontier region, which Herbert E. Bolton describes as "almost wholly military."[2]

The rationale for the defensive province was pointed out by influential Saltillo statesman Miguel Ramos Arizpe, in the early nineteenth century. He warned that Mexico should secure its hold of Texas, "particularly in the vicinity of the United States."[3] In official reports, he expressed a common Mexican preoccupation with Indian depredations and Anglo-American invasion from the United States. By this time, the name Texas had became synonymous with the word *frontera*.

Throughout the colonial period, officials in Mexico City strengthened the Texas frontier by establishing presidios, or military forts, in the province. While the total population in the province never exceeded four thousand, several communities established the Spanish presence in Texas, including San Antonio de Béxar, La Bahía (later known as Goliad), and Nacogdoches. When Mexico became independent, the government again promoted military settlements and formal civilian colonization in Texas, but without much success. As official correspondence from Saltillo noted, "The government is lacking the funds to send the four hundred farmers requested . . . unfortunately not one Mexican has applied for an impresario contract."[4] Nevertheless, Mexican settlers established the settlement of Victoria. While Texas never attracted large numbers of Mexican immigrants, the communities that did emerge provided the necessary presence to legitimize Spain and Mexico's claim on the region.

The populations in these communities established their own identity and, though small in number, maintained a certain demographic stability. Tejano communities initially formed as a result of immigration from Mexico, but later growth resulted from the marriage of presidial soldiers to local women. Most Tejanos were descendants of presidial troops, and they generally displayed a sense of responsibility to their Spanish nationality. This dedication was articulated in the memoirs of an old Bexareño, José María Rodríguez, who said, "My ancestors, both on my father's and mother's side were military men and all of them engaged in the service of their country at some time."[5]

Isolated for decades on the remote frontier, Tejanos developed a character consistent with their isolation and their sense of purpose. In keeping with Spanish colonial policy, early Tejanos saw themselves as defenders of their province against intrusion from the east. They entered the Province of Texas as *ciudadanos armados*, or soldier-citizens, and they regularly reported their movements and activities to administrators in Mexico City. They submitted frequent censuses enumerating Tejano assets and settlement efforts. Unlike Anglo-American frontiersmen, Tejanos did not develop an individualistic approach to frontier enterprise, but instead pursued their mission on the frontier with a strong sense of obligation and community. Ironically, their sense of duty tended to alienate them not only from foreigners but, eventually, from their own countrymen as well.

The defensive frontier experience produced a distinctive Tejano way of life that seemed different even to Mexicans from the south. While visiting Texas in 1828, a Mexican officer named José María Sánchez noted:

> The Mexicans who live here are a very humble people, and perhaps their intentions are good, but because of their education and environment they are ignorant not only of the customs of our great cities, but even of the occurrences of our Revolution, excepting a few persons who have heard about them. Accustomed to the continued trade with the North Americans, they have adopted their customs and habits, and one may say truly that they are not Mexicans except by birth, for they even speak Spanish with a marked incorrectness.[6]

Other Mexicans developed a condescending attitude toward the isolated Tejano. One report in 1833, for example, quoted a prominent citizen of Saltillo as speaking in a "tone of contempt" about "the poor, out-of-the-world" frontier of Texas, adding that he "could not live happily in such banishment."[7]

The decades on the remote frontier molded Tejano culture, and some of the most obvious effects were in the language. Another Mexican traveler to Texas in 1834 made a strong recommendation that Spanish be taught in Texas schools, "otherwise this language shall become null, as already little other than English is spoken in that part of the republic."[8] He might have added that the frontier Spanish was even becoming quaint. The official correspondence of Tejanos was replete with evidence of non-standard spelling and colloquialisms. Some of these terms were simple cases of misspelling, but others reflected natural etymological changes. Tejanos continued to use some words that had been dropped from common usage in Spain after the 1500s, such as *ansi* (*así*, "thus") or *vide* (*yo vi*, "I saw"). Other words were adapted, reflecting the initial development of a frontier lexicon. The word *mesta*, the designation for the Spanish stockmen's corporation, became *mesteña* for the Tejano wild cattle and horses found on the prairies of Texas.

Mexicans may have looked down on Tejano culture and language, but Tejanos were a proud people who considered their contributions important to the Mexican nation. Tejanos believed that Mexicans of the interior owed them a debt of gratitude for defending the frontier. Frequent *memorias,* or official petitions, to the federal government during these years made clear that Tejanos wanted their sacrifices and loyalty acknowledged. They continually asked for special consideration as frontier families who had for so long shed their blood to defend Mexico. In one petition, Tejanos demanded special legislation "for their worthy status as inhabitants of the frontier, who have undergone sacrifices and risks unknown to the people of the interior, and for which the latter are indebted to the former."[9]

Town and land defined Tejanos' sense of community. These two institutions were linked, since land grants had been the king's reward to settlers who founded municipalities. As Tejanos occupied their ranches, the municipality strengthened its outward grasp on the surrounding region. In time, the hostile environment was transformed into the defensive community fortress, which encompassed the legacy of land and town of their Spanish ancestors. They provided for the daily entertainment, defense, education, and farming needs of Tejanos. And their lands and towns helped define family and kinship ties, their basic form of social organization.

The frontier that had made the Tejanos so dedicated to defending Mexico from foreign intrusion bred, ironically, the very factors that eventually alienated many Tejanos from their own government in Mexico City. Their commission as defenders of the frontier made them a hardy, self-sufficient folk who became used to solving matters in their own way. In protecting their towns and lands, Tejanos understood they could not rely on support from the south and they became accustomed to defending themselves from Indians and other hostile forces. With the formation of the Mexican

Republic, Tejanos quickly came to realize that they would have to continue to protect their own interests as the new Mexican state began to cut into their autonomy as Tejanos.

TEJANOS AND THE MEXICAN REPUBLIC

During the eighteenth century, Tejanos protected community interests by fiercely defending local autonomy. This struggle for autonomy was also a constant theme during Texas's fifteen years as part of the Mexican Republic. Anglo-American expansion, Indian wars, and a scant population stirred the fears of statesmen in Mexico City, who felt that only by incorporating Texas more firmly into the Mexican nation could the region be successfully held and populated. In the end, they cast Texas as a department under Coahuila in the single state of Coahuila y Texas, a decision that Tejanos perceived as a direct threat to local interests.

Initially, it seemed that Tejanos would maintain their autonomy as a province under the Mexican Republic, but events in 1823 subverted the idea. In that year, the government of Emperor Agustín de Iturbide, Mexico's first leader after independence, collapsed. This left the nation in disarray, operating as a series of virtually autonomous provinces, until a call went out from Mexico City, known as the Plan of Casa Mata, urging the individual provinces to participate in the election of a national congress.[10]

After a short period of political uncertainty, Mexico City authorized Texas, Nuevo León, and Coahuila to establish permanent provincial deputations to participate in the drawing up of a new federal constitution. Elections on September 8, 1823, for Texas's Provincial Deputation resulted in the selection of José Antonio Saucedo as new political chief. Other members of the Deputation included José María Zambrano, Ramón Músquiz, Juan José Hernández, Miguel Arciniega, Barón de Bastrop, and Mariano Rodríguez. The next day, the Deputation selected Erasmo Seguín to represent Texas at the national Congress in Mexico City, where he went with a full slate of instructions.[11]

Among Seguín's instructions was to protect Texas's autonomy as much as possible, and he initially worked for establishing the region as a territory attached to the national government. Seguín at first felt that only Mexico City could provide the resources necessary to aid Texas financially, but by April, 1824, he had changed his mind, after seeing the intrigue and instability of Mexico's national politics. Since Texas was too sparsely populated and poor to stand alone as a state, the only other viable option was to join in a union with Coahuila. Though Seguín did not think this solution would benefit Texas very much, he reluctantly accepted and managed to obtain the national government's agreement to Texas's right to statehood when its population increased sufficiently. On May 7, 1824, the Congress in Mexico City decreed the creation of the State of Coahuila y Texas.[12]

Texas no longer had a governor and, as a mere department, had only one deputy in the Coahuila y Texas legislature. On hearing the news, many Tejanos protested vehemently, but to no avail. The new state legislature in Saltillo convened in August, 1824, and ordered the disbanding of the Texas Provincial Deputation and the immediate transfer of its archives to Saltillo. Tejanos and members of the Deputation like José Antonio de la Garza, Pedro de la Garza, José Sandoval, Fernando Rodríguez, and Manuel Yturri Castillo refused to go along and defied Saltillo until the end of the summer. To placate Tejano leaders, Miguel Ramos Arizpe wrote them a long, conciliatory letter on September 15, 1824, arguing the advantages of union with Coahuila. Ramos Arizpe pointed out that as part of a state they would continue to stand as "free men and owners of the lands that they have conquered."[13] Arguing that the union could no longer be resisted, conservative members of the Béxar *ayuntamiento,* led by Alcalde Gaspar Flores, seconded Ramos Arizpe and enjoined the more dissatisfied members of the Provincial Deputation to concede. Furthermore, in an earlier private letter, Erasmo Seguín characterized those Tejanos who objected as men "of little enlightenment," not as wise as the Navarros and the Ruizes. The Texas Provincial Deputation finally acquiesced, but not before revealing how deeply Tejanos felt about the political autonomy of their region.[14]

By October, 1824, Tejanos had recovered their composure enough to send their one representative, Barón de Bastrop, to Saltillo, where he struggled to establish the position of *jefe político,* or subgovernor, to be located in Béxar. Despite the fact that the national government had authorized Texas to have the position, the new state congress had abolished the job in its first meeting in August. But by building a coalition with politically sympathetic deputies from Parras, Bastrop managed to get the office reestablished. During the next few years, the Tejano state representatives continued to develop a fruitful relationship with the Parras delegation and gained additional appointments, including new judgeships, in Texas. By 1834, Tejanos had also managed to increase their legislative delegation to three, one for each of the districts of Béxar, Nacogdoches, and Brazos.[15]

Tejanos also had to fight to maintain the integrity of their town council, historically the most important symbol of their autonomy and defender of local interests. Toward the end of 1824, for example, the new constituent congress in Saltillo had reduced Béxar's *ayuntamiento* to half its original size. The issue became a bone of contention again in 1829, when Béxar submitted a petition requesting an additional *alcalde*. Prepared for the Béxar town council by Juan Nepomuceno Seguín and Luciano Navarro, the document demanded the additional *alcalde* and noted that Béxar had traditionally been a provincial capital and now needed a second *alcalde* to accommodate the workload and population growth. Béxar never received a favorable response.

Clearly, while Tejanos recognized the need to work within the parameters of the new Mexican nation, they did not accept the legitimacy of their subordinate status to the distant capitals of Saltillo and Mexico City without protest. They believed that Mexicans to the south were "men who are ignorant of the political state of the Department of Tejas. Men who know neither her topographical situation nor her class of inhabitants; neither in her hinterland nor on her borders." Tejanos declared that "the government cannot be convinced that the Department of Tejas is not just a newborn population which lacks the strength to govern itself."[16]

Tejanos came to understand that, since Mexican state and national leaders had little regard for their political traditions, they had to be active in the defense and promotion of their local interests; they could not allow these leaders to ignore them.

A TEJANO ECONOMIC VISION

Tejanos insisted on their political autonomy because they understood that their economic destiny depended on local control. Since the 1820s, Tejanos had seen their prosperity intricately connected to the growth of capitalism and Anglo-American colonization, both of which led eventually to the development of a liberal legislative agenda. In fact, Tejano economic interests often flew in the face of broader national considerations in Mexico.

After the establishment of the State of Coahuila y Texas, Tejanos took their liberal agenda to Saltillo. The first Tejano legislative representative, Barón de Bastrop, collaborated with the liberal political faction from Parras led by José María Viesca, a member of the Coahuila y Texas legislature, and Agustín Viesca, the state senator in Mexico City.[17] Tejanos, and their Viesca allies, promoted a federalist form of government and capitalist development in the province.

Tejanos argued that they should be free to develop their economic advantage, including uninhibited commercial interaction with the United States. Tejano economic connections to eastern markets were well established. They had sent their cattle to markets in Louisiana for almost a century, but now a new economic possibility had emerged. The U.S. cotton kingdom had moved westward and was now on the Texas border. Tejanos saw their future prosperity tied to a maintenance of open commerce, development of the cotton industry, and freedom to mold their land and labor policies locally.

A central element in the Tejano effort to attract cotton planters and other Anglo-American settlers to Texas was local control over the public domain, a right guaranteed to the states under the Mexican Constitution of 1824. Working with their liberal Viesca allies, Tejanos managed to obtain favorable land policies in Saltillo through the passage of the State Colonization Law in 1825.

Previously administered by the national government, management of the colonization program now fell to Coahuiltejanos (citizens of the State of Coahuila y Texas). They passed laws to protect landowners from creditors as a way of attracting cotton planters from the U.S. South, where competition for land made the Texas prairies all the more attractive. Tejanos passed other laws based on a Spanish colonial practice known as *denuncio*, which allowed settlers to claim unsurveyed land, and included a ten-year tax exemption as further incentive to colonize. Tejanos even appointed Anglo Americans as land agents to facilitate the application process and attract more settlers. And to further accommodate their neighbors' cultural differences, the Tejano colonization program allowed Anglo-American colonists to retain their Protestant faith as "Christians" rather than specifically as "Catholics."[18]

Capitalist expansion also required the development of ports on the Gulf coast. In the state legislature, Barón de Bastrop made this a central issue, as had Erasmo Seguín before him in the national Congress in Mexico City. Eventually, the state legislature designated Galveston a port, but it was never developed under the Mexican flag. Instead, Anglo-American merchants and settlers engaged in illicit trade and passenger transport at several unofficial ports until the national government sent customs officials, which action contributed to the outbreak of the Texas rebellion.[19]

The final element of the Tejano economic platform was to secure a viable source of labor. In this effort, Tejanos also collaborated with sympathetic representatives of the Viesca faction in the state legislature to secure favorable decrees. In one case, Tejanos obtained an exemption for Texas from a national slave emancipation decree issued by President Vicente Guerrero in 1829. But their most effective maneuver was in the state legislature. There they were able to rephrase a clause in the colonization law to assure that slavery was only vaguely referred to. Indeed, in one clause, slavery was allowed under the guise of "indentured servitude." This was clearly done to placate Anglo-American cotton planters.[20]

TEJANO POLITICS AND
THE CENTRALIST THREAT

While Tejanos worked to promote colonization and economic development, Mexico's political situation remained unstable. Having only recently established itself as an independent republic, Mexico was still in the midst of a struggle to define its political system and divide power equitably. Two major political philosophies emerged in the 1820s. The centralists favored placing power in the national government in Mexico City, while the federalists hoped to distribute power to state governments. Existing on the periphery of the Mexican state, and having already felt the wrath of central authority, Tejanos naturally aligned themselves with the federalists, led by revolutionary war veterans Guadalupe Victoria, Vicente Guerrero, and Lorenzo de Zavala, and the liberal Constitution of 1824.

During most of the 1820s, federalists struggled to implement the liberal constitution, but by 1829 severe political strains led to a conservative centralist coup against President Guerrero; this coup initiated a chain of events that deeply affected Texas. Rebel leader Anastacio Bustamante issued the Plan of Jalapa, which removed the Mexican president from office and brought a centralist administration to power.[21] Texas's two delegates to the state legislature, Rafael Antonio Manchola and José María Balmaceda, immediately opposed the new administration. Like the Tejano representatives before them, they supported a liberal agenda. But their hostility to Bustamante carried a political price; they came under bitter attack in the legislature and conservatives succeeded in having them publicly denounced by citizens in Saltillo. Finally, Balmaceda and fellow liberal deputy from Parras, Ignacio Sendejas, were officially censured and expelled from the legislature on September 18, 1830.[22]

In response to this expulsion, Balmaceda and Manchola immediately issued a call for public support. Although their opponents in Saltillo charged that the representatives from Texas did not merit the public's confidence, the Tejano deputies requested support from their home *criollos*. The city councils of Béxar, Goliad, and San Felipe de Austin responded immediately, proclaiming that only the appropriate constituents could determine a deputy's merit. The legislative session ended before this particular dispute became any more critical, but the expulsion was just another resentment Tejanos accumulated and helped confirm their belief that rulers to the south could not act in their interests.[23]

The most important immediate effect on Texas of the change in the Mexican presidency was the rise to power of people deeply suspicious of the United States and the Anglo-American colonists in Texas. By this time, authorities in Mexico viewed the increasing numbers of Anglo Americans in Texas as a direct threat to the nation, an opinion affirmed by General Manuel Mier y Terán, the military commander of Mexico's northeastern provinces. In a report to President Anastacio Bustamante, Mier y Terán noted the volume of legal and illegal Anglo-American immigration into Texas. The general charged that Anglo Americans not only imported slaves illegally, but also violated Mexican laws regarding the courts and religious practices.[24]

Bustamante's minister of foreign relations, Lucas Alamán, used Mier y Terán's recommendations to frame the Law of April 6, 1830, which, in effect, prohibited further emigration from the United States. To enforce this provision, the law also specified the establishment of military installations in the heart of the Anglo-American colonies in Central and East Texas. The law welcomed European colonists but absolutely forbade further importation of slaves. Another important provision terminated any impresario contracts still unfulfilled at the time the law was published. Finally, these same Saltillo conservative deputies prohibited foreigners from practicing retail trade. Both measures were aimed directly at the Anglo-American colonists in Texas.

As Tejanos struggled to overcome the detrimental effects of the Law of April 6, 1830, others throughout Mexico raised their voices against centralist rule. General Antonio López de Santa Anna endorsed a liberal proclamation against the Bustamante administration and proceeded to overthrow the conservative president on December 9, 1832.

Tejanos responded with support and, ten days later, the leading citizens of Béxar met in a convention and drafted a *memoria* to the state legislature protesting the previously enacted centralist actions, including the law of 1830. Intent on defending Tejano interests and autonomy, forty residents of Béxar, including many younger men like Juan Nepomuceno Seguín, Ambrosio Rodríguez, and José María Balmaceda, attended. They complained first of the national government's constant intervention in the state colonization program. Specifically, they argued that the Law of April 6, 1830 excluded useful "capitalists" from moving into Texas. The law also interfered with the growing Santa Fé trade, which was largely in the hands of "norte-americanos capitalistas" (North American capitalists).

They added that "the complete sanction" of power in the colonization program should rest with the "vecinos" and town councils of Texas, who alone had a close "topographical" knowledge of their department.[25] The Bexareños accused the centralists of having "dissolved the social compact" and unjustly expelled a Texas deputy from the state congress after the Plan of Jalapa. This insult alone, they said, "gave them another most justifiable cause to secede." At the same time, the Tejanos added demands for bilingual administrators, more judges, militia salaries, and tax exemptions.[26] The Tejanos of Nacogdoches and Goliad also drafted *memorias* in January, 1833, to reinforce the Béxar pronouncements. The Goliad *memoria* is perhaps the most revealing of Tejano sentiments at the time. It spoke for all Tejanos, addressed a wider audience, and evoked broader principles. Opening with a declaration of the social contract, the document closed with a threat of resistance and secession. In a classic Mexican phrase of protest, the Goliad leaders exhorted "Basta ya" (Enough). Their *memoria* states:

> We have had enough of these legislators who insult through their very capriciousness the sacred charter, such as those who passed the unconstitutional Decrees Numbers 50, 149, and 183; we want no more of legislators such as the one who disregarded the sacred rights of this community for no other reason than to protect the false pretensions of two colonization impresarios.[27]

While it seemed that a liberal, federalist agenda favorable to Tejano interests might triumph with the collapse of the Bustamante regime in 1832, Tejanos were disappointed when Santa Anna switched positions and threw his support to the centralist cause in May, 1834. A new Congress composed of centralist politicians then dissolved all state legislatures and abrogated the federal Constitution of 1824, to which Tejanos had been committed. Political division deteriorated into conflict as Mexican liberals throughout Mexico resisted Santa Anna.[28] Béxar's *jefe político*, Juan Seguín, representing a new generation of Tejano leaders, joined the resistance against centralist authority in support of local political and economic interests.

TEJANOS AND ANGLOS

By the early 1830s, Tejanos were clearly headed for a showdown with the new Mexican government. Though they understood well their interests vis-à-vis the Mexican government, they proceeded with caution because the authorities in Mexico City were not their only problem. Tejanos also had to contend with their Anglo-American neighbors. Initially, Tejanos accepted settlers from the United States with open arms and, for example, they considered Stephen F. Austin a great contributor to the economic prosperity of their region. But as other impresarios arrived and as their numbers increased, Tejanos began to understand that there was considerable danger in the Anglo-American presence.

By 1830, some thirty thousand Anglos had arrived in Texas and overwhelmed the Tejano population of about four thousand. As their numbers increased, so did their willingness to confront the Mexican government to promote their own interests, regardless of what Tejanos thought. Like their Tejano neighbors, Anglo Americans were enraged by the Law of April 6, 1830, but they acted with less caution. In October, 1832, the Anglo-American municipalities met in San Felipe de Austin to protest the law. They invited Tejano representation, but convened unilaterally and petitioned for the repeal of the law in question. The next year, Anglo-American colonists met again and issued a stronger petition. In each case, Tejanos declined to attend. Indeed, Ramón Músquiz, the *jefe político* of Texas whom Seguín replaced, could only apologize to state authorities for what Tejanos considered inappropriate unilateral action by the Anglo Americans.[29]

This propensity by immigrants from the United States to act independently of broader interests and desires contributed to a basic Tejano distrust of their neighbors. Even as Tejanos strove to cooperate with the colonists, crosscurrents of antagonism created tensions between the two groups. These tensions were apparent in their earliest interactions and blossomed into open animosity after 1836.

As early as the mid-1820s, conflicts between the Tejanos and non-Mexican colonists had existed in La Bahía and Victoria. The disagreements began when state authorities in Saltillo granted Green DeWitt an impresario contract in 1825 that included towns and ranches belonging to Tejanos. Tejanos protested repeatedly in Saltillo but were ignored. Moreover, the Coahuila y Texas legislature granted Irish entrepreneurs James Power and James Hewetson a tract that not only violated a ten-league coastal reserve but overlapped an already existing Tejano ranch community.[30]

DeWitt's impresario claim created an atmosphere of distrust and rivalry that erupted into open conflict within a year of his arrival. In 1826, Tejano leader and impresario Martín de León was ordered to confiscate contraband goods that Anglo-American colonists had hidden in DeWitt's colony. De León's son-in-law and local presidio commander at La Bahía, Rafael Antonio Manchola, escorted de León with an armed troop, but the immigrant colonists resisted. Only the intervention of Stephen F. Austin prevented open conflict between Tejano and Anglo-American settlers.[31]

The DeWitt colonists did not benefit from this dispute and further alienated Manchola. He not only was fully aware of the extensive illegal activities of Anglo-American colonists but he also participated as troop commander in crushing a rebellion led by Haden Edwards in 1827. The DeWitt colonists must have been dismayed to see Manchola become state deputy in 1830 and then the senior *alcalde* of Goliad in 1831. In forfeiting Manchola's favor, the Anglo-American colonists undoubtedly contributed to the restrictive Law of April 6, 1830.[32]

Manchola's attitude toward the Anglo Americans was reflected in a letter to Mateo Ahumada, the commandant of Texas, in which he reported the events of the 1826 confrontation with DeWitt. Heavily underlining his phrases for emphasis, Manchola wrote: "I have been told verbally that Gren [*sic*] DeWitt has said that if I had arrived by day instead of by night as I did, he would not have let me come near." Manchola went on to recommend that military detachments be stationed in the Anglo-American colonies to guard the rivers and bays for contraband activities. His suggestion was to "clip the wings of their audacity by stationing a strong detachment in each new settlement which will enforce the laws."[33] Indeed, shortly after Manchola's recommendations, Colonel José de las Piedras and a detachment of two hundred men arrived in Texas to enforce the colonization laws among the Anglo Americans. Tejanos who shared Manchola's sentiments began to feel that Anglo Americans were generally undesirable in society.

One Mexican diarist traveling through Texas in 1828 wrote that the Anglo Americans were a "lazy people of vicious character." When he encountered a kind and courteous Anglo American, he characterized the qualities as "a very rare thing among individuals of his nationality." The Goliad Tejanos were particularly upset at DeWitt, whom they contemptuously described as being "drunk in the streets constantly." They felt Anglo Americans to be "adventurers" who liked to engage in "fraudulent" activities. One report to state authorities said: "Let us be honest with ourselves, Sir, the foreign empresarios are nothing more than money-changing speculators caring only for their own well-being and hesitating not in their unbecoming methods."[34] Though they were relatively liberal in the Mexican political spectrum, many Tejanos nevertheless became quite nationalistic when faced with Anglo Americans.

Tejanos in Goliad also lodged protests regarding unfair treatment in the Power and DeWitt grants. After citing a series of illegal activities in connection with the new colonies, their complaint referred to don Esteban Austin as the only "true empresario" among the Anglo-American impresarios.[35] Tejanos vented their frustration with the colonization program, saying, "If [these outrages] had been committed against any other people, they would have seceded in an instant." Tejanos also protested when the Congress extended major colonization contracts for Lorenzo de Zavala, Joseph Vehlein, and David G. Burnet, who promised to settle foreigners other than Anglo Americans. These contract extensions annoyed Tejanos, who considered these impresarios to be frauds.[36]

Tensions over colonization policies, contraband, and personal relations between culturally distinct people all contributed to a distrustful relationship between the two groups. This distrust helps explain Tejanos' initial reluctance to support the aggressive actions of Anglo Americans in their conflicts with Mexican centralists. Anglo Americans had come from a capitalist society with a constitutional heritage that placed limits on government. Their grandparents had fought a revolution against England, and they themselves had been brought up in an atmosphere of skepticism about government. Tejanos, on the other hand, had long experience with a mercantilist economic system that had colonized Texas specifically to represent the Spanish government. Their approach was not to call inflammatory conventions but to use the vehicle of the *ayuntamiento* to lodge protests against actions they deemed hurtful to their interests. The Anglo American and the Tejano perceived the centralist ascendancy in different ways and from different perspectives. To the Tejano, the Constitution of 1824 was a promise, and the centralist uprising, a violation of that promise. To the Anglo American, the Constitution of 1824 was an established government, and the centralist uprising, a coup d'état, an opportunity to redesign the government according to their traditions. The two responses to the government upheaval were as distinct as their Anglo-American and Hispanic backgrounds.

CONCLUSION

During the years Tejanos lived under Mexican sovereignty (1821–1836), they moved from being an isolated, autonomous people to acting as an intermediary group caught between the growth, development, and confrontation of two nations, Mexico and the United States. Tejano culture and economic interests reflected their place between two nations. It is also true that Tejanos found themselves within a Mexican nation in transition from colonial status under Spain to an independent federalist republic. In the midst of all of this, Tejanos fought to maintain control over their destiny. They fought for their autonomy, and though they reluctantly accepted their reduced political status as a department of the State of Coahuila y Texas under the Constitution of 1824, Tejanos continued to promote their own economic vision and way of life. They forged a nascent political coalition with the liberal politicians in Coahuila, and many eventually confronted Mexico when their regional rights under the Constitution of 1824 were abrogated. Tejanos also learned to be cautious about their Anglo-American neighbors who, not very mindful of the traditions or interests of their Tejano neighbors, confronted the Mexican nation in their own bid for independence.

In the end, Tejanos faced difficult choices, none of which seemed ideal, and their decisions were varied. Some joined the Anglo-American rebels, others remained loyal to Mexico, and still others were ambivalent toward foreign soldiers roaming through their homeland. Tejanos eventually became part of the independent Republic of Texas, under whose sovereignty they initiated yet another era of defending and resisting.

FOUR

EFFICIENT IN THE CAUSE
Stephen L. Hardin

The rebellion that transformed the Mexican region of Tejas into the Republic of Texas is a study in incongruity. The commonly accepted designations — the Texas Revolution or the War for Texas Independence — are deceptive, for the struggle was not strictly a revolution, nor was it initially a bid for complete separation from Mexico. Hostilities commenced in October, 1835, as a mere revolt. Both the newly arrived Anglo-Celtic Americans and the native Tejanos fought for self-government within a federalist system established under the Mexican Constitution of 1824. Although elements of ethnic bigotry increasingly colored the propaganda on both sides as the fighting grew more intense, it did not begin as a "culture conflict." Many Texas Mexicans joined with *norteamericano* neighbors to resist the centralist regime of dictator Antonio López de Santa Anna. Others, however, resented the influx of foreign settlers, viewed opposition as disloyalty to their mother country, and flocked to the centralist banner. Yet, in a war of hard choices and uncertain allegiances, many attempted to remain neutral. Whatever path each Tejano followed, his distinctive frontier heritage had produced a proud and hard-riding trooper uniquely equipped to render efficient service to whichever cause he supported.[1]

HERITAGE

As sons and grandsons of *presidiales*, rugged members of presidio garrisons, Tejano volunteers inherited skills acquired in warfare against hostile Indians. Their military lineage bred an awareness of organization, light cavalry tactics, and a propensity for the offensive. Indian raiders rode with such speed and stealth that settlers were not able to sit idly by in a defensive posture. Tejanos learned from Comanche war parties that could strike and retire safely to their territory before a punitive expedition could muster. At the heart of the Tejano militia organization was the *compañía volante* — the flying company. These lightly armed and quick-moving squadrons of some seventy mounted troopers became the prevailing military units in the Spanish province of Tejas.[2]

In the 1770s, Teodoro de Croix, commandant general of the northern provinces of New Spain, reorganized these informal militia companies to incorporate a more formal command structure. The contingents still recruited from the local populace, which ensured a supply of tough, vigorous *rancheros* familiar with the terrain, but they were trained by professional officers who enforced strict military standards. Following this transformation, the flying companies tended to serve for longer periods as they participated in extensive campaigns deep within the Comanche and Apache territories. Observing the doctrine of "vatir y perseguir" — strike and pursue — the *compañía volante* borrowed the mobile tactics of its Indian adversaries. Not content to defend beleaguered settlements, the troopers of the flying companies took the conflict to tribesmen in their own camps.[3]

During engagements with Indians, *rancheros* incorporated range skills developed while herding cattle and defensive military techniques. A favorite tactic was to snare an enemy brave within the wide loop of a lasso, yank him out of his saddle, then drag him to death. Furthermore, since gunpowder was difficult to obtain and often unreliable, *presidiales* and militiamen tended to depend more on their lances. Their reliance on the lance is easier to comprehend when one recalls that in 1779 the regulation musket weighed about eight pounds. That same year, a Spanish inspector reporting on the Béxar garrison attested that the men found such firearms too heavy and too long to discharge from horseback. The nine-foot lance, on the other hand, proved a fearsome weapon and offered the additional benefit of never misfiring. In the hands of experienced *rancheros*, the lasso and the lance constituted a lethal double threat.[4]

The borderlanders' proficiency with the lance stemmed in large measure from long experience with a tool known as the *desjarretadera*. The instrument featured a half-moon-shaped blade, or *luna*, attached to a sturdy shaft some ten or twelve feet in length. The vaquero, holding the shaft under his right arm, rode up behind an animal until the sharp concave edge of the *luna* rested against the animal's right hind leg; a deft flick of the wrist severed the large tendon and the beast fell immobilized. The vaquero then dismounted and drove one end of the *luna* into the head to separate the spinal cord and kill the animal instantly. Vaqueros normally used the *desjarretadera* only to slaughter cattle, but occasionally they employed them to settle personal disagreements. On campaign, a more conventional lance head replaced the *luna*, but the dexterity developed on the killing fields of Texas ranches proved equally deadly against marauding warriors.[5]

Images from popular culture suggest that Tejanos lived in boots, spurs, and vaquero attire; documentation, however, tends to repudiate that notion. In matters of fashion and equipment, at least, cultural borrowing cut both ways. When General Manuel Mier y Terán conducted an inspection tour of Texas in 1828, he brought along a young sublieutenant of artillery, José María Sánchez y Tapia, who made rough sketches of the various Tejanos he encountered. Lino Sánchez y Tapia, probably a relative of José María, later fleshed out the drawings. These marvelous watercolors portray even common laborers adorned in the tall American hats typical of the period, which likely came from New Orleans or points east. Juan Nepomuceno Almonte traveled to Texas prior to the outbreak of the fighting and later filed a report on the activities of the American settlers. The flood of trade goods pouring into Texas from the United States alarmed Almonte. Writing of Stephen F. Austin's hometown of San Felipe, he reported: "There are only one or two artisans; everything comes from New Orleans ready made, and there are shops well supplied with clothing, notions, etc."

Yet, even earlier, the impact of American merchandise was substantial even in the predominately Hispanic town of Béxar. In 1832, the *ayuntamiento* dispatched a petition, to interior officials complaining about conditions on the frontier: "Although it grieves us to say so, we should state that the miserable manufacture of blankets, hats, and even shoes was never established in Texas towns. Lack of these articles has obliged us to beg them from foreigners or from the interior of the republic, two or three hundred leagues distant." This evidence suggests that Juan Seguín's Tejanos mixed their native serape attire with imported garments.[6]

While many ethnocentric Americans who flocked to Texas in the 1820s and 1830s proclaimed their preeminence in practically every aspect of human behavior, nearly all Anglo-Celtic Americans readily conceded that Tejanos were the superior horsemen. The sanctimonious Mary Austin Holley believed Mexicans to be "ignorant and degraded, and generally speaking, timid and irresolute," but granted that they were "universally acknowledged to be the best hands that can be procured, for the management of cattle, horses, and other live stock." Mary S. Helm scorned Mexicans as the "debris of several inferior and degraded races" who were "demoralized by a long course of indolence and political corruption." Mrs. Helm's bigoted philippic represented the accepted viewpoint of many Americans of her era, but her sentiments were by no means ubiquitous. Indeed, her first husband, Elias R. Wightman, lauded "Spaniards" as "most admirable horsemen" who were, furthermore, "noble, generous and brave, and great friends to the Americans." U.S. volunteer John C. Duval observed that his countrymen "were all . . . pretty good horsemen, as the term is understood in the 'old states,'" but upon witnessing a group of vaqueros break a herd of wild mustangs, he proclaimed them "unsurpassed by any people in horsemanship."[7]

General Austin further recognized *rancheros* as masters of guerrilla warfare. Years of bitter conflict with horse-borne Comanche and other hostile tribesmen had engendered within Mexican borderlanders cunning, stealth, agility, endurance, mobility, skill with weapons, and the ability to exploit their habitat to military advantage.[8]

FEDERALISTS ON CAMPAIGN

On October 2, 1835, angry passions ignited revolt at Gonzales, an American settlement on the banks of the Guadalupe River. Impresario Stephen F. Austin, the newly elected commander of the "Army of the People," could not ignore the somber reality that his unruly volunteers were unprepared to face trained *centralistas* (centralists) on the battlefield. For Anglo-Celtic militiamen out of their accustomed element, the assistance of their Tejano allies would prove crucial.[9]

Austin was especially deficient in cavalry. Considerable combat experience in the North American woodlands had not equipped Texians (Texans of Anglo heritage) for mounted warfare on the open grasslands below the Guadalupe River. There, broken Texian infantry would find no cover, no escape. With that nightmare scenario in mind, one adviser warned Austin that he should "fight [the centralists] from the Brush all the time." Another concerned Texian avowed: "The enemy have a well appointed cavalry, who are volunteers . . . Our riflemen are a deadly species of troops but in the prairies they will be powerless against cavalry."[10]

Despite the many uncertainties confronting them, Texian rebels mounted the offensive. Heartened by initial victories at Gonzales and Goliad, "On to Béxar" became their battle cry. "But one spirit and one purpose animates the people of this part of the country," General Austin reported, "and that is to take Bexar, and drive the military out of Texas." Not only was San Antonio de Béxar the political center of Mexican Texas, it was also the location of General Martín Perfecto de Cos and his centralist army.[11]

Austin conducted a wide sweep below the town, ostensibly intended to sever communications between the enemy garrison and the Mexican interior. In truth, Cos's cavalry patrols routinely slipped through gaps in the Texian cordon. Austin did not possess enough horsemen to cover every approach into the town. Even if he had boasted a full complement of horse, the enemy knew the local terrain better than the American rebels, an advantage Cos exploited with impunity.[12]

Seasoned Tejano cavalrymen rushed to Austin's assistance. On October 15, Guadalupe Victoria *alcalde* Plácido Benavides joined federalist ranks with some thirty of his mounted *rancheros*. Then on October 22, Juan N. Seguín entered the rebel camp with thirty-seven federalists, a few of whom had previous experience in a militia company that Mexican commandant Domingo Ugartechea dispersed after it had backed the state government of Coahuila in an earlier quarrel with centralist authority. Seguín also brought intelligence that many Mexican citizens of Béxar — Bexareños — supported the federalist cause. Some, he reported, were ready to fight alongside the Texians. The validity of that assessment revealed itself a few days later when more than forty volunteers under Salvador Flores and Manuel Leal arrived from ranches below town.[13]

On October 23, General Austin appointed Juan N. Seguín a captain and authorized him to raise a company of federalist *rancheros*. Austin assured his American volunteers that Tejanos would provide "essential service" as mounted troopers. William T. Austin, the general's aide, elaborated on their qualifications: "These mexicans being well acquainted with the country, were of important service as express riders, guides to foraging parties, &c." Tejanos provided much-needed rangecraft to an army whose ranks were brimming with scions of the southern woodlands. Thus did Austin blend the military traditions of two distinct frontiers.[14]

As rebels tightened their siege around Béxar, the Tejano light cavalry did provide "essential service." By patrolling the approaches to the town Seguín's cavalry hampered Cos's communications. Furthermore, on November 14, 1835, Austin dispatched Lieutenant Salvador Flores with instructions to "burn off the whole country from the other side of the Nueces to the Medina on the roads from Laredo and the Rio Grande." Mounts that could not graze could not advance. By depriving enemy cavalry of forage, Austin revealed that he was beginning to fathom the dynamics of mounted warfare. Flores had additional orders to reconnoiter the river crossings along the Rio Grande and to report any centralist movement toward Béxar.[15]

For its splendid service, Austin commended Seguín's company in an affidavit: "his company altho not a full one was very efficient in the cause. It intercepted two expresses from the interior to Genl Cos which were of the highest importance, and Cap Seguin and his men were at all times ready and willing to go on any service they were ordered. They uniformly acquitted themselves to their credit as patriots and soldiers."[16]

While Austin's volunteers were preparing to march from Gonzales to Béxar, a unit of Matagorda colonists under Captain George M. Collinsworth entered Victoria on their way to assault the centralist garrison of La Bahía on the outskirts of Goliad. While camped on the banks of the Guadalupe River, they drew up a "Compact of Volunteers under Collinsworth, dated Victoria, October 9, 1835." The signatories asserted devotion to the federalist Constitution of 1824 and to local Tejanos who remained loyal to its principles:

> The volunteers under the command of Capt Geo. M Collinsworth, being about to take up a line of March for Goliad, and to give the population of the town protection against military domination, deem it duty which they owe to themselves to their fellow soldiers embodied else where in the same patriotic cause, but more especially to the citizens of Guadeloupe Victoria, to declare in a clear and unequivocal manner, their united and unalterable resolution to give ample and complete protection to the citizens of this town, and to those also of every other which they may enter—requiring only, that, the citizens of said towns stand firm to the Republican institutions of the Govt of Mexico and of Coahuila & Texas under the constitution of 1824; and for the redemption of this resolution, we pledge our lives, our property, and our sacred honour.

Some sixty-two American colonists ultimately signed the document, but three local Tejanos also added their names to the list: J. A. Padilla, M. Carbajal, and A. Constanta.[17]

Though only three signed the document, Mexican officials viewed Victorianos as Texian supporters and turncoats and expressed bitter indignation toward them. General Vicente Filisola's judgment was fairly representative. "All the individuals of the [Victoria] families were the most assiduous collaborators in the Texas revolution," he fumed, "persuaded that they would gain great advantage from the triumph of the usurping colonists against their own country. However, they were miserably mistaken and received their reward. They trusted all they had, and instead of reward they received scorn, persecution, wounds and even expatriation.

Their only refuge was that very country which they had so betrayed, and in which they now found themselves refugees." He concluded his denunciation with a Spanish translation of an adage from Tacitus: "aun á los mismos que reciben el beneficio son desagradables los traidores" (even the very ones who receive the benefits find traitors disagreeable).[18]

Back in Béxar, Mexican federalists provided logistical support. Far from the concentrations of Anglo-Celtic settlements in eastern Texas, Austin's rebels soon found themselves short of crucial supplies. Seguín and others scoured the countryside to secure corn, beans, beef, salt, and other provender. In addition to their service in ranks, many wealthier Tejanos supplied goods to the revolt. The Seguíns alone eventually donated more than four thousand dollars' worth of grain and livestock.[19]

Early in December, 1835, federalist Texians and Tejanos united to storm Béxar. Although recruited for their vaunted equestrian abilities, *ranchero* cavalrymen dismounted and fought as infantry in bitter house-to-house street fighting. The exact number is difficult to determine, but perhaps as many as 160 Tejanos participated in the siege and subsequent assault. When heavy enemy fire cut federalist troops off from their logistical support, several Bexareños risked their lives to supply food, water, and ammunition to soldiers on the line. At least one Tejana, María Jesusa de García, was seriously wounded by centralist fire and received a pension from the Republic of Texas.[20]

On December 10, 1835, General Cos surrendered Béxar to the rebels and, in accordance with the terms, marched his defeated army to a position south of the Rio Grande.

With Béxar taken and Cos fleeing south, many Texians were confident that they had seen the last centralist in Texas and, true to their North American militia tradition, volunteers returned to the comforts of hearth and home. The early fighting had been almost too easy. Most American volunteers held enemy soldiers in contempt. Recounting the action at Concepción, veteran Noah Smithwick cheerfully recounted how Texian riflemen had "mowed down the Mexicans at a rate that might well have made braver hearts than those encased in their shriveled little bodies recoil."[21]

Amid all the self-congratulation, a few understood that the fighting was far from finished. Even as complacent Texians disbanded, Santa Anna was mustering his battalions to reconquer the presumptuous province. While most Anglo-Celtic settlers naively returned home, Seguín, Benavides, and other Tejano leaders maintained a vigil along the Rio Grande for the centralist army they knew would be coming.[22]

As Santa Anna's dusty legions marched northward, Texian officials reduced frontier garrisons to skeleton forces. Colonel James C. Neill commanded the Béxar garrison that fortified the old mission fort on the outskirts of town. Locals had named the abandoned compound after the flying company of San José y Santiago del Álamo de Parras. The townspeople understandably condensed the name; by 1835 it was simply the Alamo. Once again federalist Bexareños joined their Anglo-Celtic comrades in a common cause. "We can rely on great aid from the citizens of this town in case of an attack," Neill assured. "They have no money here, but Don Gasper Flores and Louisiano Navaro have offered us all their goods, Groceries, and Beeves, for the use and support of the army." James Bowie also affirmed that the "citizens of Bejar have behaved well."

Despite Neill's assertion that the local civilians had no cash, some evidence exists that their town council approved a loan of five hundred pesos "to Col Neill to pay for Texas troops." Even more support might have been forthcoming, but many Bexareños were justifiably skeptical that so few men could defend the Alamo. On January 28, 1836, Neill reported: "I shall consult with some of the influential Mexicans known to be attached to our cause, about obtaining the effectual assistance of these citizens of whom I judge that 4/5 would join us if they entertained reasonable expectations of reinforcements."[23]

Texian officers understood that they must rely on Béxar for sustenance and were careful to sustain its goodwill. They tried to build a cooperative relationship with the community. On January 16, 1836, the General Council of the Provisional Government, finally acknowledging the privations of the Béxar garrison, instituted procedures to allow Colonel Neill to employ local Tejanos to supply his men. The "Resolution Providing for the Troops at Bexar" resolved that he was "authorized and empowered to employ as many Mexicans, or other citizens, for the purpose of driving up beeves and procuring provisions for the troops under his command, as may be required for their support; and that this Government shall respect the drafts of said commandant for the pay of the said men in his employ." The second section of the resolution decreed in clear and forceful language that the government intended to compensate Bexareños for their goods and labor. Texian officials authorized a sum of twenty dollars a month to each of "the Mexicans employed by the commandant at Bexar, for the purpose of getting beeves and other provisions for the use and support of the troops under his command." It further empowered Neill "to draw for the pay of the said Mexicans, citizens, for their services as aforesaid."[24]

The Texas government did eventually "respect the drafts" of Bexareños.

On February 19, 1836, Lieutenant Colonel William Barret Travis, who assumed command of the fort in Neill's absence, authorized a receipt to Felipe Xaimes. It certified that during the siege of Béxar he had sold sixty-five head of cattle to the army. In an addendum to the claim, Travis praised Xaimes for his support of the federalist effort: "He is said to be a good man & was actually engaged in the service of our army for a short time [and] gave of his Beeves freely of his own accord."[25]

On February 22, Travis also lauded the heroic actions of another Tejano, Antonio Cruz. In a testimonial attached to a certificate, Travis noted:

I certify that from the statement of Captain Seguin & the best information, I can get, Antonio Cruz was one of those who entered Berrimendi's [Veramendi's] house in the storm of this town & was one of the few [Mexicans] who rendered us essential service in the late campaign — I give this certificate because I think a distinction ought to be made between those who lost property while in our service & those who were against us or were neutral.[26]

Travis's confidence in the Tejano federalist leaders was so firm, in fact, that on February 28, he dispatched Captain Juan Seguín and Antonio Cruz (the same individual whom he had commended a week earlier) with a crucially important plea for assistance. From the beginning of the revolt Seguín had been a prominent supporter of the federalist cause and had proven invaluable as a liaison between town and garrison. The pair were also the best couriers available; they were familiar with the surrounding terrain, spoke Spanish, and would be less conspicuous riding through the countryside.[27]

The cooperation between Texians and Tejanos had its limits, however. An 1860 claim lists the names of eleven Tejanos who petitioned the state for payment for service during the revolution. All profess to have been members of Juan Seguín's company, all claim to have participated in the 1835 Béxar campaign, and all declare to have terminated their service on the same two days: February 20 and 21, 1836. Significant dates, for it was then that word of Santa Anna's imminent arrival reached Bexareños and several began to evacuate the town. Many, after all, well recalled the horrors of General José Joaquín Arrendondo's 1813 visit.[28]

Before or soon after the seige began, Santa Anna offered amnesty to all Tejanos. Enrique Esparza, son of Alamo defender Gregorio Esparza, maintained that "quite a number" of the garrison's Mexicans took advantage of the offer and left the fort. These men probably departed sometime between February 29, when Seguín and Cruz went out as couriers, and

March 3, the date of a Travis letter in which he condemns Bexareños for supporting the centralists. According to Esparza, the departing Tejanos discussed the matter with Bowie, who advised them to get out while they could.[29]

The fighting had severely tested the loyalty of Texas-born Mexicans, most of whom resisted the inexorable movement toward independence. While many were willing to fight, even to die, for the Constitution of 1824, they were understandably hesitant to support an open break with their mother country. The politically astute among them realized that in an independent Texas they would be woefully outnumbered by *norte-americanos* and thus relegated to minority status in a land dominated by foreigners who possessed little knowledge of or appreciation for their culture. Bowie, a longtime friend of the Béxar community, sympathized with their dilemma and understood their reasons for abandoning the Alamo garrison and the rebel cause. Indeed, the knowledge that they had permission to leave renders the dedication of those Tejanos who remained to the end all the more heroic. Still, more abandoned the fort than remained at their post for the same reason that Texians did during the subsequent Runaway Scrape — to protect their families.

On March 11, General Sam Houston arrived at Gonzales to personally take command of the effort to relieve the Alamo. That same day, however, two Bexareños, Anselmo Bergara and Andrés Barcena, rode into town with intelligence that the fort had fallen on March 6. They stated that they had not actually witnessed the final assault, but relied on the account of Antonio Pérez, who had. According to Seguín, "their report was so detailed as to preclude any doubts about that disastrous event." Even so, since portions of their reports were contradictory, Houston arrested the pair as centralist spies. While publicly disparaging the intelligence, the general privately admitted, "I fear a melancholy portion of it will be found true." On March 13, Texian scout Erastus "Deaf" Smith escorted into town Gonzales resident Susannah Dickinson, her infant daughter, and Joe, Travis's slave. Mrs. Dickinson confirmed what Houston already suspected: Almeron, her husband, and the entire Alamo garrison had been slain. Mrs. Dickinson further reported that Santa Anna and his centralist army were on the march to Gonzales. Houston, acutely aware that his meager force could not defend the settlement, ordered it burned and withdrew toward the Colorado River.[30]

As the rebel army retreated along the Gonzales–San Felipe Road, Seguín's men performed as a rear guard. In that capacity they assisted the evacuation of both Anglo-Celtic and Tejano families who joined the exodus Texians labeled the "Runaway Scrape." The company continued in that assignment until it reached Arenoso Creek near the Brazos River. There Seguín's troops were detached with Captain Moseley Baker to San Felipe de Austin to hold the vital crossing of the Brazos River.

General Houston was vocal in his dislike of cavalrymen. He wanted one army concentrated under his undisputed command, not bands of independent horsemen bounding over the countryside. Nevertheless, in acknowledgment of their proven ability as scouts, he allowed a number of Seguín's troops to remain mounted.[31]

Like many of the Texians, Seguín's company lacked essential supplies. Although some Tejanos remained on horseback as scouts, the majority served as infantry during the punishing march to San Jacinto. Trudging through the mud was especially hard on shoe leather. On March 28, Seguín obtained twenty-two pairs of shoes "for the use of the company [under] my command at two dollars a pair" from San Felipe merchant Joseph Urban.[32]

Prior to the battle at San Jacinto, Houston ordered the Tejano company to guard the baggage, thus denying them a combative role. Seguín and Second Sergeant Antonio Menchaca dashed to confront Houston. With Menchaca acting as interpreter, the captain asserted that "when he had joined the Americans, he had done so with a view for fighting." As Houston listened in stunned silence, Seguín added that his men had not enlisted to herd livestock and, if that was all the Anglos believed them good for, he would disband his company and assist his family, who had joined the Runaway Scrape. "Spoke like a man," Houston exclaimed. Stirred by Seguín's fighting spirit, the general countermanded his earlier order.[33]

Seguín was eager to prove the loyalty of his men, especially since the Texians had captured one of them riding with the enemy. "Deaf" Smith and Henry Karnes had captured a Mexican captain, a centralist courier, and a Tejano who had been acting as their guide. When the bilingual Moses Austin Bryan arrived to interrogate the prisoners, the Tejano related a remarkable tale: "The guide said he belonged to Captain Juan N. Seguin's company; that he had a furlough at Gonzales; had been arrested by the Mexicans at San Antonio and forced to act for them as guide. Captain Seguin being summoned recognized the man and confirmed his statement." Since Santa Anna had reportedly pressed a number of Bexareños into service, Bryan believed the captured guide and observed that he subsequently "rejoined his company and participated in the Battle of San Jacinto."[34]

Notwithstanding their reputation as superior horsemen, Seguín's company fought at San Jacinto as infantry attached to Sidney Sherman's second regiment on the Texian left. Menchaca recounted that Texians insisted that their Tejano friends take precautions to identify themselves:

> Santa Anna was strongly hated by Texas volunteers on account of his brutality in murdering the men who were in the alamo when it was carried by storm. During the battle of San Jacinto the battle cry of the Texans was *"remember the Alamo"* and they made me take my men who were mexicans and put large pieces of white paste board on their hats and br[e]asts, least they should be mistaken for Santa Anna's men and killed.[35]

Several Texian officers later testified that Tejano soldiers pitched into the thickest part of the fight and acquitted themselves gallantly. An anonymous correspondent (who sounds like Stephen F. Austin) reported the valiant deportment of Seguín's men in a dispatch printed in the Richmond *Inquirer*: "I am pleased to say, that Capt. (now Col.) Inan Nepemucene Seguin, a native of Bexar, and whom I have known from a boy, commanded 25 men, all natives of the same place, and performed wonders; every man signalized himself in the most distinguished manner. One of them, with a Bowie knife, killed 25 of his countrymen."[36]

The battle, however, soon degenerated into wanton slaughter. As Second Sergeant Antonio Menchaca stormed through the enemy camp, a terrified centralist officer he had known in Béxar begged him as a "brother Mexican" to save him from the bloodthirsty *gringos*. A group of American volunteers milled about, eager to hear Menchaca's reply. "No, damn you," he snapped, "I'm no Mexican — I'm an American." Turning to his Anglo-Celtic comrades, Menchaca instructed: "Shoot him." A fusillade of musketry summarily ended the pleading. Such incidents indicate that Tejanos killed centralists with every bit as much relish as did vengeful Texians. They further demonstrate the lengths to which they went to confirm their loyalty.[37]

One Tejano youth particularly distinguished himself during the fighting. Juan López, a sixteen-year-old orphan, had joined the rebel army as a cart driver. When the battle opened, however, he abandoned his cart and, "brandishing on one hand an old rusty sword, holding on the other a gun stick at the top of which was fastened a red kind of rag," he charged the centralist camp. Seguín later testified that he ordered the boy to throw away the stick and supplied him with a rifle. Armed with a real firearm, López "fought as bravely as any man in the Army and recd. a slight flesh wound in the left knee."[38]

Such obvious devotion swayed several Texians. Following San Jacinto,

even those who had earlier expressed doubts concerning Tejano participation raised their voices in commendation. Houston avowed that Seguín's "chivalrous and estimable conduct won for him my warmest regard
and esteem." Years later he continued to praise the "brave and gallant bearing" of the Tejanos who had fought on the banks of Buffalo Bayou. Houston's second-in-command, Colonel Edward Burleson — certifiably a better
fighter than speller — also noted "Capt Seguins company and himself . . .
has bin honestly Engaged in the noble cause of freedom." [39]

Such commendable service did not cease at San Jacinto. Seguín's men
resumed their traditional role as partisan cavalry and shadowed the fleeing
centralists until they crossed the Rio Grande. Texian officials, however,
feared that the Mexicans might mount another offensive to reclaim the
rebellious province. On May 30, 1836, General Thomas Jefferson Rusk,
who had assumed command of the Republic's army in the absence of the
wounded Houston, authorized Seguín "to recruit for the service of Texas
a Battalion of men in whom you can place confidence not to exceed in
number 112 men rank and file for the purpose of being stationed in Bexar."
Rusk "particularly enjoined" Lieutenant Colonel Seguín to "be vigilant in
keeping lookout upon the different roads towards the Rio Grande, for the
purpose of ascertaining the movements of the enemy, communicating
fully and frequently all the information you may collect to the commandant of the army." Texian officials remembered the Alamo and Goliad;
they finally grasped the hazards of being surprised in an isolated location
and cut off by a highly mobile enemy. Rusk selected the right men for the
job — Bexareños had patrolled those roads for generations. Rusk concluded by expressing his faith in Seguín's loyalty and competence: "This
will be a responsible, ardious, and important duty and I know of no one
to whose hands it may be committed with more confidence than your-
self." Rusk did not misplace his trust. In short order Seguín had organized
the requested battalion of volunteers.[40]

CENTRALIST TEJANOS

While Seguín and Benavides joined the rebel cause, Texas loyalists rallied
to the centralists. Captain Manuel Sabriego, a career officer stationed at
the Presidio La Bahía, had married a local woman and enjoyed close ties
to the Tejano community. Early in October, 1835, Sabriego traveled to
Victoria to appropriate a cannon belonging to that settlement. He learned
to his dismay, however, that the citizens of Victoria were staunch fed-

eralists who refused to relinquish their ordnance. They also declined to hand over two federalist leaders, José M. J. Carbajal and Juan Manuel Zambrano.[41]

Sabriego was especially eager to seize Carbajal. In September, General Cos had issued arrest warrants for several War Party rabble-rousers, including Samuel M. Williams, R. M. "Three-legged Willie" Williamson, and William Barret Travis. The list, however, also contained the names of three outspoken Mexican federalists: Lorenzo de Zavala, Juan Zambrano, and José M. J. Carbajal. Chagrined, Sabriego left empty-handed and returned to Goliad.[42]

Not all Tejanos around Victoria were federalists, however, for Captain Sabriego mustered a company of loyalist vaqueros from the ranches along the Guadalupe River. This unit, the Guardias Victorianas, played a decisive role during General José Urrea's subsequent 1836 campaign and remained operational well into the Texas Republic period.[43]

On October 10, 1835, George M. Collinsworth and his Matagorda contingent captured Sabriego along with the Presidio at Goliad. Not knowing what to do with his centralist prisoners, Collinsworth transferred them to General Austin in Gonzales. Once there, Sabriego swore that both he and his wife were sincere federalists—he only wanted to return to her and live out a peaceful life as a civilian. The tender-hearted, if somewhat gullible, Austin paroled Sabriego and sent him home to his wife.[44]

Sabriego, however, had no intention of honoring the terms of his parole. Immediately upon his release, he rode to Matamoros to report to centralist officials. His superiors recognized Sabriego as a resourceful officer. They also realized that his marriage ties to the Tejano community placed him in a position to provide essential intelligence. Captain Sabriego soon returned to the Goliad-Lipantitlán area, where he organized loyalists into an espionage network. As one leading authority observed: "[Sabriego] was cunning and crafty and planted false and misleading information designed to deceive the Texian leaders. His agents intercepted many messages exchanged between Texian officials."[45]

Phillip Dimmitt, the new rebel commander in Goliad, soon learned of Sabriego's clandestine activities. Ironically, like Sabriego, he had married a local Tejana and one of his in-laws may have tipped him off. Dimmitt declared Sabriego a public enemy and was eager to terminate his operation. Indeed, Dimmitt cited apprehending the enemy operative as among the chief objectives of an expedition on Fort Lipantitlán. A rebel force captured the fort on November 3, 1835, and the following day defeated the centralist garrison at the Battle of Nueces Crossing. Still, the antagonist the Texians sought most eluded them. As the skirmish at Nueces Crossing ensued, Sabriego bolted for Matamoros. The Texians never managed to capture him. He soon returned to the area, where his spies continued to gall the federalists and supply valuable information to centralist authorities. As scout, spy, and supplier of vital intelligence, Sabriego had no parallel, unless, of course, one considers the federalist Tejanos who were performing the same assignment on behalf of the *norteamericanos*.[46]

As effective as Sabriego was, Dimmitt probably did more to deliver recruits to centralist ranks. Although married to a Mexican, he harbored a suspicion of all those he labeled "creole" troops. He dispatched all his Tejano recruits to Austin's army around Béxar, where, as already noted, they served with distinction. Dimmitt was a petty and heavy-handed martinet who brooked no disagreement. He ordered a policy of impressment on Goliad's civilians, poor frontier folk who in the best of times had little to spare. The spiteful commander also forced local Mexicans to perform back-breaking labor without pay, or even a promise of future compensation. Predictably, Goliad's civilians began to take refuge in the countryside to avoid such harsh demands. John J. Linn, a friend of the Tejano community, angrily reported Dimmitt's multiple "acts of tireny" to Austin. As Linn explained, all but twenty citizens had abandoned the town, afraid to return. He further remonstrated: "they do not want to be made hewers of wood and Drawers of water."[47]

Such indignities forced Tejanos in the Goliad area to reconsider their commitment to the rebellion. In the main, they had gotten along with Austin's original immigrants, but more and more troops pouring into Goliad were volunteers fresh from the United States. Most of these newcomers expressed contempt for Roman Catholics and made no distinction between federalists and centralists — to them all Mexicans were the enemy. On December 22, 1835, the unruly rebel garrison declared the so-called Goliad Declaration of Independence. Although rejected as premature by officials of the Texas provisional government, who still maintained some hope of assistance from Mexican federalists, this document demonstrated that these men had no loyalty to Mexico. Despite their ignominious treatment, Plácido Benavides, Mariano Carbajal, and Francisco García remained with the rebel garrison, but all other Tejanos faded away. They could not support independence, but neither could they abide centralist despotism; neutrality seemed their only course. Others, however, came to the conclusion that Sabriego had been right all along and joined his underground movement.[48]

As federalist Tejanos defended the Alamo, other dedicated *rancheros* were proving decisive to the southeast. Unfortunately for Colonel James W. Fannin, Jr., and his Goliad garrison, most of them rode with the centralists. Organized under Carlos de la Garza, Manuel Sabriego, Juan Moya, and Agustín Moya, they kept General José Urrea well informed of Fannin's movements and harried Texian outriders to the extent that the rebel commander had no knowledge of their enemy's position. The Guardias Victorianas, now under Carlos de la Garza's command, carried out successful guerrilla operations against the Texians. Urrea brilliantly deployed his regular cavalry and Tejano auxiliaries, who effectively screened Mexican movements and forced Fannin to operate in the absence of timely intelligence.[49]

With a lightning thrust from Matamoros, Urrea achieved the momentum and never lost it. After much delay, the indecisive Fannin finally ordered a retreat toward Victoria. Notified of the Texians' sluggish withdrawal, Urrea led his cavalry in rapid pursuit. Mexican lancers intercepted Fannin's command on the prairie near Coleto Creek. Caught in the open without natural cover, the rebel infantrymen could only form square and defend themselves. Greatly outnumbered, Fannin's riflemen held Urrea's cavalry and infantry at bay for an entire afternoon, but lack of food and water rendered their position hopeless. Outgeneraled at every turn, Fannin had no choice but to surrender when Urrea brought up artillery that would have obliterated the beleaguered square.[50]

Assisted by centralist Tejanos, General Urrea won a brilliant victory that Santa Anna would stigmatize by an act of savagery. Urrea marched the survivors of the Coleto battle back to Goliad and held them for a week. Then, on Palm Sunday, Fannin and the majority of his men were executed on Santa Anna's peremptory orders. Among the victims was federalist insurgent Mariano Carbajal. Tejano auxiliaries—Urrea called them "spies"—had been critical to his success and he acknowledged their contributions as "indecible"—inexpressible.[51]

LOYALTIES, VIOLENCE, AND SURVIVAL

Those Tejanos who took advantage of Santa Anna's amnesty and left the Alamo have already been discussed. It appears, however, that even in the federalist bastion of Béxar some did more than seek a neutral course. On March 3, 1836, acting Alamo commander William Barret Travis reported that many Bexareños had defected to the centralists as active combatants: "All the citizens of this place that have not joined us are with the enemy fighting against us." Many Bexareños had become what may be termed conditional centralists. Even before the fall of the Alamo, Santa Anna pressed Tejanos into service. Andrés Barcena related that his mother entreated Anselmo Bergara to "take her son . . . to the Colorado River to avoid the [centralist] military who was gathering up all they could and making soldiers of them."[52]

The circumstance of shifting loyalties was not confined to the Béxar area. Many of Fannin's U.S. volunteers regarded their Mexican allies with misgiving, and on at least one occasion their mistrust was justified. Captain Luis Guerra and his company of Mexican artillery deserted centralist ranks to join Fannin's Goliad garrison in the fight for the Constitution of 1824. Like other patriotic Mexicans, they were dismayed by the Texas independence movement. Appreciating the moral impasse of Guerra and his men, Fannin granted them permission to sit out the hostilities in New Orleans. Only Guerra, however, left Texas. The rest of his company subsequently joined Urrea, and members of the Georgia Battalion observed them fighting against their former comrades at Refugio. For the Anglo-Celtic Texians, such actions seemed to confirm stereotypical presumptions of the duplicitous Mexican.[53]

With news of Fannin's defeat, many Texas Mexicans who had earlier proclaimed their devotion to the federalist cause now sought to demonstrate their allegiance to Santa Anna's centralist regime. Henry Reilly, in Victoria at the time, later described the narrow escape of a Doctor Benjamin Harrison, reputedly the son of President William Henry Harrison:

> The inhabitants [of Victoria] became extremely insulting to the few Americans who remained, and as soon as they ascertained Fanning's defeat, they, headed by the second Alcalde, bound Dr. Harrison's hands behind him, in conjunction with two other Americans, and commenced butchering them; they began on the others first, and by the time they had finished their damned work, Dr H had succeeded in separating his hands, and immediately ran into the Guadaloupe timber which is uncommonly thick and secreted himself.

Terrified at being caught on the losing side, Victorianos opted for survival by executing a few helpless *norteamericano* rebels, an act they hoped would prove their loyalty to Urrea.[54]

Another encounter is especially illustrative of the acrimony generated by factious conditions. Isaac D. Hamilton, although bayoneted and shot, managed to escape the so-called Goliad Massacre. For nineteen days he wandered the prairie attempting to find "some little substance to live upon." Plácido Benavides came across the wounded fugitive, placed him in his cart, and pledged to take him to safety. Benavides, still a staunch federalist, could not countenance Texas independence and had retired to his ranch near Victoria, where he attempted to remain neutral. Finding the wounded Hamilton severely tested that newly proclaimed neutrality. He had known Hamilton from the time they had served together at Goliad and Benavides felt obliged to assist a wounded friend, whatever his politics. Benavides and Hamilton had traveled only a short distance, however, when a Mexican cavalry patrol approached.[55]

The arrival of the centralist patrol threatened both men. Benavides could now do nothing to save Hamilton. Indeed, he might not have been able to save his own life had the centralists believed he was helping a condemned rebel escape. Benavides opted for self-preservation. He called out that he had captured one of the rebels, coolly demanded a receipt for his prisoner, and handed Hamilton over to Urrea's lancers. Hamilton, incensed by what he could only interpret as reprehensible deceit, was "placed on a bare backed horse and was most cruelly beaten through the prairie until we arrived at Victoria." There he awaited the firing squad.[56]

Hamilton, however, was not executed. He was one of those fortunate Texians saved by the intercession of Francisca Álvarez, the "Angel of Goliad." Hamilton subsequently escaped and made his way back to Texian lines. He never forgave Benavides and frequently related the "treachery of the Mexican who betrayed him" to all who would listen. Many did. According to descendant C. L. Hamilton, "Family tales picture Isaac thereafter as embittered, and under driving compulsion to find and kill Placido [Benavides]." He even went so far as to commission a rifle, "which he told friends he was going to use in killing this Mexican, when he found him." Hamilton, however, was never able to wreak his vengeance. In the face of mounting hostility—much of it no doubt fostered by Hamilton's vituperation—Benavides fled with his family to Opelousas, Louisiana, where he died in 1837.[57]

The unfortunate encounter proved a tragedy for both men. Benavides was forced from his ancestral home by newcomers he had attempted to help; Hamilton, his health ruined by his ordeal, remained bitter until his death in 1859. What might have been an example of friendship and loyalty across racial lines became a legacy of enmity and misunderstanding.[58]

Despite the atmosphere of suspicion that accompanied them, a few federalist Tejanos willingly continued their fight against Santa Anna's centralist regime; others did so less willingly. Even before the fall of the Alamo, Antonio Menchaca and other Bexareños made their way to Gonzales, where they joined the force that was to provide the nucleus of the Texian San Jacinto army. Actually, some were pressed into service. Certainly, Menchaca had no intention of enlisting in the rebel army. As he was about to ferry across the Guadalupe River, Colonel Edward Burleson approached. As Menchaca recalled, he was attempting "to pass to the other side with families, but was prevented by Burleson, who told him that the families might cross, but not him; that the men were needed in the army." On the basis of Menchaca's account, it appears that there were also conditional federalists.[59]

Forbidden to leave the settlement, Menchaca and fourteen other Bexareños formed an informal association until they could structure a unit. For the following six days, Tejanos continued to trickle into town. As he told it, Juan Seguín was unable to cut his way through the enemy cordon around the Alamo; he rode instead to Gonzales, where Colonel Neill and Colonel Burleson were attempting to organize a relief column. The day following Seguín's arrival, twenty-two Tejanos formed a company, elected Seguín captain, and Manuel Flores first lieutenant. On March 4, news reached Gonzales that delegates at Washington-on-the-Brazos had declared independence on March 2. Texian officers called on the some 350 volunteers camped on the banks of the Guadalupe to swear allegiance to the new government. All did so. By this deed, Seguín's men broke with Mexican federalists, bowed to the inevitable, and took up the banner of the Republic of Texas. Whether they did so out of conviction or expediency remains in question.[60]

Menchaca's *Memoirs* constitute one of the chief sources of the Texas rebellion, but few appear aware of its inconsistencies. Dictated when Menchaca was an old man, the narrative claims that he avoided the fate of the Alamo defenders only because Bowie and Seguín insisted that he leave Béxar. According to Menchaca, the rebel leaders were aware that, "should Santa Anna come, A[ntonio] and his family would receive no good at his hands." Enrique Esparza, however, minced no words when he identified Menchaca as one of those who availed themselves of Santa Anna's amnesty and abandoned the Alamo garrison.[61]

Esparza's version appears the most credible. Would Seguín have thought Menchaca to be in more danger from centralist wrath than any other insurgent Tejano? Why would he have insisted Menchaca escape while other Bexareños, better known for their federalist sympathies, remained in harm's way? One can easily appreciate why Menchaca may have been less than forthcoming. After the revolution he became involved in local politics, served as alderman for several terms, and as mayor pro tem in 1838. He was also a member of the Texas Veterans Association. Respected by Tejanos and Anglo-Celtic residents, he remained a stalwart of San Antonio society. In the days immediately following the War between the States, when Menchaca dictated his memoirs, San Antonio had come thoroughly under Anglo-Celtic control and the Alamo battle had emerged as the premier symbol of patriotic sacrifice. It would have been political and social suicide for Menchaca to admit that he had left the Alamo.[62]

Throughout the revolt Tejanos practiced better discipline than their Anglo-Celtic comrades, but they also committed abuses. During the storming of Béxar, James Bowie — already infamous along the Mississippi Valley for exploits with his deadly blade — and Plácido Benavides patrolled south of town in search of enemy mounts. Bowie's company found no horses but detained a local herder upon information provided by one of his Tejano neighbors. The informant insisted that the herder had concealed the animals, but the suspect steadfastly disavowed any knowledge of their whereabouts. Samuel C. A. Rogers, one of Bowie's volunteers, recounted what transpired next:

> Benevidas [*sic*] prevailed upon Colonel Bowie to hang the Mexican till he was not quite dead and he would tell us. We tied the Mexican['] s hands behind him and put a rope around his neck and brought him to a tree . . . Then they pulled the Mixican [*sic*] up and held to the rope until he nearly quite [*sic*] kicking. We then let him down and with our guns cocked [and] pointed at him, [explained] that we would shoot him to pieces if he didn't tell us where the horses were. I remonstrated with Colonel Bowie and told him I didn't [participate] in such cruelty. I didn't have anything more to do with it. They had to hang the Mexican three times before he would tell.

This sordid episode mortified the compassionate Rogers, later a Methodist minister — although he insisted that, by rights, one of the captured horses should have been his for standing guard over the prisoner. In his reminiscences he avowed that he was "no advocate for lynch law" and further asserted: "I shall always believe that those horses were the Mexican['s] private property and he gave them up to save himself."[63]

What should one make of this account? The first reaction is to recoil at the casual brutality, but modern sensibilities dictate such a response. While one does not acclaim such abuses, the objective historian realizes that on the frontera, where formal institutions were few, independent pobladores commonly relied on extra-legal means. Such action was, of course, by no means unique to the Mexican frontier; a period of vigilantism appears to have been characteristic of most frontier regions.[64]

No, the puzzling aspect of this episode is not the violence itself — brutality was common in revolutionary Texas — but rather its distinctive nature. One ought not dismiss this incident as merely another case of Anglo-Celtic racism against Tejanos. Jim Bowie was among the few immigrants from the United States to have sincerely embraced Mexican culture. He had, after all, married Maria Ursula de Veramendi, the daughter of one of Béxar's leading families, he had won the admiration and affection of Juan Seguín, Antonio Menchaca, and other Bexareños, and finally some of Bowie's Mexican relatives remained with him within the walls of the Alamo. Bowie seemed to have liked and been liked by Tejanos. How then does one explain this manhandling of one of them?[65]

One ought not forget that this violation was not initially Bowie's idea, but was rather suggested by Benavides. Furthermore, a fellow Tejano had informed on the unfortunate herdsman in the first place. Indeed, it is possible that a personal vendetta could have been the motive behind the entire episode. That in no way excuses Bowie's approval. He was the commander of the expedition and must ultimately bear responsibility for this misfortune. Nevertheless, the willing participation of Benavides implies a complex disposition of loyalties among the native Mexican population in Texas. It is, of course, axiomatic that combat tends to dehumanize its practitioners, that men in the name of military necessity commit atrocities they would never contemplate in civilian life. Even so, to attribute this lamentable incident solely to the depreciation of humanity generated by combat fails to properly consider a distinctive Tejano social structure.[66]

Tejano society consisted of *ricos* and *pobres*. Military commandants, government officials, successful financiers, and large ranch owners constituted an influential ruling elite. Providing stark contrast were the mixed-blood *peones*, common laborers who lived out their lives in drudgery and service to the *patrones*. Bowie had joined one of the wealthiest and oldest families in Texas; it was only natural that he would have adopted their attitudes towards the lowly *pobres*. One of the province's leading oligarchs, Plácido Benavides (or more properly, Don Plácido, since his position as an alcalde and land owner entitled him to the honorific) would have had few qualms about abusing a herdsman, a creature clearly his social inferior.[67]

We will probably never know whether the unnamed herdsman was a civilian agent of the centralists or, as Rogers believed, an innocent who surrendered his own horses to save his life. It is certain that the incident is illustrative of the plight of many Tejanos caught amidst a swirl of changing politics and shifting loyalties.[68]

Wealthy land owners like José Antonio Navarro, Erasmo Seguín, and Plácido Benavides had been early proponents of American emigration. They were even willing to abet slavery to promote the cotton trade and economic growth for the province. Erasmo Seguín himself owned a mulatto slave woman. In May 1836, Juan Seguín shadowed the retreat of Mexican General Pedro de Ampudia to reclaim slaves attempting to escape under the protection of the centralist army. The Seguín family clearly harbored few moral reservations concerning the "peculiar institution." Thus, having placed their economic and political bets on their new allies, when open revolt erupted federalist Tejanos could only play out their hand.[69]

LEGACIES

Tejanos had little choice but to be part of the momentous events of the mid-1830s. Their reactions varied. Some saw their destiny linked to the Texian separatist movement; others remained loyal to Mexico; yet others sought neutrality to protect their families and communities. Whatever their responses, Tejanos weighed political, economic, and cultural considerations in determining their path as the United States and Mexico converged to compete for Texas.

These turbulent times left Texas with many legacies, but one was the convergence of cultural traditions that had their origins on the bloody battlefields of the Texas Revolution. American immigrants who instigated the revolt, for instance, initially embraced the tactical modes of the North American woodlands. But when Texian officers tested those methods below the Guadalupe River — in what Travis designated "enemy country" — they proved sadly deficient. At that juncture, Texians welcomed those local Mexican federalists who came to their assistance. Although their numbers were never sufficient to completely alter the North American complexion of the rebel army, by the time of the Battle of San Jacinto, Austin, Houston, Rusk, Burleson, and other Texian commanders had begun to adapt their thinking to incorporate Tejano precepts.[70] Before long, backwoodsmen from the United States were swapping their mocassins for vaquero boots, their coonskin caps for sombreros, and their Kentucky long rifles for Colt "Paterson" five-shot revolvers. Admirers later claimed a Texas Ranger could "ride like a Mexican, trail like an Indian, shoot like a Tennessean, and fight like a devil."

Still, that description would not have been accurate prior to 1835. Anglo-Celtic Americans had to be taught how to ride like Mexicans, and allies such as Juan Seguín and Plácido Benavides proved able instructors; their American friends respected them. Although he spoke no English, Seguín, for example, was Béxar's senator to the Texas Congress and, during the third and fourth congresses, served as chairman of the Committee on Military Affairs.[71] Texians recognized his abilities as a soldier and administrator.

These and other kinds of interactions, sometimes strained and other times collaborative, brought together Tejano and Anglo-Celtic American traditions and in this way Tejanos clearly influenced the direction of the cultural legacy that is Texas.

BETWEEN TWO WORLDS
Timothy M. Matovina

T he period of the Texas Republic
was a time of significant change for San Antonio's predominantly Tejano
population. Military conflicts in the town during the Texas Revolution
and afterward precipitated a dilemma for local Tejanos. They were native
Texans who had consistently promoted regional interests in their dealings
with state and national officials. But they were also Mexican Catholics
who valued their cultural and religious heritage. To side with the Anglo
Americans of Texas would mean fighting against those with whom they
shared that heritage; to side with Mexico might mean expulsion from
their Texas homeland. Anglo Americans and Mexican officials pressured
Tejanos to support their respective efforts for control of Texas, further
exacerbating the Tejano dilemma of choosing between their opposing armies. With Texas independence, a new political order was also established,
along with the promulgation of religious freedom in a region that for-
merly had a legal prescription of Catholicism.

The response of San Antonio Tejanos to these changes included both
accommodation and resistance. On the one hand, local Tejanos adapted
to Texas independence and the consequent change in the political system.
This enabled them to promote their own interests and live in tenuous
harmony with the Anglo-American population of Texas which had vastly
eclipsed them in size. At the same time, San Antonio Tejanos retained
their Catholic allegiance and continued to celebrate Mexican Catholic
feasts and other public festivities. Thus they resisted the diminution of
their religious and cultural heritage even after they were separated from
Mexican political jurisdiction. This process of accommodation and resistance shaped San Antonio Tejano identity during the period of the Texas
Republic.

THE TEJANO DILEMMA

The Tejano dilemma of choosing between their Texas homeland and the Mexico of their cultural heritage was evidenced by their divided loyalties in the various battles of the Texas Revolution.[1] At the siege of San Antonio by Texas troops (December, 1835), the battle of the Alamo (March 6, 1836), and the decisive battle of San Jacinto (April 21, 1836), citizens of Mexican descent fought on both sides of the conflict. As difficult as the decision to take up arms against one's friends and neighbors must have been, for Tejanos the divisions between family members were undoubtedly more distressing. San Antonio native Gregorio Esparza fought for Texas in the siege of his town and in the Alamo, while his brother Francisco fought on the Mexican side. At the battle of San Jacinto, San Antonio resident Ambrosio Rodríguez fought on the Texas side, while his kinsman Mariano Rodríguez was in Santa Anna's army. Others, such as the Navarro family of San Antonio, did not have combatants enlisted on both sides, but remained divided in their loyalties.[2]

The accusations of traitorous conduct directed at Tejanos by both Anglo Americans and Mexican authorities added to the dilemma Tejanos faced. In December, 1835, Governor Henry Smith warned General Edward Burleson not to trust the "false friends" among San Antonio Tejanos during the Texan siege of their town. A month later, Doctor Amos Pollard warned Smith from San Antonio about "our most formidable foe—our internal enemy—the Mexican Tory party of the country." Colonel William Barret Travis wrote a letter from the Alamo declaring all San Antonio residents who had not joined him there "public enemies." While Anglo Americans were making these accusations, Mexican officials wished a "thousand curses on the Mexican who should be dastardly enough to join in that murderous and anti-national plot [the Texas revolt]" and asserted that anyone who did not oppose the loss of Texas was a traitor who deserved death. Those of Mexican descent who sided with the Texas cause, such as Lorenzo de Zavala and native San Antonians Juan Nepomuceno Seguín, José Antonio Navarro, and Antonio Menchaca, were also accused of being traitors to their own people.[3]

The accusations and pressures directed at San Antonio Tejanos by both sides continued after the Revolution. In November, 1836, a press report in a Texas newspaper labeled Tejanos who remained at San Antonio "pretended friends" of Texas. A visitor to the town in 1837 observed that "a small military force is stationed at San Antonio to prevent treasonable intercourse with the inhabitants beyond the Rio Grande." Such "treasonable intercourse" was actively promoted by Mexican authorities, who considered it the duty of all patriotic Mexicans to assist in the reconquest of Texas. Mexican authorities also had clandestine negotiations with persons of Mexican descent in Texas and attempted to win their support for a reconquest effort in exchange for the promise of future privileges under Mexican rule.[4]

The continued pressures placed on Tejanos to choose for the Mexican or Texan cause reached a pinnacle in 1842. San Antonio was occupied twice that year by Mexican forces, first in March by an expedition under the leadership of General Rafael Vásquez, and again in September by General Adrian Woll. These invasions were preceded by a proclamation from General Mariano Arista of Mexico, which promised amnesty and protection to those who did not resist the upcoming invasion and threatened to direct "the sword of justice against the obstinate." Arista's proclamation was distributed to residents of Mexican descent at San Antonio, who would presumably be counted among the "obstinate" if they refused to align themselves with the Mexican cause.[5]

While Arista pressured Tejanos to revivify their Mexican allegiance, Anglo Americans claimed that San Antonio Tejanos encouraged the Vásquez raid and advised the enemy about the movements of the Texas militia.[6] They also alleged that one of the primary purposes of Woll's expedition was to escort two hundred San Antonio families who were faithful to Mexico back across the Rio Grande. After Woll withdrew from San Antonio with these two hundred families in late September, a Houston newspaper claimed:

> Some of the most intelligent and respectable citizens of [San Antonio de] Béxar assert that a petition was forwarded to Santa Anna a few months since. It was signed by a large number of the Mexican citizens of Béxar, and in it they complained that they were constantly subjected to impositions and exactions by marauding parties . . . They stated moreover that they had never been satisfied with the Texian government, and that they desired to be placed once more under the laws of Mexico.

While contemporary witnesses like Catholic Bishop Jean Marie Odin held that these families were forced out of their homeland by the Texas militia, Anglo-American accusations and suspicions of Tejanos continued.[7]

The Tejano population of San Antonio responded to the events of 1842 with ambivalence. As in the 1835–1836 struggle for Texas independence, in the 1842 conflicts San Antonians of Mexican heritage were reportedly represented in both the Mexican and the Texan military forces. Tejanos also offered assistance to the wounded and captured of both sides.[8] Woll stated that four San Antonio Tejanos went out and asked him to turn back, claiming that if he did not, residents of Mexican descent would be compelled to join Anglo Americans who were preparing to defend the town. Before these representatives met with Woll, another group of San Antonio Tejanos had already voluntarily joined the Texas militia. This group disbanded at the sight of Woll's numerical strength, however, and were seen a few days later greeting him peaceably. One Tejano defender of the city, Antonio Menchaca, a veteran of the Texas Revolution, later claimed he successfully resisted Anglo Americans who proposed to burn San Antonio. While Anglo Americans argued that San Antonio's isolation enabled the Mexican army to plant spies there and easily capture it, Menchaca reminded them that his aging mother and others would be left destitute by their proposed action. In the space of just a few weeks, then, Menchaca defended his home town against both Mexican attack and Anglo-American destruction.[9]

The response of San Antonio Tejanos to the 1842 conflicts and other battles is in part explained by the instinct to survive. Local Tejanos had reason to fear dire consequences if they supported a losing army. The survival instinct accounts for the neutrality that the Houston press noted in local residents: "They [the Tejanos near Victoria, Texas] appear, however, to be inoffensive, and probably temporise with both parties like the Mexicans of [San Antonio de] Béxar, in order to maintain their homes undisturbed." An Anglo American who visited San Antonio in 1842 commented that local Tejanos "profess to be friendly to the Texans, but are also obliged, for safety, to make similar protestations to the Mexican soldiery, when they see fit to visit them." The number of families that moved back and forth to Mexico and ranches in the San Antonio area during times of hostility is further evidence of Tejano neutrality.[10]

Not all Tejanos were neutral, however, and many participated actively in the cause of Texas or Mexico. Whether neutral or active in the Texan-Mexican conflict, San Antonio Tejanos were caught between Mexican and Texan demands. Depending on the circumstances, some Tejanos employed alternately the strategies of neutrality and participation. Others changed sides when they thought it convenient or necessary.[11]

THE POLITICS OF ACCOMMODATION

The victory over the Mexican army at San Jacinto won Texas independence and made the Texas Constitution and subsequent legislation the law of the land. San Antonio Tejanos, who constituted only a fraction of Texas's population by the 1830s, had exercised a political influence disproportionate to their numbers under Mexican rule. As might be expected, however, with the advent of Texas independence, Tejano political clout in the national legislature declined. Only two Tejanos were elected to the Texas senate during this period, Francisco Ruiz (1836–1837) and Juan Nepomuceno Seguín (1838–1840). Two others, José Antonio Navarro (1838–1839) and Rafael Calixto de la Garza (1842–1843), served in the house of representatives. On the local scene, only one Tejano mayor was elected during this period, but Tejanos retained control of the city council. Decreasing Tejano representation in political bodies necessitated a strategy of accommodation in order to promote Tejano interests within a new Texas political system.

At the national level, San Antonio Tejano leaders demonstrated their allegiance to the Republic of Texas in various ways. Senator Juan Seguín, for example, introduced a resolution in 1838 that would allow the government to confiscate the property of collaborators in "the present Indian war." This legislation was directed at participants in the Córdova Revolt, an unsuccessful attempt by Nacogdoches Tejanos and their allies to restore Mexican rule over Texas. Seguín's resolution showed his willingness to oppose fellow Tejanos who did not accept Texas independence. Three years later, José Antonio Navarro served as a commissioner in the Santa Fé expedition, an effort to incorporate New Mexican residents into the Republic of Texas. Navarro was captured along with other members of this ill-fated expedition, and subsequently imprisoned for four years in Mexico. While Navarro's rationale for accepting the role of commissioner in this venture is subject to debate, clearly his participation indicates pro-Texas sentiments.[12]

More frequently, however, San Antonio leaders lobbied for the concerns of their Tejano constituency in Texas national politics. They were not always successful in their efforts. In 1836, Senator Francisco Ruiz argued that Tejanos who accepted Santa Anna's offer of pardon after the Alamo battle did so "in the midst of confusion, terror and affright," and pleaded that the First Congress of the Republic of Texas "adopt some measure which will give them the assurance that they may return without the fear of harm or molestation" to their homes. But no such legislation was passed by the Congress.[13]

One of Senator Juan Seguín's first acts in the 1838 sessions of Congress was to present a bill that would have provided relief for widows and orphans of Tejanos slain in the defense of the Alamo. As late as 1860, the

Bexar County Court of Claims was still debating the grants due by law to the families of these Tejano veterans; some never received their justified claims.[14] In 1840, Senator Seguín asked when the laws of Texas would be translated into Spanish for the benefit of his constituency. Claiming that the lengthy delay in providing these translations was a violation of Tejano rights, Seguín argued that "the Mexico-Texians were among the first who sacrificed their all in our glorious Revolution, and the disasters of war weighed heavy upon them, to achieve those blessings which, it appears, [they] are destined to be the last to enjoy." Despite Seguín's urgent appeal, translations of this legislation were not immediately forthcoming. Seguín also introduced legislation at that Congress to provide national funds for a jail in Bexar County, but once again was unsuccessful.[15]

In 1839, San Antonio congressional representative José Antonio Navarro pleaded in vain for the enactment of another piece of legislation; it would have aided San Antonio Tejanos who had no title to their lands, could not speak English, and lacked the finances and familiarity with the legal system necessary for lawsuits. At the Texas Constitutional Convention before U.S. annexation in 1845, Navarro moved that the seat of government for Texas be located in Béxar. He even offered a league of land to encourage this decision, but his motion was defeated.[16]

In some instances, Tejano legislative efforts on the national level were successful. A bill presented by Senator Seguín in 1839 established a mail route from Austin to San Antonio. In 1840, Seguín reported, as chairman of the Senate Committee on Military Affairs, that the laws to provide military defense for the border settlements of Texas "have been carried out but partially, and that but very limited protection has been afforded to the frontier settlers." The legislation that Seguín endorsed was passed a month later.[17]

At the 1845 Texas Constitutional Convention, there was heated debate about the proposal that suffrage be extended exclusively to the "free white population." A speech made by F. J. Moore of Harris County left no doubt that for some delegates this was meant to disenfranchise Tejanos:

> Strike out the term "white," and what will be the result? Hordes of Mexican Indians may come in here from the West, and may be more formidable than the enemy you have vanquished. Silently they will come moving in; they will come back in thousands to Bexar, in thousands to Goliad, perhaps to Nacogdoches, and what will be the consequence? Ten, twenty, thirty, forty, fifty thousand may come in here, and vanquish you at the ballot box.

José Antonio Navarro contended that including the word "white" in electoral legislation was "odious" and "ridiculous." In the end, the position of Navarro and others held sway, as Tejanos were not denied voting rights in the Constitution of the State of Texas. Perhaps in response to the suffering the Texas army inflicted on Tejanos during the period of the Texas Republic, Navarro also successfully promoted the following statute in the state constitution: "No soldier shall, in time of peace, be quartered in the house, or within the enclosure of any individual, without the consent of the owner; nor in time of war, but in a manner prescribed by law."[18]

The influence of the change from Mexican to Texan rule, and on Tejano response to those affairs, was demonstrated in a series of events following the Texas Revolution. With threats of a renewed Mexican invasion after the Texas victory at San Jacinto, Colonel Juan Seguín left San Antonio with his troops in June, 1836. He also urged local Tejanos to do the same and take their livestock to keep it from any advancing Mexican army. Seguín led his troops back to San Antonio in November at the order of President Sam Houston. Claiming that the threat of Mexican attack continued, a Texas newspaper called for the evacuation and destruction of San Antonio, thus preventing enemy use of its resources. General Felix Huston concurred with this strategy and ordered Seguín to abandon and destroy the town. Seguín did not comply with General Huston's orders, however. Instead, he successfully petitioned President Houston to rescind them.[19]

As commander of San Antonio, Seguín encouraged Tejano citizens to cooperate with the Texan defense against a threatened Mexican reconquest effort. But upon receiving an order that was clearly harmful to his home town and its inhabitants, he petitioned the president to join him in defending Tejano interests. His attempt to promote Tejano interests while demonstrating loyalty to his new nation illustrates Tejano political strategy during the period of the Texas Republic.

This strategy is also evident in local elections at San Antonio. Tejanos continued to be the majority population and won the majority of city council seats in all elections held during this period. In the first municipal elections after Texas independence, all but one of the forty-one candidates were of Spanish-Mexican descent. Continuing Tejano control of the city council was reflected in the council minutes, which were kept exclusively in Spanish until 1838, and in both Spanish and English from 1838 to 1844.[20]

Nonetheless, Tejanos accommodated to the reality of an increasing Anglo-American population. Indeed, it is striking that despite the Tejano electoral majority, Anglo Americans consistently won election to the mayoral office in San Antonio during the Texas Republic. The sole exceptions were the elections of 1841 and 1842, when voters selected Juan Seguín for mayor. In 1837, John W. Smith, the only Anglo American in a field of forty-one candidates, was elected mayor![21]

David Montejano has argued that Anglo-American control of Tejano strongholds like San Antonio was consolidated by means of a "peace structure." By "peace structure" Montejano refers to "a general postwar arrangement that allows the victors to maintain law and order without the constant use of force." One of the primary elements in this structure was "an accommodation between the victorious Anglos and the defeated Mexican elite." This accommodation did not substantially alter the traditional authority structures of Tejano society, but, rather, placed Anglo Americans atop the existing hierarchy. Often, marriages between Anglo-American men and daughters from the elite families of a locale played a key role in this arrangement. These marriages offered Anglo Americans the advantages of land, inherited wealth, and social status. They offered local Tejanos allies to help protect familial interests and landholdings. After Texas independence, such allies were particularly useful as many Tejanos did not speak English, were unfamiliar with the legal system, and were vulnerable to accusations of disloyalty.[22]

It is not surprising, then, that during this time of transition "at least one daughter from almost every *rico* [rich] family in San Antonio married an Anglo." Anglo-American elected officials often had Tejana wives. A daughter of José Antonio Navarro, for example, married the adjutant general of the state, while daughters from the De la Garza family wed the county clerk and the sheriff, respectively. Among the mayors of San Antonio during the Texas Republic, John W. Smith (1837–1838, 1840–1841, 1842–1844) and Edward Dwyer (1844–1845) had Tejana wives.[23]

Other Anglo-American mayors such as Samuel A. Maverick (1839–1840) maintained social contacts with Tejanos. The Mavericks exchanged social calls with prominent Tejano families like the Navarros, Sotos, Garzas, Garcías, Zambranos, Seguíns, Veramendis, and Yturris. Samuel Maverick's wife, Mary, wrote in 1838 that "our only society are Mexicans." The Mavericks participated at local festivities in honor of our Lady of Guadalupe, including a dance held by "the more prominent families" at the Flores residence, and also attended a dance at the Yturri home given in honor of Mirabeau Buonaparte Lamar, the president of Texas. While Samuel Maverick did not marry a daughter from a local family, his election as mayor was accompanied by his incorporation into the social circle of the Tejano elite. This is consistent with Montejano's concept of peace structure.[24]

CATHOLIC ALLEGIANCE
AND LOCAL TRADITIONS

After Texas independence, Protestant denominations quickly established official structures to coordinate ministries in the new Republic.[25] Most Protestant activity was in settlements to the east of San Antonio and conducted predominantly among Anglo-American residents. Protestant leaders recognized that the possibilities of success were greater among Anglo Americans from Protestant backgrounds. Furthermore, a scarcity of resources prevented much initial outreach to Tejano Catholics at San Antonio and elsewhere. As one Methodist missionary wrote in 1838: "I have hitherto [been] prevented from visiting [San Antonio de] Bexar and its vicinity, as I had intended; but it seems, in some instances, more needful to supply and occupy places which we have explored, than to explore others which we cannot occupy." The danger of Indian attack on the journey to San Antonio was another obstacle; an Episcopalian priest canceled a trip to San Antonio in 1843 because of this threat. Denominational life at San Antonio during the period of the Texas Republic was summarized well by Baptist minister Z. N. Morrell, who claimed after an 1839 visit that Catholicism "reigned [there] without a rival."[26]

Some Protestant clergy interpreted the independence of Texas as divine sanction for the spread of their missionary influence among people of Mexican heritage. Reverend A. B. Lawrence wrote in 1840:

> To Protestant Christians the events of Texas are further deeply interesting, as an indication of Providence in relation to the propagation of divine truth in other parts of the Mexican dominions. . . . Viewed then as the beginning of the downfall of Antichrist, and the spread of the Saviour's power of the gospel, the history and relations of Texas must furnish to the mind of the ardent Christian subjects of deep enquiry, delightful contemplation, and fervid thanksgiving.[27]

Along with the pressure of demonstrating their Texan loyalty to suspicious Anglo Americans and adapting to a new political system, then, Tejanos were also confronted with an Anglo-American approach to religion that saw Mexican Catholicism as inherently inferior and Protestantism as a force that would inevitably conquer the continent. This view of religious "manifest destiny" was reinforced by expanding Protestant ministries in other areas of the Republic. As Catholicism was the prescribed religion at San Antonio de Béxar throughout the Spanish and Mexican periods, these attitudes challenged an assumed element of Tejano life and identity. There are no recorded instances of San Antonio Tejanos becoming Protestants during this period. But their continued practice of Catholicism becomes more significant in light of the Anglo-American assumption that abandoning their Catholic heritage would enable Tejanos to comply with divine providence and improve themselves as a people.

Within the Catholic Church, other changes influenced the religious life of San Antonio Tejanos. In 1840, Pope Gregory XVI removed Texas from the Mexican diocese of Linares and declared it a prefecture apostolic under the diocese of New Orleans. He appointed Father John Timon, a Vincentian, as prefect apostolic. Since Timon was unable to undertake the responsibility personally because of other duties within his congregation, his French confrère, Jean Marie Odin, assumed the leadership of the church in Texas as vice prefect apostolic. The following year, the pope elevated Texas to a vicariate apostolic and named Odin the vicar apostolic. Texas remained a vicariate apostolic under the diocese of New Orleans until the establishment of Galveston as the first Texas episcopal see in 1847, with Odin as first ordinary.[28]

This shift in ecclesiastical jurisdiction led to a change in clergy at San Antonio's San Fernando parish. During his first visit to the city in 1840, Odin removed the two native San Antonian priests, Refugio de la Garza and José Antonio Valdez, claiming that their ministry was ineffective and that they had broken their priestly vows by having wives and children. In their place, he appointed his Spanish confrère Miguel Calvo as pastor of San Fernando.[29]

Some foreign priests who encountered Tejanos for the first time opined that their knowledge and practice of the faith were inadequate. Former prefect apostolic Timon stated that "the poor Mexicans would die for their religion, yet they hardly knew what their religion was; how could they? Their faith was rather a divine instinct that grew from their baptism, than a faith of knowledge." Recalling his first years in Texas, Odin later wrote that the Catholic population he encountered "kept no more than a slight vestige of faith."[30]

Catholic clergy were not always critical of Tejano Catholicism, however. Odin, for example, participated in Tejano religious feasts like the 1841 San Antonio celebration in honor of Our Lady of Guadalupe and, in contrast to his later statement about Tejanos' lack of faith, spoke enthusiastically of the religious zeal demonstrated in these celebrations. Many priests also made heroic efforts to serve the Spanish-speaking segment of their flock. Odin learned Spanish and was insistent that those coming to minister in Texas do the same, including his episcopal successor, whom he said should be "acquainted with the English and Spanish languages."

Calvo's Vincentian confrères later claimed that, during his twelve years as pastor of San Fernando (1840–1852), he "consoled and defended the native-born [Tejanos] against the cruelty of the yankees." The efforts of Catholic priests to participate in Tejano religious feasts, learn Spanish, and offer pastoral service and support to the Tejano community encouraged Tejanos to retain their Catholic allegiance.[31]

Another impetus for enduring Catholic affiliation among San Antonio Tejanos was their own initiatives to continue celebrating Mexican Catholic feasts. Even though Odin and others may have been caring pastors, their lack of familiarity with local traditions meant Tejano leaders had to assume much of the responsibility for continuing those traditions. While local leaders had organized communal celebrations since the eighteenth century, frequently they had done so in conjunction with clergy like Father de la Garza, who were accustomed to Tejano feasts and practices. Odin and Calvo may have been familiar with feasts like Our Lady of Guadalupe, but some local practices in celebrating these feasts were undoubtedly new to them.[32] By Odin's own account of San Antonio's 1841 Guadalupe celebration, Tejano leaders collected funds for purchasing gunpowder, which was used in firing salutes as an expression of devotion. He also wrote that Tejanas exercised a leadership role, assisting in the decoration of San Fernando Church and the Guadalupan image used in processions. Odin asserted that he had "seen few processions more edifying" than the one prepared by the local Tejano population. His cooperative approach did not detract from Tejano initiatives to celebrate the feast of their patroness in the customary manner. These initiatives revealed the value of local traditions to the Tejano community.[33]

Two contemporary accounts of the San Antonio Guadalupe celebrations from primary sources are extant. One is Odin's account of the 1841 celebration; the other, taken from the memoirs of Mary A. Maverick, who was Protestant, provides an account of the celebration in 1840.[34] In both Odin's and Maverick's descriptions the most noteworthy activity mentioned is the Guadalupe processions. Maverick describes one procession, Odin two (one in the afternoon and the other in the evening). Although there are minor discrepancies between the two accounts, there is enough agreement to suggest some general patterns for the ritual performance of the processions. An elegantly adorned image of our Lady of Guadalupe was the principal ritual object. Odin also mentions a cross, a banner of Mary, and the ornaments offered by local women for the decoration of the church. Priests and the general populace both took part in the processions. Young girls dressed in white and bearing candles (some carried flowers, according to Odin) were the immediate attendants of the Guadalupan image. Maverick adds that fiddlers also participated, Odin that sixty members of the militia served as escorts. The rosary was prayed, and, according to Odin, religious hymns honoring the mother of God were sung. Both observers recall guns being fired as part of the devotion, and Odin writes of cannons and bells sounding as well. They also mention religious ceremonies at San Fernando Church in addition to the processions.

These colorful Guadalupe processions exemplified the Mexican heritage of local Tejanos and perpetuated a devotion prevalent in San Antonio from the early years of the settlement's history. The continued celebration of the Guadalupe feast in the traditional manner showed that Tejano signs of allegiance to the Texan cause did not indicate a rejection of their Mexican Catholic heritage.

Anglo-American participation in the Guadalupan feast showed the strength of local traditions at San Antonio and the Tejano desire to incorporate newcomers into those traditions. As has been mentioned, the Maverick family attended the 1840 Guadalupe celebration, while Odin wrote that Anglo Americans from as far away as Austin attended in 1841.

Anglo Americans also joined with Tejanos in other public events at San Antonio. The popular *fandangos* (dances) were attended by numerous visitors to the town.[35] In 1841, both Tejano and Anglo-American residents participated in a twenty-one-gun salute and dance given in honor of visiting Texas president Mirabeau Buonaparte Lamar. The 1837 interment ceremony for the ashes of the Alamo dead also brought Tejanos and Anglo Americans together. Juan Seguín led the ceremony and was accompanied in procession by other members of the military, civil authorities, clergy, musicians, and the general populace. Seguín gave a speech in which he stated: "The venerable remains of our worthy companions as witnesses, I invite you to declare to the entire world, 'Texas shall be free and independent, or we shall perish in glorious combat.'" While the procession resembled similar communal efforts in the town's past, the rationale for gathering and the sentiment of Seguín's speech demonstrated loyalty to the Texas Republic.[36]

The Mexican background of San Antonio Tejanos was reflected in other communal events. Despite claims to the contrary by Mexican officials, the celebration of Mexican Independence Day continued in San Antonio even after Texas independence. Apparently, Tejano separation from Mexico as a political entity did not sever the bonds of national sentiment they held in common with others of Mexican heritage. A British traveler wrote the following in his diary entry for October 1, 1843: "The Maromeros, or Mexican rope dancers, are jumping about this evening. Although San Antonio is governed by Texan laws, Mexican customs prevail; rope dancing, tumbling, and plays on a Sunday!"[37]

CONCLUSION

When asked in later years if he loved Texas more than Mexico, San Antonio resident Enrique Esparza reportedly stated that he was of mixed Indian and Spanish blood and "proud of that ancestry." He then added that he saw his father "die for Texas" in the battle of the Alamo and that he was "proud to be a Texan and an American."[38] This statement reflects Tejano response to the dilemma they faced during the Texas Republic. Caught between demands, accusations, and pressure from both Anglo Americans and Mexican officials, Tejanos tried to sustain themselves during a series of attacks and counterattacks. Conflicting allegiances among San Antonio Tejanos are indicative of their desire to remain loyal to both their Texan homeland and their Mexican cultural motherland. The choice for neutrality was an attempt to avoid violence and harm by remaining in peace with both sides. In either case, the pressure to choose sides led Tejanos to forge an identity that could resolve the tensions inherent in being caught between two opposing armies.

As the prospects of permanent separation from Mexican political jurisdiction became more probable, however, Anglo Americans increasingly pressured Tejanos either to abandon their homeland or to align their national sentiments with those of the Texas Republic. The flight of San Antonio Tejanos with General Woll illustrates that many Tejanos felt the pressure of Anglo-American animosities. While Tejanos like Antonio Menchaca resisted Anglo-American military objectives such as the destruction of San Antonio, this resistance was possible only for those who, like Menchaca, had demonstrated loyalty to the Texan cause through military service or by other means. Faced with the dilemma of choosing sides in the Texas-Mexico conflict, Tejanos who chose to remain in Texas increasingly presented themselves as a people of Mexican heritage who were loyal (or at least unopposed) to the cause of Texas.

Diminishing influence in national affairs after Texas independence forced Tejanos to accept a new political reign in which Anglo-American interests consistently won out over Tejano claims. While actions like José Antonio Navarro's participation as commissioner in the Santa Fé expedition supported Anglo-American political aspirations, Tejano legislative efforts more typically promoted their own concerns. The suffrage debate at the 1845 Texas Constitutional Convention is evidence of the Tejano political struggle, as Navarro had to fight for voting rights that never would have been challenged under Mexican rule. Limited potential influence did not deter Tejano representatives from championing the rights of their constituency, however. They accommodated themselves to Texas law and procedures but struggled within that framework to advance the interests of Tejano citizens.

Juan Seguín's response to General Felix Huston's 1836 order for the abandonment and destruction of San Antonio illustrates Tejano political strategy during the Texas Republic. Seguín demonstrated his allegiance to Texas in his efforts to protect the frontier but defended Tejano interests by counteracting his superior's potentially damaging order.

The election of Anglo-American mayors during this period was also part of Tejano accommodation to a new political reality. Tejanos incorporated Anglo Americans into local leadership by consistently electing Anglo-American mayors. But they also tended to select Anglo Americans who were aligned by marriage or other ties to local families, while Tejanos themselves retained a majority among the members of the city council. By choosing Anglo-American mayors, San Antonio voters demonstrated that they were not sustaining a Tejano enclave that was hostile to its Anglo-American neighbors. By choosing mayors tied to local families, they gained potential allies in the broader network of a new and unfamiliar political system.

Despite increased religious pluralism in Texas and Protestant inducement to change religious affiliation, the Mexican Catholic identity of San Antonio Tejanos remained intact throughout the period of the Texas Republic. Following the removal of their native clergy, continuing Tejano initiatives perpetuated local traditions for feasts like Our Lady of Guadalupe. The celebration after Texas independence of the Guadalupan feast, Mexican Independence Day, dances, and Mexican entertainments like the *maromeros* showed that Tejano signs of allegiance to the Texan cause did not indicate a rejection of their Mexican heritage. Anglo-American participation in Tejano celebrations like the Guadalupe feast and *fandangos* demonstrate the vitality of Tejano traditions at San Antonio and the Tejano desire to incorporate newcomers into the celebrations of their religious and cultural heritage. At the same time, ceremonies such as the interment of the Alamo dead and social events like the dance for President Lamar indicated that Tejanos were also part of Anglo-American Texas. Intentionally or not, San Antonio Tejanos' religious and other celebrations provided a means to express their emerging identity as citizens of the Texas Republic who proudly retained their Mexican Catholic heritage.

It is not surprising that San Antonio Tejano accommodation during the Texas Republic was most evident in the realms of national loyalty and the new political system. Flagrant resistance to the national security of Texas or its political procedures undoubtedly would have evoked a vigorous response from Anglo-American settlers in the Republic. On the other hand, weak Protestant proselytizing efforts, the Spanish language ministry of Catholic priests, Tejano initiatives to continue local traditions, the numerical majority of the local Tejano population, and the constitutional guarantee of religious freedom facilitated continuing Tejano Catholic allegiance and the celebration of Mexican Catholic feasts and other public festivities at San Antonio. Anglo-American participation in Tejano celebrations shows the extent to which San Antonio's Mexican population maintained its religious and cultural heritage.

Separation from Mexico removed Tejanos from political alliance with others of Mexican culture and raised the question of whether they would abandon that heritage altogether. Andrés Tijerina has said that Tejanos caught in this historical conflict "increasingly defined themselves as an entity different from Mexico and separate from the Anglo." [39] In the face of changes brought about by Texas independence, the identity of San Antonio Tejanos was increasingly shaped by their efforts to sustain their religious and cultural heritage while adapting to a new political order.

SIX

THE CÓRDOVA REVOLT

Paul D. Lack

Tejanos responded to their declining status in the Texas Republic with varied forms of resistance, some creative or adaptive and others direct. The most far-reaching and blunt rebellion broke out in the region of Nacogdoches in the summer of 1838 under the leadership of Vicente Córdova. It had the potential for undermining the tenuous legitimacy of the new Texas political order by combining all the minorities of the region—Mexicans, Indians, disaffected Anglos, and even blacks—with additional support promised by the central government of Mexico. Because of this last element, analysis of the Córdova rebellion has generally focused on the conspiratorial dimension as an episode in Texas-Mexican border warfare.[1] The perspective of the rebels themselves suggests an alternate view: that of a rebellion born of desperation following years of worsening isolation, political decline, unremitting tensions, and failed halfway alternatives.

Vicente Córdova was born in 1798. His generation came to maturity in a small community (strategically placed near an international border) swept by far-reaching changes in an age of revolution. Mexico's struggle for independence began in 1810 as he became a teenager and did not end until he was twenty-three. During these years plots hatched and power shifted abruptly. Amid this political scheming and land speculation, a major demographic changed occurred. In the 1820s, Mexican colonization laws invited settlers into Texas in order to spur its development and to provide a buffer against expansion from the United States. Individuals seeking the promised land and various impresarios with dubious or overlapping claims scrambled for firm titles.[2]

The native Mexicans in East Texas competed directly for property and power with non-Hispanic colonists. Most Tejanos in the region lived in and around Nacogdoches. Until 1834, the approximately six hundred Tejanos dominated or at least shared governmental offices. Subsequently, with votes cast along fairly rigid ethnic lines, Anglo candidates won nearly every political race along with economic leverage for resolving the maze of conflicting land claims. Increasingly, the Tejanos of the Nacogdoches area retreated into a separate community. A traveler from the United States observed that "there is no social intercourse between [Anglo Americans] and the Mexicans." Seething animosities and segregation combined to hurt the potential for reconciliation.[3]

NACOGDOCHES TEJANOS AND
THE TEXAS REBELLION

The Texas revolt against Mexico, which formally established a goal of independence in March, 1836, posed greater dilemmas for the Mexican population than any previous political crisis. What became the Texas Revolution began as a preventive movement to protect the system of limited government and local autonomy that had prevailed since the beginnings of Anglo colonization. Under the federalist Mexican Constitution of 1824, Texas had been successful in defending its interests from every challenge that arose in Mexico, thereby maintaining policies such as liberal immigration and de facto tolerance of slavery. The centralists, who gained power in 1834 under Antonio López de Santa Anna, promised firm government, thus threatening both the material interests of Texas and the tradition of virtual self-rule.[4]

At the local level, in East Texas this political controversy became nearly inverted. To the Tejanos, centralism held out a promise of external protection against the Anglo majority. In actual practice, though, the Nacogdoches Mexicans operated as a lonely minority, for meaningful centralist support was beleaguered and isolated four hundred miles away in Béxar at first and even farther south thereafter. Further, their political choices were never perfectly clear.

Several elements contended for local power during this period, including leaders who had been appointed or elected under Mexican authority and officers of the committees of vigilance and safety that emerged in the summer. This latter faction contained many recent immigrants, often impatient with Mexican institutions that they considered alien and backward. Thus, even though Anglos controlled most of the machinery of government, when resistance to the government of Santa Anna emerged in Nacogdoches in the late summer of 1835, it took the form of extralegal popular meetings. These groups threatened to confiscate the property of residents who refused to cooperate with vigilance committee measures, such as statements urging the dissolution of political connection with Mexico.[5]

The local Tejano population recognized the threatening turn of events and refused to participate. The only question seemed to be whether they would actually attempt to block the rebellious movement or would acquiesce in a kind of nervous neutrality. Efforts by Nacogdoches Mexicans to obtain outside aid failed badly. *Procurador* Antonio Menchaca informed the governor that Anglos had taken the law into their own hands to oppose Santa Anna and planned to "disarm all the Mexicans so that they cannot help defend the Government." He concluded with a plea for protection of "the Mexican citizens who love their Country." Centralist officials, however, promised only that treason would eventually be punished and order restored.[6]

This response left the Tejanos with but one meaningful source of power—the local militia. But would its captain, Vicente Córdova, attempt to involve the militia in the political contest? His opinions, as demonstrated in an address to the company at the end of August, leaned toward defense of the government of Mexico. He favored continuing the tradition of obedience to "the orders of our authorities" and "sustaining the laws" rather than heeding the voices of discontent. His rhetorical appeals—to God, the law, tradition, tranquillity, and preservation of property—all reflected mainstream conservative ideals.[7]

However strong these leanings, Córdova was isolated from centralist support, and it became impossible to defend the established order after other officials committed to the rebellion. Córdova's militia company declined in numbers and refused to participate in public rallies against centralist rule, but he did not make an open political commitment. A kind of informal understanding came about, with Mexican militiamen becoming a permanent guard to protect local families and preserve order. In essence, Córdova agreed not to resist the Texas Revolution, whose leaders, in turn, did not insist on Mexican participation in the war against other Mexicans.[8]

The Tejanos' unity as a community allowed them to avoid the war but perpetuated potential for Anglo-Tejano conflict. By November, rebel spokesmen expressed disappointment that the Tejanos remained, as one Nacogdoches leader explained to Sam Houston, "just as ever—[that is] to say unwilling to afford aid." On November 10, Córdova ordered his company to dissolve, thus maintaining the silent disobedience of the Nacogdoches Tejanos.[9] By early 1836, Texas leaders abandoned talk of defending Mexican federalism and moved toward independence.

Nacogdoches divided bitterly over the issue. Citizens of Mexican descent once again entered into public affairs against independence, but dubious voting procedures ensured the failure of their cause. The Nacogdoches election on February 1, 1836 (to choose delegates for the convention that would decide the independence issue) was determined by the votes of a military unit from the United States. These soldiers threatened force to gain the ballot and cast the deciding votes for pro-independence candidates.[10]

Tejanos had relied on constitutional processes that were swept aside by bolder methods. Their open opposition to independence and the worsening military position of Texas in March made them suspect in the eyes of the Anglo majority. When centralist forces advanced eastward in April, a panic erupted over an alleged plot of Nacogdoches Mexicans conspiring with Santa Anna and the Cherokee. Rumors of such a plan had existed since December, 1835. Details varied, but in most versions the uprising was to culminate in a joint attack timed for the arrival of the regular Mexican army.

Tensions nearly erupted in armed conflict during the week following April 9, 1836. On that day, Alcalde David A. Hoffman issued a notice that abruptly terminated the unwritten understanding of Tejano neutrality. The Texas convention on March 12, in providing for military conscription, had specified that Nacogdoches Mexicans should be organized into a separate unit. Hoffman ordered "every Mexican Citizen liable to Militia duty" to "take up the line of March, to the headquarters of our army" or to move to Louisiana or west of the Brazos within ten days. "Any failing to comply with this order, . . . or in any manner corresponding with the Indians to the prejudice of our cause, shall be dealt with as enemies, and treated according to the usual custom in time of war."[11] The Tejanos did form an active militia force under Córdova, but their purpose was self-defense rather than fighting against Mexico. As many as 250 Anglo-American volunteers also assembled under the vigilance committee.

The forces of each ethnic group engaged in what the other viewed as provocations. Anglo recruits set out to disarm Tejanos. This created fear among Córdova's men that an attempt would be made to burn the town, which they determined to prevent. On April 12, Córdova sent scouts toward Nacogdoches; this party, "full of passion," as their commander wrote, because of an impression that the town had been set on fire, arrested an American on suspicion of arson. Near clashes abounded as Anglo soldiers inspected Córdova's camp.[12]

Despite these incidents, Córdova and his opposites on the Anglo side negotiated their way to, first, a truce and, then, an understanding. On April 14, Córdova pointed out that the actions of his men in defense of the property of Nacogdoches could not be regarded as disloyalty and expressed willingness to find ways of "reconciling our people." However, the Tejano leader made it clear that confiscated weapons had to be returned as evidence of faith. Otherwise, "if the Mexicans are thus to be treated and suspected — I beg it may be remembered that they have it in their power if they are so disposed to do much mischief."[13] That same day the local Texas military commander accepted Córdova's terms and asked the Mexican militia to come forward to protect the town. "It is not intended," he wrote in contrast to the *alcalde*'s previous order, "that your duties will call you out of the municipality." These actions restored an uneasy peace.[14]

On April 17, the local commander wrote a reassuring review of the situation to General Houston and outlined details of the agreement with Córdova: "The Mexicans are organized and seem willing to do all they can in defence of the country against Indians who are pillaging." Yet, he added, the Nacogdoches Mexicans "will not fight their countrymen in the present instance." Houston continued to view the Tejanos as a threat and, in the summer of 1836, he opposed either enrolling them in the army or attempting again to disarm them.[15] Clearly, while the Mexicans of East Texas did not rise in armed rebellion against the Texas cause in 1836, they refused to support war against the central government of Mexico.

Tactically, their armed neutrality during 1835–1836 had preserved a form of community autonomy. Strategically, the outcome of the war for independence left East Texas Tejanos in an untenable position — more than ever isolated geographically, overwhelmed demographically, weakened militarily, and alienated politically. For the next two years, Córdova and his people persevered in their careful disaffection. Until proclaiming rebellion on August 10, 1838, they held to a studied silence of quiet dissent. On August 10, the Nacogdoches Tejanos declared that they had never accepted the legitimacy of the Texas Republic.

UNEQUAL BEFORE THE LAW

For its part, the new government made no effort to effect reconciliation with the non-Anglo populations of East Texas. Rather, encroachments on traditional lands grew more serious, threats to political privileges gained repeated expression, and rumors of the Tejano-Indian-Mexican conspiracy refused to die. The story that can be pieced together from testimony left by the Nacogdoches Mexicans tells of apprehension about attacks on home or family, unheeded complaints of mistreatment, and intolerable pressures of living as a suspect people. In the end, these cumulative tensions mixed with their passive political disloyalties to produce exactly the kind of rebellion that the Anglos had prophesied for three years.

The end of the military phase of the Texas Revolution brought scant respite to underlying Anglo-Tejano tensions in the Nacogdoches area. In June, 1836, military authorities considered again the issue of drafting Mexicans, and the local vigilance group discussed using force to make them join the cause. Later that month, Houston wrote to the head of that committee urging him "not to adopt any harsh measures towards the Mexicans in the neighborhood of Nacogdoches. Treat them kindly and pass them as tho' there was no difficulty or differences of opinion. *By no means* treat them with *violence*." This advice forestalled group conflict, but, individually, the Tejanos suffered at the hands of the law. They were detained illegally by private citizens and punished by whippings and forced labor for minor infractions.[16]

From the time of the first official election held under the Republic, the basic political rights of the Nacogdoches Mexicans came under challenge. In September, 1836, a group of eighty-two "american citizens" prepared a petition to Congress urging the disfranchisement of "the Mexican Population residing in the Municipality of Nacogdoches." The rationale of this meeting maintained that these people

> have been since the present struggle for liberty and Independance in Texas opposed to [the] greate cause in which all good Citizens have been Ingaged. They have uniformly refused their servises or to Contribute in anyway to aid the Cause of their suffering Country ingaged in one of the most fearful contests in the history of *Man* although they have had repeated calls from those appointed to muster them into servis and to ask their ade [illegible] They have by their repeated acts shown that they ware the friends of our enemies and the enemies of our friends. That they refused to aid the country whare their property is situate and whare institutions protect them in their political and cival rights . . . in the opinion of your petitioners they had by their Conduct in the present struggle completely forfeited those rights.

Local officials had kept and returned a separate polling of the Mexicans. The petitioners urged Congress to reject these votes, "beleaving that it would be a dangerous principle as well as a violation of the rights of the patriotick Citizens of the republick to admit persons to exercise the right of suffrage who are unfrenly to our Cause and who have allways been opposed to the Independance of our Country."[17] It appears that majority local sentiment prevailed; no further record of controversy regarding Mexican voting occurred in 1837 or 1838.

The political order also threatened the economic well-being of the Nacogdoches Tejanos. Anglos used the court system in debt collection suits, gaining judgments for cash payments and seizure of chattel or real property.[18] Throughout the new Republic, Andrés A. Tijerina has shown, Tejanos lost their land through bogus lawsuits, fraudulent sheriff's auctions, and other forced transfers of title. Outside the Rio Grande district, few persons of Mexican origin completed new land grants. In the Nacogdoches region, only 18 percent managed to patent their claims.[19]

CONSPIRACY RUMORS AND RISING TENSIONS

Conspiracy rumors continued to poison relations as concerns over another insurrection panic emerged again in the spring of 1837. President Houston's inability to implement treaty recognition of Cherokee land in the area kept Indian discontent alive, and reports circulated of delegations from Northeast Texas visiting with Mexican officials in Matamoros and of "a party of Spaniards" stimulating Indian attacks on Anglo families. One such warning came from the U.S. Army in Louisiana and provided the names of alleged conspirators, including Córdova.[20] The local authorities reacted energetically, communicating with the Cherokee and their defender, President Houston. A citizens' meeting on March 11 gained corroboration from local Mexican informants and formed a new vigilance committee and an emergency military company. No one initiated direct communication with the Tejanos, though it became clear that one of the informants was a personal enemy of Córdova.[21]

Belief in such a conspiracy loomed real not only because the charges seemed to arise annually as a rite of spring but also because violence formed such an integral part of the fabric of racial and ethnic relations. Cases of horse thievery, disputes over possession and title to land, and similar incidents erupted continually in the region north and west of town and often led to killings. Some of the president's correspondents attributed these "difficulties" to "the rascally manner in which" whites picked quarrels with Indians. Seldom could Anglos discern exact responsibility among the different groups living in the area because of the close relationships that existed among them. Runaway slaves took refuge among Indians who often held long-standing friendships with Tejanos; a Senate committee noted that the Caddoes "all understand and speak the Castilian Language."[22]

One particularly significant conflict centered around Richard Sparks, who attempted to settle on a tract of disputed frontier land. In March, 1837, he lost fourteen horses to a band of "Nadico" Indians reputedly headed by Telesforo Córdova; Houston's correspondent feared that indiscriminate retaliatory depredations would be carried out. Any such activities went unrecorded, but Sparks persisted in surveying near the headwaters of the Trinity until an unidentified group killed him and Indian agent Jess Watkins in the spring of 1838. A Nacogdoches meeting of 115 men, professing fear of a wholesale effort to drive Anglos from the area, requested that the Congress adopt either offensive or defensive measures. After the legislative body tabled this petition, another meeting demanded that Congress authorize and arm "an Independent Volunteer Corps, to be styled *The Nacogdoches Guards*," of men who pledged "to be ready at *all times*." In a veiled manner, this gathering defined Tejanos as enemies by arguing that hostile tribes had made an "unfriendly alliance with those of less doubtful pacific characters," which would "imminently endanger the safety of our town and the lives of our women and children."[23]

By the early spring of 1838, the leaders of the Tejano community had also reached the point of exhaustion with the relentless atmosphere of tension. Vicente Córdova, Antonio Menchaca, and three others wrote a letter requesting assurances that "we may retire and attend to our private affairs." Though this document survives only in garbled translation, it basically summarizes the travail of the Nacogdoches Mexicans. They sought "tranquility," "more security of their property," and an end to the attitude that held "that they should be considered as Enemies." The letter expressed chagrin at the antipathy directed toward them despite their adherence to the promise of peace. It renewed a pledge "to do no harm to persons who have treated us" in a worthy manner, but criticized the prevailing Anglo attitude. The document reads like a plea for some kind of official reassurance, but renewed outbreaks of violence and military mobilization took place instead. Houston appended a note to this document that described its fate: "The enclosed Translation was promised by Genl [Thomas J.] Rusk to be handed over the month of March . . . but never was sent previous to the 30th Augt [after the Córdova rebellion began] — Had the facts been communicated to the President, he might have prevented the evils which have resulted so destructive to that section of the Country."[24] Receiving no official response to their letter, the leaders moved forward on a cataclysmic path.

During the time of the Córdova rebellion, Anglo evaluation of Tejano motivations generally reflected the approach taken by two major leaders. One, General Rusk, who had headed the military response, attributed the affair simply to evil Mexicans. He described the rebels as "reckless desperados," "infernal scoundrels who have meditated the death of women and children," and who had previously done nothing to defend their country but now attacked it "without provocation."[25] The other, President Houston, also considered their cause unjust. His official proclamation derided the "pretext that they apprehend danger at their homes." Privately, he wrote that the affair had been brought on by mere horse stealing. At the same time, Houston on August 11 informed Andrew Jackson that "a commotion broke out which had been long preparing. The violence of the American character was one cause, and measures were taken without my knowledge or consent."[26]

The explanation of the Córdova rebels themselves emphasized preservation of their familial and political traditions. The ones who made the first hostile moves against Anglo residents explained their behavior as defensive: "the Americans were taking their people."[27] The official proclamation of rebellion on August 10, signed by Vicente Córdova and eighteen others (including a black and three Anglos), asserted:

> The citizens of Nacogdoches, tired of suffering injustices and the usurpation of their rights, cannot but state that having gathered together with their weapons in hand, they are determined to shed their last drop of blood in order to protect their individual rights and those of the Nation to which they belong. They confess, as they have in the past, that they have no knowledge of the current laws by which guarantees of their lives and property are offered. They ask only that their families not be molested, in return promising their good conduct toward yours.[28]

Oral tradition passed down the words of another rebel that captured the mood of one of the rank and file. Guillermo Cruz responded to the questioning of his former employer, Joseph Durst, by explaining: "they were going to fight for their rights, they had been dogs long enough."[29]

The conditions for success must have seemed as favorable as they were ever likely to be. The isolation of the Nacogdoches rebels had no remedy, and each day their minority status grew more pronounced as emigration from the United States continued. The timing must have seemed good — the spring of 1838 passed without the usual alarm of conspiracy being sounded. In fact, a sense of near complacency existed among Texas authorities regarding matters of defense. From the city of Houston, Ashbel Smith informed a correspondent: "There is nothing of a general character interesting. The Mexicans Indians. & ourselves are all quiet. Our Army is dwindled to a mere circumstance and I should not be surprised were it wholly disbanded."[30] The Cherokee and other Indians had recently seen their hopes dashed regarding Texas willingness to honor treaty promises. Agents from Mexico brought encouragement, ammunition, and military instructions. "Send word that Tejanos and Indians had taken up arms and give estimates of the strength of your forces," wrote Vicente Filisola, general-in-chief of the northern department, so "that I may be enabled to direct the forces that are to leave from this place [Matamoros] to the assistance of those who are to operate in that quarter." His message promised "a forced march" to the region of battle should there be a "sudden reverse" of military fortunes.

The Filisola memorandum came by way of a small, poorly supplied party headed by Pedro Julián Miracle that wound its way from Mexico across the Texas frontier during June, 1838. This group made it to Choctaw Indian country east of the Trinity River. Córdova arrived on July 5, read the communiqué, and waited for the various Indian chiefs to gather. The Mexican emissaries and Nacogdoches leaders talked to individuals but, as Miracle recorded in his diary, "nothing was done." The group went to Cherokee Chief Bowl's village and waited. Finally, on July 20, enough representatives had gathered to provide at least a fair evaluation of their options. No firm commitments existed from any Indians acting as a tribe, thus limiting manpower to a potential force of 540. Prevailing sentiment favored remaining in a state of preparedness until an army from Mexico arrived. After asking for reinforcements in a letter to Manuel Flores, who also held a commission from Filisola, Córdova departed. He claimed the chiefs had promised "to unite as soon as possible for action," but the strategy also provided that "in case our plans should be discovered in the mean time, they then will commence operations with the force we may have at command." Córdova also grasped for the rumor that an invasion force had begun hostilities in Goliad. After Córdova departed on the twentieth, Miracle moved on to try more recruiting at the Kickapoo and Chickasaw villages, waited without reward for the Kichis, Wacos, or Tahuacanos, and continued the journey in August toward Caddo villages. On August 20, he was killed in an engagement at the Red River; the incriminating journal and other papers fell into the hands of the Texas government.[31]

Córdova may have suspected that help from Mexico would not come but probably did not know what little chance existed. The Texas government, in fact, felt unusually secure largely because of renewed civil war in Sonora and Tamaulipas, which diverted the focus of the Mexican military away from the *norteamericano* nemesis. Whether the Nacogdoches Tejanos in July had made a firm choice to initiate rebellion hardly mattered, for by this time the momentum of events was too great to turn back. The open discussion of the plot by the Miracle party as it moved through the frontier had alerted the Texas government two weeks before contact had been made with Córdova. From Bastrop an army officer wrote the president on June 18 that the Comanche had rejected an invitation to join in the Mexican-Cherokee-Tejano "confederation." Houston quickly set out for Nacogdoches but first wrote the Cherokee agent that hostilities could be imminent. Further instructions called for keeping this news "confidential"; only Rusk and Joseph Durst were to be informed. The agent should quietly "ascertain whether any Spaniards have absented themselves from the vicinity . . . , or whether any Indians are absent at this time . . . This matter must be managed with great industry, prudence, and Secrecy." Rusk had sources of his own. Durst had been observing the movements of area Mexicans for some time before the rebellion, and Juan Piñeda had been spying for the Texas government since 1836.[32]

THE REVOLT

With both sides preparing for war but moving covertly, the question of who initiated battle remains a matter of perspective and mystery. This issue is complicated by the absence of documents left by Tejanos; except for the proclamation of rebellion, all contemporary accounts come from Anglo Texas sources. The first incident of violence involved an expedition of eight to ten Anglos who left Nacogdoches on August 4, in the words of an unnamed newspaper correspondent, "to recover some stolen horses, known to be secreted in a neighboring Mexican settlement." Mounted Tejanos fired on this party, killing one. A posse from town found a trail but broke off pursuit when the signs indicated that the number of Tejano horsemen had grown with distance, arousing "suspicion of some ulterior design."[33]

In some respects, the facts of this initial incident suggest that each side believed it acted in retaliation for attacks by the other, an impression reinforced by the next set of events. At sunrise on August 6, a party of eighteen Nacogdoches-area Mexicans rode up to the house of William Finley, about fourteen miles from town. They demanded that he and his brother-in-law surrender "as the Americans were taking their people." According to subsequent testimony, the captives "never returned," having been "murdered." The widow added that the Tejanos "said they intended to take the country from the Americans and drive them across the Sabine." [34]

At the same time, Rusk had already begun to scour the countryside and, accompanied by an interpreter and an emissary to the rebels, reached a point about five miles from Nacogdoches. The emissary, Antonio Menchaca, reportedly agreed that "the Mexicans were doing wrong and that he would get as many of them to leave Córdova as he could and return to their homes." Menchaca returned to town on the seventh, presumably with some assurances, but other news arrived that same night in the person of John Durst. He reported personal contact with a Tejano rebel patrol and gave other details of a general uprising. [35]

Newly arrived in Nacogdoches, the president on August 8 took action similar to Rusk's. However, Houston made a strange choice of messengers in José María Madrano, whose reports the previous year had initiated that revolt scare and who was widely known as a bitter enemy of Córdova. Houston ordered his envoy to "salute them in my name" and warn them that having "assembled with arms" was "contrary to the orders of the Government." His letter offered an armistice — they could "return to their several homes as good citizens, where they will be under the protection of the constitution of the Republic" — and promised redress of grievances. "The President has learned all the causes which exist and assures the citizens of the county that he will have them carefully examined and justice done to those who have been oppressed or wrongfully treated." To those who defied his offer, Houston threatened "the penalties of the crime of Treason, which will be a forfeiture of life, and property." His official proclamation, published in English and Spanish, leaned on the forceful side. It referred to "misapprehension and unnecessary alarm" of the armed Tejanos and repeated the opportunity to receive "plenary atonement" from the civil government, repent, return, and "enjoy their homes without molestation." Yet, in a tone that emphasized "the vile and monstrous crime of Treason," Houston flatly forbade "all unlawful assemblages of persons, and associations of armed men" and threatened retribution on any "who shall remain in a hostile attitude" for even a day after August 8. [36]

While the Texas leaders made these last grabs for peace through diplomacy, they also prepared for war. The first step aimed at splitting the enemy confederacy by warning the Cherokee not to support Tejano rebels.[37] Meanwhile, Rusk raised the Nacogdoches militia on August 8 and set out for Córdova's camp, thirty-two miles away on the Angelina River. Both Houston and Rusk ordered out other militias from all over East Texas, and the president requested arms from the U.S. Army.[38] The public expressed grave concern over the Mexicans' capacity as fighters. "A great multitude," numbering over one hundred (as the subsequent grand jury indictment read), the rebels were "armed and arrayed in a war-like manner, that is to say with Guns, rifles, shot Guns, pistols, swords, sabres and Bowie knives and other warlike weapons." A correspondent explained on August 9, "I have fought side by side with these Mexicans. They are brave men and Sharp shooters."[39]

These measures by the Texas government helped limit the potential of the rebellion. Córdova gained Indian recruits, but more as individuals than as tribes. Rusk's prompt show of force disrupted the difficult process by which the Cherokee had to build the consensus required for collective participation in the revolt. In the face of the Texas government's preparatory efforts and its measures to keep Mexican and Indian apart, Córdova found himself isolated on the Angelina River.[40] For several days beginning on August 9, the Tejanos successfully slipped through the scouts as well as the main deployment of Rusk's army and moved toward Cherokee town. Nevertheless, the Nacogdoches Mexicans were outnumbered by between four-to-one and eight-to-one, a ratio that indicated the success of government emissaries who got through to Indian leaders Chief Bowl and Big Mush. The Tejanos had little recourse but to break camp to get away from the Texas militia.[41]

Disagreement among the Texas leaders aided Córdova's repeated escapes. Houston favored defensive measures to guarantee the safety of Nacogdoches; Rusk chafed at these restraints but executed the policy well enough to block the Indian-Tejano militia. In any case, he seemed unable to strike a hard blow at Córdova,[42] who divided his two hundred followers into small groups and in this way avoided being attacked as they left Cherokee lands. Some of these men returned to their homes and families, but Córdova reassembled his remaining followers in Northeast Texas, again avoiding Rusk's chase by forced marches over difficult terrain. Assuring Houston that the Tejanos had not been able to recruit Cherokee, Kickapoo, Delaware, or Shawnee in tribal units, the Texas commander gave up pursuit on August 20.[43]

Córdova lacked both allies and desirable options, but during late August and September he managed to hold a substantial remnant of his force together while concealing his soldiers from the Texas authorities. His enemies proposed several unsuccessful military plans but did not really know of the whereabouts of the Tejano rebels.[44] Ultimately, Córdova had little choice but to force the action, and in the fall of 1838 the rebellion reached its military climax. Hunger led him to initiate military contact again by raiding farms for corn fourteen miles from Fort Houston on September 27. The Tejano-Indian army routed a company of fifty mounted Texans who had trailed it for two days and forced another command of forty men to take defensive measures. This incident led to renewed concern by Texas leaders over a possible attempt to rescue the Mexican families, attack Nacogdoches, and reactivate the Cherokee alliance. In early October, Rusk again mobilized a larger force against Córdova.[45]

On October 5, parts of Córdova's army launched another violent foraging expedition against settlers near the Neches River. The raiders seized corn, cattle, horses, wagons, and household utensils valued at $20,650. Fifteen Anglos died in this attack. Rusk then abandoned the defensive. The Texas militia had enrolled about 500 by October 4 and grew by one-half in the next ten days. Its commander complained, however, that he could not put 500 men in the field and set out with a force of 230 "to exterminate these cowardly robbers from the face of the Earth."[46]

The Texans marched to Kickapoo town, approximately twenty-five miles from the fort, expecting to surprise a force of two hundred Tejanos and Indians. Rusk made camp on the evening of October 15, but Córdova gave the Texans no time to organize an attack. At 10:00 P.M., his followers set fire to the woods around the Texas position. With the next morning's mist providing added cover, he concealed riflemen on three sides of the Texas camp. Córdova's move may have been designed to force Rusk into a retreat that could then be routed by Tejano-Indian cavalry held in reserve. The firing from the woods in heavy rain confused the Texans, who hastily formed a defensive square.

Casualties mounted for several minutes before the Texas commander brazenly seized back the initiative. One participant reported: "General Rusk with a view to draw them out, as he was entirely ignorant of their force, advanced about 20 paces & shouted — 'You damned cowardly sons of bitches, come out & show yourselves like men.' They made no reply except the yell & their rifles. . . . In about 15 minutes their fire began to slacken, and a charge was ordered." This attack lasted for only one-half to three-fourths of a mile but gave Rusk enough room to conduct an orderly retreat back to Nacogdoches with eleven wounded men.

The battle made it clear that Córdova's army, though it had suffered eleven known deaths and left a trail of bloodshed, could not be taken lightly. One of the Texas survivors explained that "nearly every man in the head of the Square had his clothes cut, it was the closest shooting I ever saw to do so little execution." The Tejanos had failed to raise entire tribes to their side, but militant Coshatto, Caddo, a Cherokee, "& some thought Keechies" had fought alongside Mexicans and a few Anglos and blacks. Córdova gave no indication of leaving the region and in fact continued to operate there until the following spring.[47] Rusk remained more or less constantly active, either in recruitment or in the field. However, the general's offensive planning gave way to defensive execution.

Time worked against the Tejano rebels. Still isolated from real or potential Indian and Tejano supporters, Córdova received another blow in March, 1839, when word reached him from Matamoros that the assistance he had been promised would not be coming. Valentín Canalizo, successor to Filisola as general-in-chief of the Division of the North, sent a variety of instructions to East Texas by way of messenger Manuel Flores. Flores carried both excuses and promises. Seven Indian chiefs received renewed assurances of land. When Mexican troops did come it would not be in the form of "flying invasions" but as more permanent operations to recover lost national territory. Canalizo advised the Texas supporters of the Mexican government to conduct relentless guerrilla warfare ("to burn their habitations, to lay waste their fields"). He also ordered all operations to focus on a line north and west of San Antonio de Béxar, where only Mexico would be in the rear, and to avoid eastern Texas, with its dangerous U.S. border.[48]

This shift in position ostensibly rested on its safety: "there is no danger, as you will be supported by the forces of this army, which occupies a convenient and advantageous position to furnish immediate relief to the line of operations which is designated." In fact, the movement removed Córdova's tiny force from the familiar, forested terrain in which it had repeatedly taken refuge and placed it in open, unfamiliar territory, still hundreds of miles from Mexican army support. It also reduced Córdova's numbers. Fewer than seventy-five went with him in March, 1839; mostly they were Tejanos and blacks, as few Indians made this trek to the land of the Lipan and Comanche.

These liabilities suggest another possibility: that Córdova's move may not have been entirely voluntary. Chief Bowles insisted that all the Tejanos' intended Indian allies—confronted by Rusk's persistent presence— had decided to hold a peace conference. According to this version, "Córdova, the Mexican renegade and traitor, wished to attend the meeting but was driven away. After this repulse, he retired westward." Some of the captives from Córdova's party suggested a third explanation: that the expedition sought ammunition in Matamoros to rearm a new Tejano-Indian rebellion in East Texas.[49]

Whatever its motivation, the expedition was ill-fated. Córdova ran into trouble in late March before reaching the Béxar region. Venturing too close to the Anglo settlements on the upper Colorado, his presence alerted Texas Ranger companies. About half his force of 53 men were casualties of a surprise attack while they rested in camp near the Guadalupe River. Those captured included a wounded black named Raphael, who reported that Córdova and many others had been wounded. Two other fresh companies, totaling 130 Texans, pursued the survivors. Córdova, reeling in his saddle from loss of blood and a broken arm when last seen, divided his remaining followers, eluded both units, and made it to Matamoros. Soon the Texans heard that he had vowed to return. Córdova's rebellion had failed but not because of its leader's want of courage.[50]

CONTROLLING THE PEOPLE

While all but a handful of those who followed Córdova into rebellion died during the next eight months, those who refused to join or who accepted promises of amnesty were also shattered by the conflict. The Tejanas, elderly, and children left behind became de facto hostages to the Texas government. Houston immediately recognized the military significance of these civilians. On August 10, he wrote to Rusk: "it is impossible to divine what course the Mexicans will take. I hope those least offending will go to their houses, and take care of their families & substances. A famine in the land must ensue, unless the Mexicans go to their houses, and take care of their property." The next day the president published an order regarding treatment of civilians:

> The army and soldiers of the Republic will in no case molest the peaceful citizens who remain at their homes . . . property of every kind is to be respected and protected, when found in the hands of peacable citizens. The families, and the women and children of all Mexicans and Indians, will be treated with the greatest humanity and kindness, and will be special objects of the soldiers care and protection.

Houston subsequently ordered the return of property and threatened prosecution of thieves.[51]

On August 22, the Texas president outlined his policy to Rusk, who, as usual, adopted a more militant stance but had not yet issued directives regarding Tejano civilians. Houston explained that a policy cloaked in humanitarianism would undermine the rebellion. "You will exercise the power of given permits, to the delinquent Mexicans to return to their homes, and attend to their stock & little farms — They are going to waste and those of the inferior order if made examples of will deter those of most importance from coming in, or harboring about their homes, so that they may be placed in arrest, and at the disposition of the law." The next day from San Augustine he repeated these orders and again advised that "much prudence will be necessary, or the consequences growing out of the eruption will drive the miserable Mexicans to desperation, and while the serviles are suffering, it will have a tendency to place the most guilty beyond the reach of justice. The more leniency that you extend . . . and protection to their famalies, the better."[52]

During the first two weeks of the rebellion, the president's "prudent" policy went unimplemented. Tejanas and children fled into the woods four miles from their town. Houston's emissary, John Applegate, finally made contact, asking "the cause of them leaving home. They state it was through fear. I invited them to return home letting them know that it was your orders that I should protect them," he continued, "but they refuse to return." Once he returned to Nacogdoches, Rusk complied with his orders. He published an order in Spanish, proclaiming that destitute women and children "having no men to protect them," would be provided for from public stores administered by Quartermaster John S. Roberts. This same official received authority to care for Tejano property, which Rusk admitted was still, "unfortunately," being plundered. The general also began issuing passports to lure those disposed to renounce the rebellion. The next week, Rusk appointed a special agent to the Mexican families as a liaison between them and Roberts. This may have been necessary because the quartermaster, having overseen a roundup of two hundred cattle and thirty to forty horses from the ranches of Córdova and his neighbors, favored "disposing of that part belonging to the ringleaders." In that way, "the government would realize something from it." He made no provision for harvesting Tejano crops, merely noting that they would soon go to waste.[53]

Sentiment grew for expulsion of the surviving East Texas Mexicans. Bernard Bee on September 6 wrote matter-of-factly, "the leaders if they can be had must pay the penalty. The rest must be sent to Louisiana or Mexico." Near the end of the month, the president issued a proclamation from Nacogdoches designed to encourage this exit: "I . . . hereby grant permission to all Mexicans with families who wish to leave the country, to retire with such personal estate as may be necessary to their comfort." Destitute dependents of traitors would be similarly supplied at public expense. He repeated the order that personal property stolen from the "delinquents" should be returned but made no promises regarding Tejano real estate.[54]

During these early months of the rebellion, the leaders of Texas also made deceptive promises for protection to all but the major leaders of the rebellion. In practice, the authorities arrested, jailed, and tried nearly all the adult male Hispanics who could be located, regardless of their loyalties or behavior. Even Juan Piñeda, who served as a government spy for two years, received this treatment. The ranks of the group brought to trial also included Antonio Menchaca, who had been dispatched to quell the uprising, failed, and then written back for assurances. "The President will be glad to see him in town," came the reply, and further, all who "remain at their homes in tranquility . . . will be under the protection of the law, and shall not be molested."[55]

"Protection of the law" at best meant civil prosecution rather than the vigilante or military style of justice that many called for. By August 26, according to one of Rusk's aides, "the jail and a guard house in Town [were] crowded with prisoners — Several of them important — None of the mainsprings of the affair, however, are yet taken." Others concurred that only "the subordinate actors in this bold insurrection have been captured." Yet, the Nacogdoches Tejanos all remained either in rebellion in the field or in detention in town.[56]

TRIALS

On October 10, the authorities brought thirty-three Tejanos forward for trial (they soon added three more).[57] The charge centered on treason. The prisoners violated their allegiance to Texas, it read, and "wickedly" attempted "to disturb, and to stir, move and excite insurrection, rebellion & War against the said Republic." Prosecuted in three groups but all on the same charge, the prisoners received a court-appointed counsel, who gained a change of venue to San Augustine, perhaps in part because the prosecutors agreed that "the distracted state of public feeling" would make it impossible to secure a jury in Nacogdoches. This move delayed the trial until January 7, 1839, but the court remanded all prisoners to the custody of the San Augustine county sheriff in the interim. It took two days to select jurors and three raucous days (defense counsel William C. Duffield received two stiff penalties for contempt of court) to conduct the trial. The state presented documentary evidence, including Córdova's proclamation (which none of those on trial had signed), and called six witnesses.

Two of these testified that some of the prisoners had been in the rebels' camp in the Cherokee Territory on August 11 and 12. Five of the accused were singled out. They "did not appear to be forced there and mingled freely and cheerfully" among the three hundred men, though none of those on trial could actually be identified as having borne arms at that or other times. Neither had heard the prisoners utter words of support for the rebellion or advise Córdova. Rather, they "were standing about and looking on." Cross-examination revealed that one of the defendants had been sent to the scene as Rusk's informant. Another witness, José Neato, swore that some of the prisoners bore arms but had stated that they had gone to the camp "to hear orders from General Houston." Others had "said they were brought there against their will."

Two witnesses gave testimony on the Finley incident rather than the specific charge of treason. They made allegations against Menchaca, but Adolphus Sterne (another state witness) provided Menchaca an alibi, as he was with the accused in the company of General Rusk on that date. Further, according to Sterne, "Menchaca said the Mexicans were doing wrong and that he would get as many of them to leave Córdova as he could."

Duffield and his assistant knew that the prosecution not only failed to make its case but also introduced evidence that vindicated all of the accused. The defense thus confined itself to points of law and a long closing argument. The jury deliberated for three days until, in exhaustion on Sunday January 13, it came forward with a ludicrous verdict: all the accused were not guilty except Menchaca. One other was detained on another charge; the remainder were released.

The trial of the second set of defendants began on Monday but lasted only one more day and resulted in not guilty verdicts. The district attorney then announced that he would not prosecute the remaining Tejanos.

On January 16, the court brought Menchaca forward for sentencing. Judge Shelby Corzine ruled against defense motions for an arrest of judgment or a new trial. Instead, Menchaca would "be returned in the Goal [jail] . . . until Friday the 22nd of February . . . be taken from thence to the Gallows and . . . hanged by the neck untill he is dead."

Several citizens petitioned President Lamar to set aside this judgment. One argued for a reprieve on the basis that the acquitted "were equally guilty," the humanitarian grounds of Menchaca's wife and children, and the promise that the entire family would "leave the county immediately."

This correspondent claimed to represent the views of several San Augustine residents, including the sheriff. These petitions had some effect, but the telling statement came from seven of the jurors, who "certified that they were of the opinion that the said Menchaca should be wholly acquitted . . . and they only yielded that opinion after two days of confinement . . . as the only means" to render any verdict. Lamar issued a pardon on February 18.[58]

In March and April, the sheriff arrested three Anglos and two more Tejanos on charges related to the Córdova rebellion. He presented them for trial with a notation that none of the others named in various warrants could be found. The district attorney refused to prosecute their cases or that of one other who surrendered. Two more—Jesús Gamos and José Antonio Pérez—escaped punishment on the basis of procedural irregularities that overturned their guilty verdicts on April 19, 1839. These cases ended the criminal prosecutions arising from the insurrection.

CONCLUSION

Extensive trials, appeals, and acts of clemency eventually freed all those arrested, but the judicial process left the Tejanos broken, impoverished, and physically set apart in East Texas. Forced land sales occurred, property holdings declined, and court procedures (including one against the Córdova family's stone house on the square) plagued their economic well-being. The survivors persisted in a kind of defensive segregation in the small community of Mora near town.[59]

For the Indians of East Texas, the Córdova revolt also signaled a fork in a long road of treachery by the Texas government. Disregarding the fact that individual Indians rather than tribal units had joined in the Córdova uprising, General Rusk, Secretary of War Albert Sidney Johnston, and President Lamar decided to punish the alleged disloyalists and to end this potential conspiracy forever. They argued that the Mexican government's efforts during the Córdova affair to enlist Indian support served as proof of collusion by the various tribes. Public opinion seemed to support this view, in spite of Houston's point that no evidence demonstrated that the Indians initiated any communication, agreed to the alliance, or by other word or deed encouraged the uprising. Given a choice of eviction or war, some of the Indians resisted. The fighting that ensued in the summer of 1839 led to the death of Chief Bowl and the removal from Texas soil of most of the surviving Cherokee, Delaware, Shawnee, and others.[60]

From Mexico, Córdova relentlessly kept up his war against the Texas government. In the winter of 1839 and spring of 1840, he and fifty to one hundred Indian, Mexican, black, and Anglo followers attacked military units and harassed businesses in South Texas. Victoria residents attempted without much success to raise volunteers to check him. In September, 1842, Córdova returned again as a member of the Woll expedition and died on the eighteenth of that month in the battle of Salado.[61]

His rebellion has not been understood from the perspective of the Tejano experience. Most contemporary Texas leaders like Rusk dismissed the rebels as mere renegades or bandits. One who attempted to probe more deeply, Bernard Bee, expressed wonderment in a letter to Lamar on September 6, 1838: "A Revolt against a *Republican* Govt in these days — is something unexpected. No forms of govt are after all ideal — and Pope was doubtless true to nature — when he said 'that gov't which is best administered is best."[62] Intended no doubt as a slur of Houston, Bee's analysis nevertheless touched the essential factor.

Despite boasting to the contrary, the government of Texas provided few benefits of citizenship to the Mexican residents of East Texas. It allowed economic, social, and political power to be withdrawn with no promise of return. It failed to secure their property from petty thieves or their persons from violence. It treated them as suspected traitors, setting up a kind of self-fulfilling prophecy. For their part, the Tejanos first fell into that form of passivity that comes from unpalatable alternatives. Throughout the 1820s and 1830s, they found themselves acting as conservatives on ground that constantly shifted. Unlike the Mexicans of Béxar, those in Nacogdoches did not join heavily in the upscaled mercantile initiatives that accompanied Anglo migration. They suffered from the intrigues of border adventurers and learned to hesitate before rallying to yet another flag of aborted revolution. In 1835–1836, the Tejanos sat out the conflict that ended up being the real turning point. This set in motion a cycle of suspicion that only worsened their status until Córdova finally launched a rebellion of desperation and hastened the destiny of his people.

SEVEN

FINDING THEIR WAY

Ana Carolina Castillo Crimm

A s control shifted from Mexican
to Anglo-American hands during and after the Texas Revolution, the
Mexicans of South Texas struggled to find a place in the new society. The
stories of two Texas-Mexican families, the de Leóns of Victoria and the de
la Garzas of Goliad, are representative of the difficult decisions and the
even more difficult adjustments made by many Tejano families during this
period. The choices they made provide a more complex view of a world
often seen only in black and white.

For Tejanos in 1836 to actively support the predominantly Anglo-
American independence movement was risky, but to side with Santa Anna
was equally dangerous. By the end of the war, as Mexican forces abandoned them, the Tejanos who remained on their ranches faced growing
antagonism from newly arrived Anglo Americans. For some, such as the
de la Garzas, giving up family lands was simply out of the question. For
others, such as the de León family, survival meant leaving Texas. Each
Tejano family found ways to endure, and even prosper, in an often antagonistic society.

Scholarly studies of the fortunes and misfortunes of Tejanos during
and immediately after the Texas Revolution have concentrated on their
acculturation and assimilation into the Anglo-American world. Some historians have maintained that most of the Tejano families did not succeed
at all. Threatened by incoming, often racist, Anglo Americans, they were
driven off their lands and fled to Mexico.[1] Others have claimed that some
Mexicans remained in Texas, but have dismissed them as a relatively insignificant minority divided into two groups: a handful of rich landowners
who allied themselves with the dominant Anglo-American culture; and a
mass of *peons* who had few ambitions and fewer possessions.[2] Still others

see the Tejano families, in particular, those given the sobriquet "old Spanish families," remaining on their ranches, living quietly out of the mainstream of the political upheavals created by the Anglo Americans, and refusing to assimilate.[3] This latter view is borne out by this study, which uses county and local sources to study the lives of these two Victoria County families and their kinship network.

FAMILY AND COMMUNITY

In 1829, Mexican settlers in Goliad and Victoria, two towns in South Texas, had become embroiled in the growing conflict over Anglo-American settlement of Texas. The Carlos de la Garza family at Goliad was conservative and opposed to the continuing immigration of Anglo-American settlers. The Martín de León family at Victoria, although not necessarily don Martín himself, reflected the pro-American views espoused by Mexican liberals. Both took an active part in the Texas Revolution. The de la Garza clan at Goliad remained loyal to Mexico and joined Santa Anna to fight against Texas independence; the de León family and most of the Victoria Tejanos sided with the Anglo Americans in their fight for Texas independence.

The two towns had histories as different as the attitudes of their residents. Goliad had existed on the Guadalupe River as the mission and fort of La Bahía del Espíritu Santo de Zúñiga since 1749. Residents of the area were civilians who served the fort or soldiers retired from the military garrison. Knowledgeable about the country and its advantages and disadvantages, these soldiers chose the best locations along the river, staked out their claims, and settled down on their ranches. Their sons and grandsons entered military service and their daughters and granddaughters married into local families. Their society, small though it was, was stable.[4] In and around Goliad, the only lands not already claimed were the extensive pasturelands belonging to the Mission of La Bahía del Espíritu Santo and Mission Refugio.

The town of Nuestra Señora de Guadalupe Victoria, in the Guadalupe River Valley to the north, had been in existence for only four years. Martín de León had arrived in 1824 from the northern Mexican state of Tamaulipas with a grant from the Provincial Deputation of Texas, the first and short-lived state government. The permit authorized de León to create a colony and establish settlers on land extending from the Guadalupe River to the Lavaca River and from the Atascosito Road on the north to a line ten leagues from the coast. Acting as a government land agent, Martín de

León divided the land up among the colonists by granting each family a league of land (4,428.4 acres) for cattle ranching and a *labor* (177.1 acres) along the river for farming.[5] For every one hundred families that de León settled, he received a grant of 5 leagues, or 22,142 acres. Not surprisingly, de León and his family welcomed any and all settlers, including Anglo Americans, Canadians, the French, and Irish.[6]

A THREAT TO TRADITION

The arrival in 1821 of Anglo Americans in Texas, led by Stephen F. Austin, created a problem for the region's Hispanic settlers—land speculation. When Austin began advertising the league and *labor* grants of over 4,600 acres in the United States, farmers found the amount almost inconceivable. Land in the United States in 1820 was selling for $1.25 per acre, with no credit available to help ease the $200.00 cost for a government quarter section of 160 acres.[7] An entrepreneurial farmer, by joining the growing flood to Mexico, even though one had to become Catholic, could acquire almost 5,000 acres for approximately $100.00, the cost of the Mexican taxes and titles. Without slaves, no single farmer could ever hope to clear and plant that much land. The excess land could, however, be sold for a tidy profit. Farmers-turned-speculators were soon outdone by would-be impresarios. Doctors, lawyers, merchants, and, especially, government officials from both Mexico and the United States (including U.S. Ambassador Joel Poinsett) applied for impresarial grants.[8]

An impresario did not own the land; he was a land agent for the government, responsible for supervising a large area, usually many thousands of acres, where he was to introduce and care for a minimum of one hundred families. The duties involved were onerous and expensive. The impresario surveyed the land, granted titles to his colonists, created a town, set up a government, acted as judge, built a church, and commanded the militia. The over 20,000 acre payment of land for his own use was what interested the speculator, not the noblesse oblige requirements that went along with it. Speculators in the United States and in Mexico had no intention of coming to Texas to colonize. Their motives in signing the contracts with the Mexican government were quick profit.[9]

The ranchers of Goliad were directly threatened by an 1828 impresario grant to James Power and James Hewetson, both of Monterrey, Mexico. Many of the residents of Goliad had held their lands, a few with titles but most without legal land titles, for two, three, or more generations. James Power and James Hewetson, both of Irish origin and residents of Monterrey, received a contract to bring four hundred Irish families to the San Antonio River Valley near Goliad.[10] Since most of the land along the river was already taken, they had been authorized to settle their families on lands that had belonged to the old mission of La Bahía and the adjacent Refugio Mission. The mission lands, in 1829, were in the process of being secularized and distributed to private owners. Goliad residents, who had long had their eyes on the valuable mission properties, appealed desperately for protection to the Mexican government of Coahuila y Texas. They "manifested great discontent" at two strangers being granted land that the local ranchers felt they deserved.[11] Since Power and Hewetson were well connected in Mexico, however, Goliad residents complained to little avail.[12]

The Mexican governor in Saltillo, who accepted the need to protect the local residents, made some concessions. Power and Hewetson would accept all Mexican families in the area as legal colonists, their lands were to be respected, and they were to be given legal titles to the ranches on which they lived if they had none.[13] Among those who did not have titles was Carlos de la Garza.

In spite of the governor's directives, Power and Hewetson did not immediately accept the local Mexican ranchers as settlers. They also prevented the longtime settlers from expanding onto the mission lands when these became available. By 1831, some of the disgruntled Mexican settlers around Goliad threatened to leave the area entirely "so long as the impresarios Power and Hewetson are preferred in all matters of progress."[14] There is no indication in the land records that any ranchers actually carried out their threat.

Although the mission lands were not free and clear until 1830, James Power brought the first thirty Irish families to the San Antonio River in 1829. The small group of Irish immigrants, who arrived from Ireland via New York and New Orleans, landed in a pathetic condition, sick from the long voyage, with no food and little knowledge of acquiring any in what seemed to them a terrifying wilderness. For want of any other shelter, they took refuge at the Refugio Mission. The Goliad Tejano ranchers may have opposed the new settlers but they would not let the Irish Catholic families starve. Mexicans from the ranches near the old Refugio Mission brought food and supplies to their new Irish neighbors.[15] With the help of the Tejanos, including the Carlos de la Garza family, the Irish settlers carved out their small farms along the San Antonio River near the old mission. Among the new Irish families were Nicholas Fagan, John Dunn, George C. McKnight, Antonio Sideck, Edward McDonough, and Peter Hyne; they would become important during the Texas Revolution.[16]

Just as the Mexican settlers had feared, the first two land commissioners authorized to grant land titles for Power and Hewetson refused to
consider the local Mexicans' claims to land and their requests for titles.
Tadeo Ortiz de Ayala, the new director of colonization in 1830, received
more than one hundred petitions from the Goliad settlers whose titles
were "not being taken up for consideration or were being refused
altogether."[17]

Meanwhile, however, James Power was finding it difficult to bring
settlers from Ireland. Word may have gotten back to the old country
about Indian raids and the dangers of the new land. Many of those who
arrived in 1833 died of cholera contracted while they were at New Orleans,
and those few who did survive were wrecked on the coast while attempting to land.[18] Others found the wilderness overwhelming and chose to
leave Texas. When Power realized how unlikely it was that he could actually complete his promised contract of four hundred families, he added
the dozens of Tejano families settled in and around Goliad to count toward his required total.[19] Under orders from Power in 1833 and 1834, Land
Commissioner Santiago Vidaurri finally granted titles to over fifty local
families, including the Carlos and Julián de la Garza families.[20]

EMBRACING LIBERALISM

At Victoria, only two days' ride to the north, the attitude toward land
grants and immigration was completely different. Although Martín de
León was not new to the area, having first moved from northern Mexico
to a ranch on the Nueces River in 1801 for which he never received a title,
the de León family was, in comparison to Goliad families, a recent arrival.
As an impresario whose success depended on granting land to at least one
hundred families, the sixty-year-old de León needed settlers. Although the
archives are replete with problems between Martín de León and the increasing numbers of Anglo-American colonists coming to Austin's or
Green de Witt's colonies, de León appears to have gotten along well with
his own Anglo settlers.[21] It was in his best interests to favor liberal land
policies and increasing immigration. In 1829, Martín de León had requested an additional grant of land on which to settle 150 new families.[22]
In order to complete the contract, keeping the borders open was impera-
tive. De León, regardless of how he might have felt about Anglo Americans in general, allied himself with those pro-American liberals in Mexico
who favored continuing immigration.

In addition to attitudes over immigration, a further difference of opinion between Victoria and Goliad developed over governmental control. The creation of towns under the Spanish and, after 1821, the Mexican governments was carefully controlled. Under the Spanish Constitution of 1812, ten married men could form a town as long as it was at least five leagues from any existing town.²³ Nine years later, as Mexico became independent, the government changed the requirement to twenty-five families of free men and allowed for the creation of an *ayuntamiento,* or town council, made up of the town members, or *vecinos,* under the watchful eye of the *jefe político (subgovernor)* at San Antonio.²⁴ Towns considered too small or underpopulated answered to the next closest town with a formal council. For most of its existence, La Bahía had remained under the control of San Antonio, but by 1821 the town had been permitted to create its own town government, and in 1829 it received a new charter and changed its name from La Bahía to Goliad.²⁵

When Victoria was founded in 1824, the Mexican government had granted Goliad jurisdiction, since it was the closest town with an *ayuntamiento.* This control meant that all judicial rulings, all government acts, and all legal papers had to go from Victoria to Goliad before being passed on to San Antonio and then to Saltillo, the state capital for the combined states of Texas and Coahuila. When Goliad received its new town charter in 1829, Martín de León felt Victoria, too, should receive its own government. His two sons-in-law, José Miguel Aldrete and Rafael Antonio Manchola, were closely involved in the Goliad government but they were opposed by the conservative ex-military members of the town council who were hostile to any more immigration and the potential threat to their land and titles. What de León feared was not bureaucratic control, which was an accepted fact under the Mexican bureaucracy, but the anti-immigrant attitudes of some of Goliad's leaders.²⁶ De León's request for a separate government was turned down, and the most that he could achieve was the right to have one representative for the town of Victoria sit on the Goliad town council and protect his interests.²⁷ This, evidently, he already had.

Just as Martín de León was planning an expansion of his contract, a governmental overthrow in Mexico City shifted the balance of power from the liberals, who favored immigration, to the conservatives, who opposed it.²⁸ In 1830, Goliad residents were pleased to find that the new conservative government opposed the continuing land speculation and settlement of Anglo Americans in Texas. The Law of April 6, 1830, closed the borders to any more colonists from the United States. To the dismay of the Goliad government, however, and to the joy of de León and Power and Hewetson, there were exceptions. Under Article 10 of the law, colonies that already had successful establishments (such as those of Austin, de León, and Power and Hewetson) were exempt from the law. Both Austin and de León completed their contracts with the settlers who arrived in the next two years. Power and Hewetson, however, were unable to find enough Irish willing to come to the wilds of Texas and failed to supply the four hundred families that they had promised. Although they continued to apply to the Mexican government and, later, the new Texas Republican government, they never received their hoped-for ninety-two thousand acres.[29]

When the aged Martín de León died of cholera in 1833, his family was comfortably settled as the largest landholder in the Victoria area. While twenty-eight-year-old Carlos de la Garza remained removed from politics in Goliad, the de León family, now led by the eldest son, thirty-seven-year-old Fernando, became more closely involved with the pro-American liberals. In 1834, the separation from Goliad was finally completed when Victoria received its own town charter. By that time, the de León family had fulfilled the second contract and, although they did not necessarily need more colonists, they retained their pro-immigration, liberal-leaning attitudes.[30]

Fernando and some of the de León family were drawn more closely into the pro-Anglo-American camp by the marriage of their sister Refugia to José María Jesús Carbajal, one of the leaders of the Mexican pro-liberal movement in Texas. Carbajal was born in San Antonio in 1809, one of eleven children, and the descendant of a long line of San Antonio soldiers. By 1821, his widowed mother, perhaps suffering from a lack of funds, was introduced to the newly arrived Stephen F. Austin and Ben Milam and accepted their suggestion to send her eleven-year-old son to the United States for an education.[31] When Carbajal returned in 1830, Austin needed a surveyor who could interpret for the Mexican land commissioner, who spoke no English, and the surveyors, who spoke no Spanish.[32] Carbajal became the first bilingual land surveyor for Texas and was assigned to work with the newly appointed land commissioner, José Francisco Madero.[33]

In Mexico City, as mentioned earlier, the conservatives had taken control of the government and passed a law that attempted to stop immigration, the Law of April 6, 1830. This law was designed to halt the flow of Anglo settlers arriving in Texas without permits and without any connection to one of the legal impresarial centers. It still allowed impresarios such as Austin and de León to receive settlers. The problem lay with the many undocumented settlers on lands between the Sabine and the Trinity Rivers.

As part of the Law of April 6, 1830, a series of forts were established in Texas to control trade and Anglo-American settlement. The port at Galveston Bay was put under the control of an American-turned-Mexican, Colonel Juan Davis Bradburn. Bradburn, although willing to accept those who had arrived prior to April 6, 1830, as legitimate citizens, was concerned over those illegal settlers who arrived between April 6, 1830, and January, 1831. Land Commissioner Madero, acting under orders from the state government in Saltillo, planned to grant titles to all the colonists in the Trinity area. Bradburn, fearing that illegal settlers might receive grants, ordered Madero not to grant any titles at all. When Madero persisted, Bradburn jailed both him and his surveyor, José María Jesús Carbajal. Madero claimed Bradburn had acted beyond his authority.

It took the state government two months to sort out the problem. Bradburn was reprimanded and was ordered to free Madero and Carbajal. The months in confinement may well have politicized the young Carbajal. Whereas Madero returned to Mexico, Carbajal became deeply involved in pro-liberal Texas politics. In May of 1831, he was elected to an Anglo-American caucus to petition the Mexican government for redress from Bradburn's excesses. By November he was appointed to the civil government of San Felipe, Austin's capital, and the following year served on the Nacogdoches town council. He also worked with the newly established town of Liberty in setting up the town council. He continued as the only bilingual surveyor, making contacts with both Mexicans and Anglo Americans all over the state.[34] He was also particularly influential with his in-laws among the Victoria Tejanos.

Carbajal's popularity in Texas won him election as one of the liberal, pro-immigration representatives for Texas to the Coahuila y Texas state congress in 1835. His liberal view and his involvement with the land speculators caused him trouble with the conservatives. When Martín Perfecto de Cos was sent from Mexico City by the conservatives to close down the session of congress, Carbajal and other liberals were forced to flee for their lives. Carbajal found refuge in Victoria, where de León family members and his Anglo-American friends protected him from the troops sent to capture him.[35] A few months later, Carbajal was elected as a representative to the Texian Constitutional Convention at Washington-on-the-Brazos. Fernando and the de León kin, perhaps as a continuation of their ten years of support for the pro-immigrant, pro-Anglo-American liberal faction, joined their brother-in-law in his support of the separation of Texas from Coahuila and the more radical step of outright revolt against the increasingly conservative government in Mexico City.

TEJANOS AND THE WAR

With the beginning of all-out war between Mexico and the Texian rebels in October of 1835, Fernando de León joined Carbajal in providing monetary support for the revolt. De León and Carbajal drove a herd of horses to New Orleans to exchange for arms and ammunition for the Texian troops. Returning aboard the schooner *Hannah Elizabeth* with the supplies, de León, Carbajal, and Peter Kerr were captured by Mexican warships attempting to stop the independence movement, and their vessel was run up on the beach at Paso Caballo. De León and Carbajal lost their entire investment in the cargo and were imprisoned in Matamoros. They escaped several weeks later with the help of friends. The *Hannah Elizabeth* was recovered by the Texian forces and eventually found its way back to the growing number of Anglo-American troops. Carbajal, however, never received credit from the Anglo Americans for his efforts.[36]

As the war in Texas escalated during the fall and winter of 1835, Plácido Benavides, another de León brother-in-law, formed a cavalry company of thirty Tejanos from the Victoria area in support of Texas independence. The Benavides company fought with George M. Collinsworth's expedition against Goliad and, once the old presidio was captured, the cavalry company joined Captain Phillip Dimmitt and Colonel James Walker Fannin in their defense of Goliad. Finally, Benavides led his men in the attack on Mexican General Cos at San Antonio in December of 1835. Plácido Benavides's success in battle and as a leader of his cavalry company earned him the respect of the Anglo-American officers in the Texian army. Despite the opposition from some of the newly arrived Anglos who wanted to segregate the Mexicans living in Texas, Benavides was appointed first lieutenant of cavalry in the newly organized Texas Militia along with Manuel Carbajal, brother of José María Jesús Carbajal.[37]

Meanwhile, Carlos de la Garza, from his ranch on the San Antonio River, had abandoned his isolationist position. De la Garza, as a conservative, refused to side with the Anglo Americans who favored the overthrow of the legally constituted government. As newly arrived Anglo-American volunteer troops began to raid the homes of local Goliad residents in 1835, de la Garza offered asylum and safety on his ranch to those who believed as he did.[38] Opposing his Irish neighbors, de la Garza formed a loyal, pro-Mexican cavalry troop made up of his fellow Tejano ranchers and the local Karankawa Indians. In early 1836, Mexican forces under General Urrea arrived in the Goliad area to halt the rebellion. De la Garza put himself and his men at the general's disposal. De la Garza's

troop, the Guardias Victorianas, was well mounted, familiar with the terrain, and able to provide the Mexican general with accurate news of
Anglo-American troop movements.[39] De la Garza's Guardias controlled
the land between the San Antonio and Mission Rivers and were effective
in capturing a number of the Texian troops on their retreat from Refugio
as well as some who had gotten lost trying to find Victoria.[40] De la Garza
also attacked Refugio, where he looted and captured supplies and horses
for the Mexican army; however, he spared the Anglo-American civilians
in the town, perhaps because many of them were his neighbors.[41]

One month later, Carlos de la Garza was again facing a dilemma over
his Irish Catholic friends. On March 20, 1836, General Urrea defeated a
Texian force at Coleto Creek. The captured soldiers were taken to Goliad,
where Santa Anna ordered their execution. De la Garza learned that a
number of his Irish neighbors had been a part of the Texian army. They
were among those captured by General Urrea and held at Goliad. Dis-
obeying Santa Anna's explicit orders, Carlos de la Garza effected the release of James W. Byrnes, John Fagan, Nicholas Fagan, Edward Perry,
Anthony Sideck and John B. Sideck. His intervention saved them from
the subsequent massacre of the remainder of the Texas troop.[42]

Back in Victoria, during the last months of the war, Fernando de León
continued to have bad luck. As Santa Anna marched toward San Jacinto,
General Urrea was sent to secure Victoria. Fernando de León, as one of
the town leaders and a supporter of the Texian independence movement,
immediately came under suspicion. Urrea was informed by local conservatives that de León was hiding supplies destined for the Texian army.
Urrea jailed de León and forced him to disclose the location of the cache
of supplies.[43] The disclosure did not win de León his freedom and he
remained in the Victoria jail until the departure of General Urrea. After
the Texian victory at San Jacinto, General Thomas Rusk marched on Victoria to make sure that General Urrea and the Mexican forces had left
Texas. Upon Rusk's arrival in Victoria, de León, just having been freed
for aiding the Texian cause, was turned in to Rusk by his Anglo-American
enemies for turning over the supplies to the Mexican army. De León was
again jailed, this time by the Anglo Americans, as a traitor to the Texian
cause.[44]

A NEW ERA

With the end of the Texas Revolution, some Tejano families left with General Urrea, but many remained. Carlos de la Garza, who had opposed

Texan independence, chose to remain in Texas. By the middle of June, 1836, General Thomas Rusk, the commander of the Texian forces in Texas had been warned of another attack by Mexican forces. He ordered the removal of all citizens, in particular those Tejanos likely to help the threatening army. When Rusk's soldiers arrived at Carlos de la Garza's ranch, according to Hobart Huson, de la Garza "heard the orders read but continued his plowing and none durst molest him."[45] The attack by the Mexican forces proved to be illusory, and Rusk's orders went unheeded by the Tejano settlers of the San Antonio River Valley and the Corpus Christi area.[46]

Carlos de la Garza, in spite of his anti-Anglo attitudes during the war, was never punished for his stand nor were any of his possessions confiscated. There are some possible explanations. First, he may have received support from his Irish neighbors, who had taken control of the Refugio government at the end of the war. A second, and less likely, possibility may be that General Rusk did not want a confrontation with the many Tejano refugees from Refugio and Goliad gathered at the de la Garza ranch. A third possibility is that General Rusk was too busy trying to keep his rapidly swelling volunteer army in check to worry about the views of ranchers on the San Antonio River. It is ironic, considering the outcome for the de León family, that one of the men who had done the most to oppose Texan independence remained on the San Antonio River.

The de León family did not fare as well. According to a claim filed with the state of Texas by Fernando de León upon his return in 1846, General Rusk had ordered the removal of the whole de León clan, including the Carbajal and Benavides families, from Victoria and the Aldretes and Mancholas from Goliad. He gave them no time to gather their possessions nor did he provide any protection from Texian volunteers, who, according to de León, mistreated the de Leóns, "taking the ear rings and jewelry from the persons of helpless females belonging to your petitioners family."[47] Rusk, from his own accounts, "sent men with them to see that they went on board the vessels" at Matagorda Bay.[48]

The removal of the de León family is puzzling in light of its efforts on behalf of Texian Independence. Although Fernando had been accused of treason and of giving supplies to the Mexican army, the same could not be said about the efforts of land surveyor–turned–politician José María Jesús Carbajal, Texian army lieutenant Plácido Benavides, and José Miguel Aldrete, who had fought with Captain Phillip Dimmitt's command at Goliad. General Rusk has been accused of racism and cruelty toward the de León clan. Although he was not from the area, Rusk had to have known of the contributions of de León, Carbajal, and Benavides to the cause of independence. By removing them — the first a wealthy contributor to the Texian cause, the second an elected member of the Texas Constitutional Congress, and the third an officer in the Texian army — Rusk was losing men who were valuable supporters of the Texian movement.

Another possibility presents itself. During this period, Rusk was being overwhelmed by newly arrived Anglo-American volunteers looking for a fight. Although Rusk begged the new government for money and supplies to feed the troops, he received neither and was forced to let the soldiers forage for themselves on nearby ranches. Particularly susceptible were the ranches of the Victoria Tejanos. Doña Patricia de la Garza, the de León matriarch, protested the treatment directly to Rusk and demanded his protection from the wild and uncontrollable Texian troops. Rusk, unable to keep the troops from harassing the family, may have been trying to avoid a confrontation with the de León clan by sending them to the coast. Regardless of the reasons for their removal, the de León family left with not much more than ten muleloads of their possessions.[49] The family remained in exile in Louisiana until 1846, and when they finally returned to Victoria to reclaim their land, they found that most of their goods had been lost to marauding Texian troops.

While the de León family was in Louisiana, Carlos de la Garza became a leader in the small community of Tejano and Irish settlers on the San Antonio River. The Refugio town government found his ranch a safe place to conduct county business. A troop of the Texas Rangers operated from the haven of his ranch. During the Mexican American War, in 1846 and 1848, Carlos de la Garza sold beef to U.S. troops and supplied a camping place for General Albert Sidney Johnston's troops.[50] He also supported the Catholic Church. In 1841, Father Estany of Victoria established a Catholic boys' school at the ranch and held masses there when he could.[51] The ferry at Carlos Crossing was still operated by don Carlos as late as 1872, although for a time, he shared the ferry with his neighbor John White Bower, who lived across the Guadalupe River.[52]

When the de León family returned to Victoria in 1846, although they had lost their home and goods, they were able to regain much of their extensive landholdings. The land enabled them to return to a semblance of the lifestyle they had led prior to the Revolution. By using land as payment, Fernando hired lawyers to fight and win court cases for his brother's children, for himself, and for his family. Although he never received any recompense from the State of Texas for his losses, he was able to rebuild the family name and its position as one of the elite "Old Spanish" settlers. He passed on to his heirs over nineteen thousand acres he still retained in 1850.[53] His mother, Patricia de la Garza, matriarch and guardian of the de León family, sold one of the two large twenty thousand–acre ranches and invested the money in mortgages in both Louisiana and Victoria, which kept the family solvent during its sojourn in Louisiana. The money also enabled her to have an independent income until her death in 1849, at which time her land, money, mortgages, and claims against the State of Texas passed to her family.[54]

CONCLUSION

The Texas Revolution was a watershed for the Tejanos of what was to become Victoria County. Although some fought on the side of Santa Anna's forces and others fought on the side of the Texian army, the opposing ideologies were soon subsumed in the difficulties of making a living after the war. With little say in the new Anglo-Texan government, threatened by newly arrived and antagonistic Anglo Americans, and pressured to pay taxes on their large ranches to the insolvent Republic of Texas, the Tejanos of Victoria found a means of surviving. By retaining their ties to Mexico, their ranching heritage, their Hispanic culture, and their Catholic religion, they created a societal separation that helped them preserve their ethnic community. They did not, however, cut themselves off from the Anglo-American society. In the ten years before the war, many of the Anglo Americans and Tejanos of Victoria had come to know and respect one another as they fought the elements, the Indians, and political problems together. As the Mexican Texans had protected their Anglo-American neighbors from the invading Mexicans prior to Texas independence, so, too, did the Anglo Americans protect their Mexican neighbors from the flood of newly arrived racist Anglos to the Republic of Texas.[55] Whether this friendly relationship was the exception or the rule will only be proved by further studies of individual communities where Tejanos and Anglo Americans lived and worked side by side.

CONCLUSION
Gerald E. Poyo

Tejano history, as reflected in these essays, speaks about tradition, identity, and continuity, on the one hand, and turbulence, accommodation strategies, and change, on the other. While distinct, these processes operated together in very complex ways to guide the historical development of Tejano communities. History gave Tejanos their traditions and identity, and, although historical developments brought changes to the communities, their established ways provided a familiar and relatively defined framework within which those changes occurred. Tejanos coped with change by drawing on their frontier experience, and while they were not always successful, their strategies reflected an instinct to protect and defend their homes.

TRADITION, IDENTITY, AND CONTINUITY

During the course of the eighteenth century, the basic elements of a Tejano political, economic, and cultural identity emerged. As they gathered in communities on the northern border of New Spain, settlers formed traditions based on their frontier experiences. In creating their local way of life, they went from being Spanish colonists intent on protecting this buffer region for Spain to Mexican settlers with a special connection to this province called Texas; they became Tejanos.

Texas frontier communities evolved a culture within the context of an isolated agricultural, ranching, and military economy. Tejanos originally arrived in the region as military settlers. Always ready to defend the region and community from foreign intruders as well as from indigenous peoples who resented the Hispanic presence, Tejanos became self-sufficient settlers capable of doing whatever was necessary to survive. Aware of the hardships and twists and turns of frontier life, Tejanos relied on each other to ensure the survival of their families and communities. To make a living, they harnessed the land, a resource that became the central element of their economic prosperity. Vast territories had to be claimed and distributed in some orderly fashion. Mission and civilian ranches emerged and provided the institutional basis for developing their economy. Cattle and horses ran free on the land, and Tejanos drew from the ranching traditions of their Hispanic forebears. They adapted equestrian arts to the frontier and, with exceptional roping and branding skills, rounded up and secured cattle and horses for local use and export. They also farmed and usually produced enough to feed their families.

This reliance on a military, ranching, and agricultural economy influenced Tejano social structure, language, dress, and religion. Tejano frontier communities developed simple functional societies. A ranching and commercial elite led communities populated mostly by cowboys, farmers, and artisans. These communities were small and poor but well established. And though social stratification clearly existed, few inhabitants and austere living conditions ensured that people interacted and relied on each other. Elites lorded over the workers in a personalistic and paternalistic manner, but they usually worked shoulder to shoulder on the farms and ranches.

Tejanos developed their own peculiar frontier Spanish. Isolation and contact with numerous other cultures led to language adaptations that made Tejanos distinct. Hispanic visitors to Texas commented on the poor quality of Tejano Spanish, a phenomenon that reflected isolation and lack of formal education. In addition, other languages influenced the region. Many Tejanos, particularly those from Los Adaes and Nacogdoches, spoke French or inserted "Frenchisms" into their language. In time, it also became increasingly important for Tejanos to be at least familiar with English. Some Tejanos studied in the United States and learned English well. It is also probable that the many indigenous languages influenced frontier and border Spanish in Texas.

Tejano culture included a deep connection to the Catholic Church, and on the frontier they practiced their religion in mission and parish communities. In the vicinity of San Antonio, five missions attracted Indians from the region into settled Hispanic communities, and in the town itself residents built the parish church of San Fernando, where a parish priest attended to their spiritual needs. From the Spanish period through the 1840s, religious feasts and celebrations organized by church and city officials point to the centrality of spirituality and the church to Tejano community life and culture.

By the 1770s, Tejanos made their living in ranching and commerce. While they had trading relations with Coahuila and other markets to the south, Tejanos also found prosperity by establishing trading relations to the east. For Tejanos, a choice of market offered obvious advantages. As early as the 1740s and the 1750s, settlers in Texas survived by trading illicitly with settlers in French Louisiana. Within a generation, Texas cattle and horses were regularly traded to Louisiana, sometimes legally but mostly as contraband.

Mexican independence brought new possibilities. In the 1820s, Tejanos saw new opportunities toward the east as the U.S. cotton kingdom moved to the Texas border. Opening the vast unsettled lands in the province to colonists from the United States brought capital and a vibrant cotton industry. Prosperity seemed assured by tying Texas to the U.S. economic system. Tejanos in San Antonio and Victoria believed that they could cooperate with the Anglo-American economic interests in a way that would benefit both.

Tejanos usually understood that to effectively defend and promote their economic interests, they needed authority over local affairs and the ability to influence the larger political context. The municipality provided the political mechanism for expressing their interests to the power centers in Mexico. The municipality, introduced to the Americas by the Spanish colonial system, defined and defended local political, economic, and social interests and, at the same time, tied Tejanos to the Spanish empire and then the Mexican republic.

In their isolation, Tejanos established a community tradition of local autonomy, which was expressed through their municipal council, the *cabildo* or *ayuntamiento*. By the 1770s, this local institution had established a strong record in defense of Tejano regional interests and it continued to do so through the 1830s. The *cabildo* provided Tejanos with the channels to communicate their positions and needs to Spanish officials in Saltillo and Mexico City. Petitions, lawsuits, and other bureaucratic procedures carried Tejano concerns to the power centers. And when isolation faded, Tejanos fiercely protected their town councils, first against Spanish governors and then against the legislature of Coahuila y Texas.

Tejanos also participated in representative government when this was necessary to protect their interests. If the ability to use the town council was of critical importance for Tejanos during the Spanish period, an equal sophistication was necessary in dealing with the state legislature and national Congress after Mexican independence. The promulgation of the Mexican Constitution of 1824 and the establishment of the province of Coahuila y Texas shifted the center of authority from the governor and local government in Texas to the legislatures in Mexico City and Saltillo. Tejanos journeyed to the Mexican capital to promote their interests and also sent representatives to the state legislature in Saltillo after Texas lost its status as an independent province. Tejanos resented their loss of autonomy, but they adapted and worked within the parameters created by the Mexican constitution.

Although Tejanos engaged with sophistication in the political process, they were not unwilling to turn to insurrection when unexpected political turns threatened their interests. During the Mexican war for independence some Tejanos hoped to regain lost ground by joining the revolt against Spanish authority. Dissatisfaction existed in Texas, and conditions did not inspire wholesale insurrectionary activity, but a significant segment of Tejano society risked rebellion to protect local interests. But even this they did with considerable caution, and most found ways to reconcile with Spanish authority when the insurrection failed.

The spirit of insurrection appeared again in the 1830s, when Mexican authorities abandoned the Constitution of 1824. Faced with accepting a centralist Mexican regime under Santa Anna or supporting the rebellious Anglo-Americans, a significant number of Tejanos opted for insurrection. Tejano political, economic, and cultural traditions guided community development through the first half of the 1830s. Old Tejano communities like San Antonio, Nacogdoches, and La Bahía had a strong sense of place and historical memory, and even new towns like Victoria drew on these traditions while charting new courses. As Tejanos crossed into a new political situation after 1836, however, they confronted radically different power and social relationships and had to devise strategies that would allow them to survive.

TURBULENCE, ACCOMMODATION, AND CHANGE

While the elements of a Tejano civilization existed through the first half of the nineteenth century, changes in sovereignty and confrontations with outside forces (from the east as well as the south) brought considerable turbulence to Tejano communities. In confronting the political instability, Tejanos faced change and devised diverse survival strategies that had the common goal of seeking to protect families, communities, and a way of life.

The Texas war of independence separated Tejanos from their nation. Strains between Texas and Mexico had been apparent since the late eighteenth century, but few Tejanos had aspired for a break with the south and incorporation into the United States. Nevertheless, their own struggles for local autonomy combined with the larger political forces in the United States and Mexico to create a definitive rupture. Tejanos recognized the need to face the reality of their situation, relied on certain long-established patterns of experience, and embarked on a journey that eventually made them Mexican Americans.

Tejanos drew on what was familiar when confronted with new situations. At the same time that they looked to their historical traditions to protect and advance their communities during times of redefinition and uncertainty, they did not always choose the same strategies. Difficult times demanded flexible responses. This reflected the heterogeneity of the communities themselves. Tejanos did not have a monolithic view of what was best for them as individuals or their communities within the Euro-American environment.

As minority citizens of the Republic of Texas and, later, the United States, their position in politics changed and became marginal, their economic livelihood was constantly threatened, their social status diminished, and their culture was not valued. Most Euro-American newcomers to Texas had little regard for Mexicans and Indians, and Tejanos faced immediate threats to their position as their communities were engulfed by immigrant *norteamericanos,* who had little appreciation for Mexican historical claims to the region.

Euro-American hostility toward Mexicans had already appeared before the insurrection against Mexico and caused Tejano resentment in return. Driven by an underlying racism, Euro-Americans usually viewed Tejanos as potential enemies; after separation from Mexico, this sentiment grew stronger. The battle of the Alamo and the slaughter at Goliad had fed Euro-American animosity toward Mexicans and Tejanos regardless of their contributions to the war effort. Tejano supporters and opponents alike of the Euro-American enterprise in Texas during the 1820s and the 1830s faced imminent economic extinction after 1836. Ultimately, the promising eastward economic focus Tejanos had developed as early as the 1740s backfired and eventually brought virtual ruin to most.

While most Tejanos faced similar threats, they dealt with their reality in different ways, depending on the severity and the immediacy of the threat. In defending themselves and their communities, Tejanos drew from their historical experiences. Some Tejanos drew on their tradition of insurrection. In Nacogdoches, they saw little hope of securing a reasonable future in what had once been their community. Their status was dramatically undermined by Euro-American arrivals who showed little interest in developing harmonious relationships with Tejanos or Indians. In the end, Vicente Córdova and those he led in Nacogdoches faced two choices: they could accept the new order, which meant the loss of their lands, their economic possibilities, and their right to full citizenship; or they could revolt. Since Tejanos stood little chance of stopping the Euro-American advance, some chose to fight. In the end, their insurrection did not succeed and resulted in even greater repression. Tejanos in Nacogdoches became virtually invisible.

The instinct for rebellion among Tejanos in Nacogdoches who felt despair and a sense of helplessness did not receive support from Tejanos in other parts of Texas. In San Antonio, for example, Juan Seguín and others openly opposed Vicente Córdova's insurgency. Living in a more flexible and thus viable situation, with greater power and prestige, Bexareños hoped to advance their interests by working within the new political system. At the local level, Tejanos in San Antonio devised a political strategy to maximize the influence of the now-restructured city council. Tejanos in San Antonio had always considered their control over local government essential to protecting and promoting their interests and this instinct remained after 1836.

Tejanos also participated in the Texas Republic's national political system. Just as they had traveled to Mexico City and Saltillo to advance and protect their interests, Tejanos went to Houston and, later, Austin and defended their rights as citizens of Texas. Perhaps the most successful advocate in the national legislature was José Antonio Navarro. While Tejanos had always had to defend their political and economic rights before Mexican and Spanish authority, Navarro now found that his task included the very right of Tejanos to participate and to promote their cultural ways. During the 1840s, some in the Texas legislature hoped to disenfranchise Tejanos, but Navarro rallied support and blocked the action.

While San Antonio's Tejanos had to modify their political expectations and strategies as part of the republic, they maintained a steadfast commitment to their cultural traditions, especially in matters of spirituality and celebration. Tejanos in San Antonio engaged in religious processions and celebrated Hidalgo's revolution, for example, perhaps more fervently than ever before. These cultural expressions ensured that Tejano culture as developed under Mexico would continue to exist even as the expressions themselves changed.

Tejanos also remained connected to their land, which they struggled to retain at all costs. They felt perhaps the greatest resentments when their economic resources seemed threatened. During the Spanish and Mexican periods, they evolved a tradition of using all the available political and legal processes to defend their land. Some Tejanos successfully defended their land in similar fashion after 1836. The de León family of Victoria was one prominent case. Although forced to leave Victoria during the war, the family returned in 1846 and immediately set out to regain its position. Using land as payment, the family hired lawyers and successfully regained control of its landholdings. Like many Bexareños who learned to use the political system to protect their interests, the de León family engaged the new legal system to its advantage. Others, like Carlos de La Garza and his clan, who had remained loyal to Mexico but nevertheless stayed in Texas after independence, protected their lands and resources through sheer determination. De la Garza did not have to regain the land since he never left it; his enemies' efforts to destroy him met with defiant retaliation. Euro Americans soon learned to leave him alone. Many Tejanos survived the transition with their resources in place by keeping to themselves in isolated rural environments.

Clearly, Tejanos used a variety of strategies to cope with their incorporation into a Euro-American system. Insurrection, involvement in the political system, using the legal system to their advantage, or simply isolating themselves from the mainstream were a few reactions to the events of the late 1830s through the 1840s. It was only because they were effective actors on their own behalf who drew practical inspiration from their historical memory and traditions that they maintained the integrity of their communities. On the whole, Tejanos were not absolutely overwhelmed and demoralized because they drew on their strengths and devised ways to negotiate even the most difficult situations.

CONCLUSION

In the decades after Tejanos' incorporation into the United States, the social system became increasingly intolerant, not only narrowing their participation in the state's affairs, but also closing economic opportunities. Tejano initiatives and responses to changing times grew more sophisticated throughout the nineteenth century, as is revealed in studies by

Gilberto M. Hinojosa, Arnoldo de León, David Montejano, and Mario García. Tejanos brought the lessons of their Spanish and Mexican past to bear on their post-1836 world. Though their world was significantly transformed by new political definitions, changing demographic patterns, and restructured economic relationships, Tejano history did not begin anew, nor was Mexican American, or Chicano, history suddenly born or lived without references and attachment to the past. Though some argue that the Treaty of Guadalupe Hidalgo in 1848 is the starting point of Chicano history, and others suggest that patterns of economic development and demographic evolution define 1910 as the beginning, essays such as the ones in this book suggest that Mexican American history starts with the foundation of the first Spanish Mexican communities from Texas to California. Complex interactions that include continuity and change characterize the long and arduous Tejano and Chicano journeys from the eighteenth century to this day. Only continuing detailed inquiries into the historical foundations and intricate developments of the communities themselves will fully illuminate the many though not uniform political, socioeconomic, and cultural linkages that give Tejano historical trajectories a unity of movement across time.

NOTES

INTRODUCTION

1. See "Introduction," in Poyo and Hinojosa, eds., *Tejano Origins in Eighteenth-Century San Antonio*. See also Arnoldo de León, "Tejano History Scholarship: A Review of the Literature," and idem, "The Tejano Experience in Six Texas Regions."

2. See Gerald E. Poyo and Gilberto M. Hinojosa, "Spanish Texas and Borderlands Historiography in Transition: Implications for United States History," pp. 393–416.

3. Gilberto M. Hinojosa, "The Enduring Hispanic Faith Communities: Spanish and Texas Church Historiography"; and Robert E. Wright, "Local Church Emergence and Mission Decline: The Historiography of the Catholic Church in the Southwest during the Spanish and Mexican Periods."

4. Arnoldo De León, *The Tejano Community, 1836–1900*, p. 203.

1. COMMUNITY AND AUTONOMY

1. "Memorial from the government of the villa of San Fernando and the Royal Presidio of San Antonio de Béxar to Governor Martínez Pacheco, regarding the people's right to the *mesteña* horses and cattle of Texas," Bexar Archives Translations, Bexar County Courthouse, San Antonio (hereafter BAT), vol. 150, 1787, p. 2. Bexar Archives translations are also available at the Barker Texas History Center, University of Texas (hereafter BTHC), where the translations are prepared. A version of this essay appeared in *Recent Research* (Dec., 1991), an in-house publication of the former Department of Research and Collections, University of Texas at San Antonio Institute of Texan Cultures.

2. For the most detailed narrative discussions of the establishment and settlement of the Province of Texas, see Herbert Eugene Bolton, *Texas in the Middle of the Eighteenth Century*, and Carlos E. Castañeda, *Our Catholic Heritage in Texas, 1519–1936*, vols. I and II.

3. For information on the establishment and demographic growth of San An-
tonio during the eighteenth century, see de la Teja, *San Antonio de Béxar*; "Estado
General de la Tropa de el Presidio de San Antonio de Béxar y Vecindario de la
Villa de San Fernando," Archivo General de Indias, Audiencia de Guadalajara
(hereafter AGI), Legajo 283; and Alicia V. Tjarks, "Comparative Demographic
Analysis of Texas, 1777–1793," pp. 302–303, table 1.

4. For a detailed discussion of this process, see Poyo and Hinojosa, eds.,
Tejano Origins.

5. On the development of the cattle industry in Texas, see Jack Jackson, *Los
Mesteños: Spanish Ranching in Texas, 1721–1821*.

6. See Poyo and Hinojosa, eds., *Tejano Origins*.

7. On the Bourbon reforms, see James Lockhart and Stuart B. Schwartz, *Early
Latin America: A History of Colonial Spanish America and Brazil*, pp. 315–368; and
Colin M. MacLachlan and Jaime E. Rodríguez O., *The Forging of the Cosmic Race:
A Reinterpretation of Colonial Mexico*, pp. 251–293.

8. Max L. Moorhead, *The Presidio: Bastion of the Spanish Borderlands*, pp. 47–
74.

9. On the withdrawal from Los Adaes, see Castañeda, *Our Catholic Heritage*,
pp. IV: 273–302.

10. Governors who fit this description for Texas during the reign of Carlos III
are Hugo O'Conor, 1767–1770; Juan María Vicencio Barón de Ripperdá, 1770–
1778; and Domingo Cabello, 1778–1786. On these governors, see Paige W. Christiansen, "Hugo O'Conor: Spanish-Indian Relations on the Frontiers of New
Spain, 1771–1776"; Fritz L. Hoffman, "The First Three Years of the Administration of Juan María Barón de Ripperdá, Governor of Texas 1770–1773"; Helen
Dixon, "The Middle Years of the Administration of Juan María Baron de Ripperdá, Governor of Texas, 1773–1775"; Odie B. Faulk, "Texas during the Administration of Governor Domingo Cabello y Robles, 1778–1786."

11. For a discussion of the functions of these offices, see Mattie Alice Austin,
"The Municipal Government of San Fernando de Béxar, 1730–1800."

12. Apparently, the senior magistrate served as an appellate judge in San Fernando: Ibid., p. 317.

13. On *cabildo* resistance to gubernatorial authority, see Archivo General de la
Nación, Mexico, Provincias Internas (hereafter AGN-PI), vols. 32 and 163.

14. Early disputes over land and water between Canary Islanders, missionaries,
and soldier-settlers are included in AGN-PI, vol. 163. Subsequent conflicts are revealed in "Tanto y testimonio de una escritura de concordia entre los señores ysle-
ños y las misiones, 1745," Spanish Materials of Various Sources, 2Q237, BTHC;
and "Proceedings in Connection with the Establishment of Complaints of Monopoly by the Cabildo," BAT, vol. 30, 1756, pp. 54–62.

15. See "Certified Copy of the Proceedings Relative to the Visita made by Martos y Navarrete to the Administration of San Fernando," BAT, vol. 36, 1756–1762,
pp. 186–187; "Documents Concerning Distribution of Water and New Irrigation
Canal at San Fernando," BAT, vol. 37, 1762, pp. 27–39; Andrés Ramón to Governor, Aug. 31, 1762, Land Petition (LGS-550), Bexar County Archives, Bexar
County Courthouse, San Antonio, Texas (hereafter BCA); "Documents Concern-

ing Civil Disturbances Caused by Vincente Álvarez Travieso and Francisco de Arocha," Sept. 6–15, 1762, BAT, vol. 37, 1762, pp. 40–47.

16. Fray Juan Agustín Morfí, *History of Texas, 1673–1779*, p. I: 92.

17. Ibid., p. II: 395.

18. See BAT, vol. 48, 1770, pp. 155–172; vol. 56, Jan. 4, 1774–July 31, 1774, pp. 67–76. Also see Robert S. Weddle and Robert H. Thonhoff, *Drama and Conflict: The Texas Saga of 1776*, pp. 49–73.

19. BAT, vol. 48, 1770, p. 136.

20. Ibid.

21. Ibid.

22. BAT, vol. 49, 1771, pp. 78–93.

23. See BAT, vol. 50, 1771, pp. 5–14, 30–31; vol. 53, 1772, pp. 43–50, 56–64; vol. 54, 1773, pp. 37–42; vol. 55, 1773.

24. BAT, vol. 134, Oct. 1–Oct. 29, 1785, pp. 42–81.

25. Elizabeth May Morey, "Attitude of the Citizens of San Fernando toward Independence Movements in New Spain, 1811–1813," pp. 36–43. See also BAT, vol. 31, Nov. 13–Dec. 31, 1807, p. 199.

26. See "Protest of Don Vincente Álvarez Travieso and Don Juan Andrés Travieso against Claims of the Missions of San Antonio, 1771–1783," in Grazing in Texas Collection, Box 2R340, BTHC; and "Petition and Testimony Concerning Lands of San Antonio, Missions, 1772," Archivo del Convento de Guadalupe, reel 3, 3600–3628.

27. For a detailed discussion of these trials, see Jackson, *Los Mesteños*, pp. 125–171.

28. On Croix's visit to San Antonio, see Elizabeth A. H. John, *Storms Brewed in Other Men's Worlds: The Confrontation of Indians, Spanish, and French in the Southwest, 1540–1795*, pp. 504–505.

29. Jackson, *Los Mesteños*, pp. 155–157.

30. "Memorial from the government of the Villa of San Fernando and the Royal Presidio of San Antonio de Béxar to Governor Martínez Pacheco, regarding the people's right to the *mesteña* horses and cattle of Texas," BAT, vol. 150, 1787, pp. 54–55.

31. On local attempts to have the original ranching regulations overturned, see Jackson, *Los Mesteños*, pp. 279–319.

32. See ibid., pp. 303–308. While additional research is needed on this point, it seems that many of the prominent ranching families of the 1770s and 1780s had lost considerable economic and political influence by 1808. For example, when the cabildo was appointed by the governor, the Menchacas no longer figured as officers. See BAT, vol. 31, Nov. 14–Dec. 31, 1807, p. 199, and Manuel de Salcedo to Manuel Barerra, on orders to summon the town council to resolve several municipal ordinances, Nov. 19, 1809, Bexar Archives, BTHC.

33. On early contraband trade with Louisiana, see Bolton, *Texas in the Middle of the Eighteenth Century*, pp. 336–337, 426–431; Castañeda, *Our Catholic Heritage*, pp. III: 75–82; J. Villasana Haggard, "The Neutral Ground between Louisiana and Texas, 1806–1821," pp. 147–212.

34. Haggard, "The Neutral Ground," pp. 150–154.

35. See "Expediente sobre la causa formado en Mexico contra el Colonel Don Jacinto de Barrios y Jauregui sobre el trato ilicito que tuvo siendo governador de la provincia de Texas con los Franceses y Indios fronterizos no sujetos," AGI, 103-6-27, in Dunn Transcripts, 1756–1766, BTHC. This trial is discussed in Doris Clark, "Spanish Reaction to French Intrusion into Texas from Louisiana, 1754–1771." See also "Proceedings Concerning Confiscation of Contraband Money and Merchandise Belonging to Governor Angel de Martos y Navarette, 1767," BAT, vol. 42, pp. 114–160; vol. 43, pp. 1–39; vol. 44, pp. 13–56.

36. BAT, vol. 81, pp. 7–10.

37. BAT, vol. 55, pp. 52–53.

2. REBELLION ON THE FRONTIER

1. For the more recent writings reflecting these various historical interpretations, see David Vigness, *The Revolutionary Decades: The Saga of Texas, 1810–1836*; T. R. Fehrenbach, *Lone Star: A History of Texas and the Texans*. For a general discussion of Anglo-American historians' influence on colonial Texas history writing, see Poyo and Hinojosa, "Spanish Texas and Borderlands Historiography," pp. 393–416.

2. Timothy E. Anna, *The Fall of the Royal Government in Mexico City*; D. A. Brading, *Haciendas and Ranchos in the Mexican Bajío: León, 1680–1860*; Brian R. Hamnett, *Roots of Insurgency: Mexican Regions, 1750–1824*; Doris Ladd, *The Mexican Nobility at Independence*; John Tutino, *From Insurrection to Revolution in Mexico: Social Bases of Agrarian Violence, 1750–1940*; Luis Villoro, *El proceso ideológico de la revolución de independencia*. The best effort among Texas historians to analyze events within the context of local social and economic circumstances is Jackson, *Los Mesteños*, pp. 525–535.

3. This discussion of San Antonio in the eighteenth century is drawn from my *San Antonio de Béxar*.

4. Nettie Lee Benson, "Texas' Failure to Send a Deputy to the Spanish Cortes, 1810–1812," pp. 31–32.

5. Ibid., pp. 23–24; Proceedings concerning the election of a deputy to the Cortes, June 27, 1810, Bexar Archives (hereafter BA), BTHC.

6. The most complete account of Nolan's activities on the Louisiana-Texas frontier is Maurine T. Wilson and Jack Jackson, *Philip Nolan and Texas: Expeditions to the Unknown Land, 1791–1801*.

7. Odie B. Faulk, *The Last Years of Spanish Texas, 1778–1821*, p. 124; Mattie Austin Hatcher, *The Opening of Texas to Foreign Settlement, 1801–1821*, pp. 61–62, 70–71.

8. "Estado que manifiesta la fuerza efectiva de las tropas," May 23, 24, 1810, BA.

9. Aside from the works cited in n. 2, an excellent brief acccount of the Mexican War of Independence is Timothy Anna, "The Independence of Mexico and Central America."

10. For a general survey of Spanish policy toward Texas during this time, see Hatcher, *The Opening of Texas to Foreign Settlement*, chaps. 1–5. French intrigues and the role of Texas as an avenue to the interior is treated in Julia Kathryn Garrett, *Green Flag over Texas: A Story of the Last Years of Spain in Texas*, pp. 14–19, 25–26.

11. Lucas Alamán, *Historia de México desde los primeros movimientos que prepararon su independencia en el año de 1808 hasta la época presente*, vol. 2, pp. 379–380; Vito Alessio Robles, *Coahuila y Texas en la época colonial*, pp. 629–635; Garrett, *Green Flag over Texas*, pp. 33–35. Garrett writes that Cordero had two thousand troops under his command, while Alessio Robles sets the figure at seven hundred.

12. "Fieles habitantes de la provincia de Texas," Jan. 6, 1811, BA; Salcedo to Sebastián Rodríguez, Jan. 16, 1811, BA; "Junta convocada por el señor gobernador de la provincia de Texas . . . ," Jan. 18, 1811, BA. The details of the Casas revolt have been well told in a number of works, and documents regarding the coup are published in Frederick C. Chabot, ed., *Texas in 1811: The Las Casas and Sambrano Revolutions*.

13. The standard narrative of the counterrevolt is J. Villasana Haggard, "The Counter-Revolution of Bexar, 1811," pp. 222–235.

14. Alessio Robles, *Coahuila y Texas en la época colonial*, pp. 639–649. Garrett, in *Green Flag over Texas*, pp. 61–62, and following earlier historians, maintains that Elizondo was an insurgent convinced by Governor Salcedo to return to the loyalist fold. Alessio Robles maintains, however, that the evidence overwhelmingly points to Elizondo's having been a royalist all along.

15. Alessio Robles, *Coahuila y Texas en la época colonial*, pp. 635–654; Garrett, *Green Flag over Texas*, pp. 83–112. The Gutierrez-Magee expedition is one of the most studied episodes of early Texas history. Among the best narratives are Félix D. Almaráz, Jr., *Tragic Cavalier: Governor Manuel Salcedo of Texas, 1808–1813*, chap. 6; Castañeda, *Our Catholic Heritage*, chaps. 4 and 5; Garrett, *Green Flag over Texas*, pp. 25–39.

16. Harry Henderson, "The Magee-Gutierrez Expedition," pp. 49–51.

17. A detailed survey of the period between the Battle of Medina and Mexican independence is found in Castañeda, *Our Catholic Heritage*, pp. VI: chaps. 6 and 7.

18. A narrative of Governor Salcedo's administration is found in Almaráz, *Tragic Cavalier*; for Governor Cordero, see Fabius Dunn, "The Administration of Don Antonio Cordero, Governor of Texas, 1805–1808." See also Morey, "Attitude of the Citizens."

19. Alessio Robles, *Coahuila y Texas en la época colonial*, p. 622; my translation.

20. Jesús F. de la Teja, "Indians, Soldiers, and Canary Islanders: The Making of a Texas Frontier Community," p. 94; Morey, "Attitude of the Citizens," pp. 38–39.

21. Muñoz to viceroy, Jan. 7, 1792, Nacogdoches Archives Transcripts, BTHC (hereafter NAT). Case against Tomás Álvarez Travieso, July 12, 1805; Case against Francisco Travieso, Nov. 23, 1810; Vicente Travieso vs. Francisco Travieso, May 23, 1810; Case against José Félix Menchaca et al., Jan. 27, 1808; Case against Juan Ma-

nuel Zambrano, Oct. 27, 1802; Junta to commandant general, June 19, 1811, in copy of same date, BA.

22. Following earlier writers who misrepresented anti-Spanish sentiments in the population, and by attaching to Béxar's disturbances the same character as the insurrectionary movement in central areas of the empire, recent writers have also concluded that European and class hatreds were rampant in San Antonio. Compare, for instance, Morey, "Attitude of the Citizens," p. 46, and David J. Weber, *The Mexican Frontier, 1826–1846: The American Southwest under Mexico*, p. 9.

23. Harris Gaylord Warren, *The Sword Was Their Passport: A History of American Filibustering in the Mexican Revolution*, p. 50; Garrett, *Green Flag over Texas*, pp. 180–181.

24. [Copy of testimony taken from Br. don Feliciano Franco Vela, Dn. Guadalupe Caso, and D. Antonio Fuentes], Apr. 15, 1813, Archivo General de la Nación, Mexico, Historia (hereafter AGN-H): Operaciones de Guerra, Arredondo, vol. 422, p. 309.

25. Morey, "Attitude of the Citizens," p. 53.

26. De la Teja, "Indians, Soldiers, and Canary Islanders," p. 94.

27. The nature and workings of this group seems to fit Hamnett's description of the "local dissident groups" through which Hidalgo extended his insurrection (*Roots of Insurgency*, pp. 125–126).

28. Decree of the Junta, Mar. 3, 1811; Decree of the Junta, Mar. 24, 1811; Junta to Manuel Salcedo, Apr. 18, 1811; Decree of the Junta, Apr. 21, 1811, BA.

29. Chabot, ed., *Texas in 1811*, pp. 54–55, 58–62, 111; "Contra dn. Francisco Travieso por falta de respeto e inobediente," Nov. 23, 1810; Decree of the governing Junta, Mar. 3, 1811; Junta to Nemecio Salcedo, June 19, 1811; Antonio Cordero to Manuel Salcedo, July 4, 1812, BA.

30. Kathryn Stoner O'Connor, *The Presidio La Bahía del Espíritu Santo de Zúñiga, 1721–1846* (1984), p. 85.

31. Morey, "Attitude of the Citizens," p. 100.

32. Garrett, *Green Flag over Texas*, p. 176.

33. Alessio Robles, *Coahuila y Texas en la época colonial*, pp. 656–657; [Copy of testimony of soldier Guillermo Nabarro, of the Lampazos Company, taken at Laredo on Apr. 8, 1813], AGN-H, vol. 422, p. 242.

34. Morey, "Attitude of the Citizens," p. 106.

35. Garrett, *Green Flag over Texas*, pp. 151, 157–158.

36. Ibid., p. 170.

37. [Copy of testimony of Guillermo Saldaña], Apr. 6, 1813, AGN-H, vol. 422, p. 247.

38. [Copy of testimony from Br. don Feliciano Franco Vela, Dn. Guadalupe Caso, and D. Antonio Fuentes], Apr. 15, 1813, AGN-H, vol. 422, p. 309.

39. Ignacio Elizondo to Arrendondo, June 18, 1813, AGN-H, vol. 423, p. 80.

40. Morey, "Attitude of the Citizens," pp. 113–114, 119, 121–122; Hatcher, *Opening of Texas*, pp. 235–238; Elizondo to Arrendondo, Sept. 2, 1813, and Sept. 12, 1813, AGN-H, vol. 423, pp. 215, 218. Joaquín de Arrendondo to Cristóbal Domínguez, Oct. 10, 1813; Ygnacio Pérez to Benito Armiñán, Mar. 17, 1814; Lista de los Presos to Benito Armiñán, July 4, 1814; "Noticia de los Ynsurgentes

Yndultados, y de las familias que pueden ser sospechosas, y perjudican la quietud y pública tranquilidad de esta Provincia," Aug. 8, 1814; [Governor] to Antonio Cordero, Jan. 2, 1815, BA; John Sibley to General John Armstrong, Aug. 10, 1814, in Julia Kathryn Garrett, "Dr. John Sibley and the Louisiana-Texas Frontier, 1803–1814," pp. 607–608.

41. Petition of José Félix Menchaca, Sept. 22, 1813; [Commandant General] to Governor of Texas, Nov. 2, 1814, BA. Proceso de José Erasmo Seguín, 1813–1819, Archivo de la Secretaría de Gobierno, photostatic copy in Saltillo Archives, BTHC (hereafter SA). In inventories of property confiscated from the Spaniards during the Gutiérrez-Magee occupation, Fernando Veramendi appears as president, treasurer, or both; e.g., "Ymbentario de los enseres qe. se imbentariaron por el Presidente y Tesorero Dn. Ferndo. Beramendi en la Casa del Sor. Dn. Simón de Herrera," Apr. 17, 1813, SA. Yet, just over a year later, in an unsigned document, Fernando Veramendi is listed as the town's choice for schoolteacher, there not being a more qualified individual. See [May 31, 1814], SA.

42. Election report, Dec. 28, 1813; Dec. 28, 1814; Benito Armiñán to council, Dec. 28, 1814; council to Armiñán, Jan. 5, 1815; election report, Dec. 21, 1815; election report, Dec. 21, 1816; new election, Dec. 23, 1816; Ygnacio Pérez to council, Dec. 22, 1816; election report, Dec. 23, 1816, all in BA.

43. Governor to José Darío Zambrano, Sept. 21, 1815, BA.

44. Minutes of the council, Jan. 25, 1815, Oct. 5, 1815, BA.

45. Town council to Interim Governor Mariano Varela, Feb. 1, 1816, BA.

46. Morey, "Attitude of the Citizens," p. 122.

47. Chipman, *Spanish Texas*, pp. 238–241; Castañeda, *Our Catholic Heritage*, VI: 126–169.

48. For a discussion of the coming of independence to San Antonio, see Félix D. Almaráz, Jr., *Governor Antonio Martínez and Mexican Independence in Texas: An Orderly Transition*.

3. UNDER THE MEXICAN FLAG

1. This chapter is drawn from Tijerina, *Tejanos and Texas*.

2. Bolton, *Texas in the Middle Eighteenth Century*, pp. 4–8.

3. Miguel Ramos Arizpe to Commandant General, vol. 62, pp. 56, 58, AGI.

4. Víctor Blanco to Juan Antonio Saucedo, Sept. 9, 1826, BA.

5. José María Rodríguez, *Rodríguez Memoirs of Early Texas*, p. 45.

6. José María Sánchez, "A Trip to Texas in 1828," p. 283.

7. William Kennedy, *Texas: The Rise, Progress, and Prospects of the Republic of Texas*, p. 394.

8. Juan N. Almonte, *Nota estadística sobre Tejas*, p. 76.

9. J. B. Wilkinson, *Laredo and the Rio Grande Frontier*, p. 145.

10. Nettie Lee Benson, *The Provincial Deputation in Mexico: Harbinger of Provincial Autonomy, Independence, and Federalism*, pp. 12–13, 55–56, 64–65; idem, "The Plan of Casa Mata," pp. 51, 55; Eugene C. Barker, "The Government of Austin's Colony, 1821–1831," pp. 223–225.

11. Lucas Alamán to Luciano García, Sept. 17, 1823; Luciano García to Béxar Ayuntamiento, Sept. 24, 25, 1823; Lucas Alamán to José Antonio Saucedo, Nov. 15, 1823, BA. Benson, *The Provincial Deputation*, p. 65; Charles A. Bacarisse, "The Barón de Bastrop: The Life and Times of Philip Hendrick Nering Bogel, 1759–1827," p. 297.

12. De la Teja, ed. *A Revolution Remembered*, pp. 8–9.

13. Miguel Ramos de Arizpe to Béxar Ayuntamiento, Sept. 15, 1824, BA.

14. Erasmo Seguín to Texas Provincial Deputation, Oct. 5, 1824; Erasmo Seguín to María Josefa Seguín, Oct. 20, 1824, BA; Erasmo Seguín to Bastrop, Apr. 21, 1824, BA. Eugene C. Barker, ed., *The Austin Papers* (1919 report), II: pt. 1, 775–777.

15. John P. Kimball, comp., *Laws and Decrees of the State of Texas and Coahuila*, p. 154; Coahuila y Texas, "Actas del congreso constitucional del estado libre de Coahuila y Texas," Dec. 14, 1824, typescript, BTHC.

16. Béxar Ayuntamiento Special Committee Report, Nov. 18, 1829, BA.

17. Ildefonso Villarello Vélez, *Historia de Coahuila*, App.; Robert Andrews to Austin, Sept. 5, 1823, Barker, *The Austin Papers* (1919 report), vol. II: pt. 1, p. 694.

18. Kimball, *Laws*, pp. 154, 160; Coahuila y Texas, "Actas del congreso," Feb. 10, 1825, BTHC.

19. Estevan F. Austin to José Felix Trespalacios, Jan. 8, 1823; Barker, *The Austin Papers* (1919 report), vol. II: pt. 1, pp. 567–568.

20. Coahuila y Texas, "Actas del congreso," Nov. 30, 1826, Apr., 1832, BTHC.

21. Representación, Dec. 19, 1832, BA; Michael P. Costeloe, *La primera república federal de México (1824–1835): Un estudio de los partidos políticos en el México independiente*, pp. 243, 247.

22. Ayuntamiento of San Felipe to Ayuntamiento of Saltillo, Sept. 27 1830; Barker, *The Austin Papers* (1922 report), vol. II: 500–502.

23. Permanent Deputation to Béxar Ayuntamiento, Sept., 1830, Leona Vicario [Saltillo], BA; Barker, The Austin Papers (1922 report), vol. II: 500–502.

24. Coahuila y Texas, "Actas del congreso," Jan. 11, 1831, BTHC.

25. Representación, Dec. 19, 1832, BA.

26. Ibid.

27. Nacogdoches Ayuntamiento to State Congress, Jan. 30, 1833; Goliad Ayuntamiento to State Congress, Jan. 15, 1833, Nacogdoches Archives, Texas State Library Archives Division (hereafter NAT).

28. For details of these events, see Coahuila y Texas, "Actas del congreso," Jan.–Apr., 1834, BTHC; Vito Alessio Robles, *Coahuila y Texas desde la consumación de la independencia hasta el tratado de paz de Guadalupe Hidalgo*, p. II: 13; Costeloe, *Primera república*, pp. 381, 428, 435; Hubert H. Bancroft, *The History of North Mexican States and Texas*.

29. Juan Nepomuceno Seguín to Béxar Ayuntamiento, Jan. 22, 1833, BA; Eugene C. Barker, *The Life of Stephen F. Austin, Founder of Texas, 1793–1836*, pp. 332–333, 344–351, 356.

30. Green DeWitt to Ramón Músquiz, July 28, 1830; Francisco Flores to Ramón Músquiz, Oct. 30, 1830, BA.

31. Representación, Dec. 19, 1832; Mateo Ahumada, Military Order, Oct. 29, 1826, BA; Ethel Zivley Rather, "DeWitt's Colony," pp. 108–113.

32. Cavalry Report, Sept. 15, 1826; Mateo Ahumada to Francisco Rojo, Dec. 10, 1826, BA. Goliad Census, Dec. 31, 1831, NAT.

33. Rafael Antonio Manchola to Mateo Ahumada, Oct. 29, 1826, BA.

34. Sánchez, "Trip to Texas in 1828"; Goliad Ayuntamiento to State Congress, Jan. 15, 1833, NAT.

35. Representación, Dec. 19, 1832; Mateo Ahumada, Military Order, Oct. 29, 1826, BA; Rather, "DeWitt's Colony," pp. 108–113.

36. Nacogdoches Ayuntamiento to State Congress, Jan. 30, 1833; Goliad Ayuntamiento to State Congress, Jan. 15, 1833, NAT.

4. EFFICIENT IN THE CAUSE

1. For a brief background to events leading to the revolt, see "Revolution and Independence," in Stanley Siegel, *A Political History of the Texas Republic, 1836–1845,* pp. 3–37; for a broader perspective, see Weber, *The Mexican Frontier,* pp. 242–255, and idem, "Refighting the Alamo: Mythmaking and the Texas Revolution," pp. 138–139. A concise discussion of the early support for the federalist system appears in Hobart Huson, *Captain Phillip Dimmitt's Commandancy of Goliad, 1835–1836: An Episode of the Mexican Federalist War in Texas, Usually Referred to as the Texian Revolution,* pp. 1–6. The traditional notion of "culture conflict" is espoused in Samuel Harmon Lowrie, *Culture Conflict in Texas, 1821–1835.* For a thoughtful and readable overview of Tejano life during the period, consult Tijerina, *Tejanos and Texas.*

2. Tijerina, *Tejanos and Texas,* pp. 79–80. For the uniforms, weapons, and equipment of the presidial companies, an excellent study is Rene Chartrand, "Leather Jacket Soldiers: The 'Cuera' Cavalry of the American South-West."

3. Tijerina, *Tejanos and Texas,* pp. 80–82. For the organization of the compañía volante, see Moorhead, *The Presidio,* pp. 30, 58, 72, 91, 97, 179–180, 267.

4. Mary S. Helm, *Scraps of Early Texas History,* p. 93. Claudio Linati, a European lithographer, visited Mexico in 1828 and subsequently published a book of lithographs depicting the regional attire of the country; this book has been a treasure trove for students of material culture. One of Linati's sketches shows a ranchero horseman snaring an enemy officer within the loop of his lasso: *Trajes civiles, militares y religiosos de Mexico,* p. 104; Moorhead, *The Presidio,* p. 189.

5. David Dary, *Cowboy Culture: A Saga of Five Centuries,* pp. 18–21.

6. Jean Louis Berlandier Papers, Thomas Gilcrease Institute of American History and Art, Tulsa, Oklahoma. This outstanding collection contains the work of Lino Sánchez y Tapia, which includes watercolor studies of a presidial soldier and a teamster, both of whom are wearing American top hats; see also Richard E. Ahlborn, "European Dress in Texas, 1830: As Rendered by Lino Sánchez y Tapia," pp. 1–18; Juan N. Almonte, "Statistical Information of Texas," p. II: 270. For a view that suggests Tejanos exaggerated their poverty, see David J. Weber, ed.,

Troubles in Texas, 1832: A Tejano Viewpoint from San Antonio with a Translation and Facsimile, p. 20.

7. Mary Austin Holley, *Texas*, pp. 127, 128; Helm, *Scraps of Early Texas History*, pp. 34, 94; John C. Duval, *Early Times in Texas; or The Adventures of Jack Dobell*, pp. 47–48.

8. Stephen L. Hardin, "A Vatir y Perseguir: Tejano Deployment in the War of Texas Independence, 1835–1836," p. 163.

9. For a solid background on Tejanos, see Lack, *The Texas Revolutionary Experience*, pp. 183–207; for the skirmish at Gonzales, see "First Breaking Out of the Texas Revolution at Gonzales," in James M. Day, comp. and ed., *The Texas Almanac, 1857–1873: A Compendium of Texas History*, pp. 4–42. For Austin's role as commander of the Texian "Army of the People," see "General Austin's Order Book for the Campaign of 1835," pp. 1–56. The theme of American woodlanders in an unfamiliar prairie environment is developed further in Stephen L. Hardin, "Long Rifle and Brown Bess: Weapons and Tactics of the Texas Revolution, 1835–1836," and continued by the same writer in *Texian Iliad: A Narrative Military History of the Texas Revolution.*

10. Eli Mercer to Stephen F. Austin, Oct. 12, 1835, in Barker, ed., *The Austin Papers*, p. III: 176; *Red River Herald*, undated, in Jerry J. Gaddy, *Texas in Revolt: Contemporary Newspaper Account of the Texas Revolution*, p. 26.

11. The best study of the 1835 campaign remains Alwyn Barr, *Texans in Revolt: The Battle for San Antonio, 1835*, pp. 5–14. Stephen F. Austin to Committee of Safety of Harrisburg, Oct., 4, 1835, in John H. Jenkins, ed., *The Papers of the Texas Revolution, 1835–1836*, pp. II: 31–32.

12. Martín Perfecto de Cos to José María Tornel, Nov. 11, 1835, in Jenkins, *Papers*, p. II: 378; Stephen F. Austin to Edward Burleson, Nov. 15, 1835, in "General Austin's Order Book," p. 41.

13. Barr, *Texans in Revolt*, p. 18.

14. Commission of Juan N. Seguín as Captain in the Federal Army of Texas, Salado [Creek], Oct. 23, 1835, BA; General Orders, Head Quaters Camp Sebolo (Cíbolo Creek), Oct. 23, 1835, in "General Austin's Order Book," p. 24; William T. Austin, "Account of the Campaign of 1835 by William T. Austin, Aid[e] to General Stephen F. Austin and Gen Edward Burleson," BTHC.

15. Stephen F. Austin to James W. Fannin, Nov. 14, 1835, in Jenkins, *Papers*, p. II: 406; Austin to Salvador Flores, Nov. 14, 1835, in Jenkins, *Papers*, p. II: 407.

16. Austin's affidavit of services rendered by Juan Seguín, Salvador Flores, and Vicente Zepeda, Nov. 24, 1835, BA.

17. Mirabeau Buonaparte Lamar, *The Papers of Mirabeau Buonaparte Lamar*, p. I: 242.

18. Vicente Filisola, *Memoirs for the History of the War in Texas*, pp. II: 62–63. Tacitus's quotation in the Latin reads: "Quippe preditores etiam iis quos anteponunt invisi sunt." For the original text, see Vicente Filisola, *Memoria para la historia de la guerra de Tejas*, p. II: 151.

19. Weber, *The Mexican Frontier*, p. 209.

20. Ibid., p. 252; Barr, *Texans in Revolt*, p. 48. See María Jesusa de García file,

Memorials and Petitions Collection, Texas State Library, Archives Division, Austin (hereafter TSL).

21. "Capitulation Entered into by General Martin Perfecto De Cos, of the Permanent Troops, and General Edward Burleson, of the Colonial Troops of Texas," Dec. 11, 1835, in Jenkins, *Papers*, pp. III: 156–158; Noah Smithwick, *The Evolution of a State: Or, Recollections of Old Texas Days*, p. 80.

22. De la Teja, ed., *A Revolution Remembered*, pp. 78–79; Fane Downs, "The History of Mexicans in Texas, 1820–1845," p. 35.

23. Weber, *Mexican Frontier*, p. 53; J. C. Neill to Sam Houston, Jan. 14, 1836, in William C. Binkley, ed., *Official Correspondence of the Texan Revolution, 1835–1836*, p. I: 294–295; James Bowie to Henry Smith, Feb. 2, 1836, in Jenkins, *Papers*, p. IV: 238; Minutes of the City Council of San Antonio de Béxar, July 2, 1840, Book II, p. 702; Neill to Government, Jan. 28, 1836, in Jenkins, *Papers*, p. IV: 175. See also Neill to Governor and Council, Jan. 6, 1836, in Binkley, ed., *Official Correspondence*, pp. I: 272–275.

24. "Resolution Providing for the Troops at Bexar," General Council of the Provisional Government of Texas, San Felipe de Austin, Jan. 16, 1836, in H. P. N. Gammel, *The Laws of Texas, 1822–1897*, pp. I: 1037–1039.

25. Republic Payments for Service, Record Group 304, Felipe Xaimes file, Feb. 19, 1836, oversize box no. 21, TSL. For other examples of repayments, see Republic Payments for Service, Record Group 304, Ignacio Pérez file, TSL; Susan Prendergast Schoelwer with Tom E. Glaser, *Alamo Images: Changing Perceptions of a Texas Experience*, p. 128; and Memorials and Petitions, Ignacio Pérez file, compensation for beef furnished to Texas Army, June 17, 1841, box no. 100-445, TSL.

26. Republic Payments for Service, Record Group 304, William B. Travis affidavit, Feb. 22, 1836, Antonio Cruz file, TSL. For a different view, see Lack, *Texas Revolutionary Experience*, p. 167.

27. De la Teja, ed., *A Revolution Remembered*, pp. 79–80, 191–192, 194–195; Schoelwer, *Alamo Images*, p. 122. See also Stephen L. Hardin, ed., "The Félix Núñez Account and the Siege of the Alamo: A Critical Appraisal."

28. Republic Payments for Service, Unpaid Claims, Juan Seguín file, no. 2, box no. 304-301, TSL. The individuals in question were Clemente Bustillo (left Feb. 21, 1836), Luis Castañón (left Feb. 21), Agapito Cervantes (left Feb. 21), Carlos Chacón (left Feb. 21), Domingo Días (left Feb. 20), Francisco Días (left Feb. 20), Clemente García [?] (left Feb. 21), Jesús García (left Feb. 21), Antonio Hernández (left Feb. 21), Gregorio Hernández (left Feb. 20), and Pablo Mansolo (left Feb. 21).

29. "Alamo's Only Survivor, Enrique Esparza, Who Claims to Have Been There during the Siege, Tells the Story of the Fall," San Antonio *Daily Express*, May 12, continued on May 19, 1907. The article is Charles Meritt Barnes's interview with Enrique Esparza. See also "The Story of Enrique Esparza," San Antonio *Daily Express*, Nov. 22, 1902.

30. Seguín recorded that Bergara and Barcena were "both soldiers of my company whom I had left in the vicinity of San Antonio for purposes of observation,"

but remembered Bergara's name as "Vergara": de la Teja, ed., *A Revolution Remembered*, pp. 80–81. See Sam Houston to James W. Fannin, Mar. 11, 1836, in Amelia W. Williams and Eugene C. Barker, *The Writings of Sam Houston 1813–1863*, pp. I: 364–365; E. N. Gray to [?], Mar. 11, 1836, in E. N. Gray file, Republic of Texas General File, Archives and Manuscripts Collection, box no. 2B41, BTHC; Sam Houston to James T. Collinsworth, Mar. 18, 1836, in Jenkins, *Papers*, pp. V: 82–84; "Examination of Andrew Barsena and Ansolma Bergara at Gonzales, 11 March, 1836," in Frederick Chabot, ed., *Texas Letters*, pp. 146–147; Walter Lord, *A Time to Stand*, pp. 181–183.

31. De la Teja, ed., *A Revolution Remembered*, p. 81; Ralph W. Steen, "Analysis of the Work of the General Council, 1835–1836," pp. 330–342; Llerena B. Friend, *Sam Houston: The Great Designer*, p. 64.

32. Republic Payments for Service, Record Group 304, Joseph Urban file, claim for shoes signed by Juan N. Seguín, San Felipe, Mar. 28, 1836, TSL.

33. Antonio Menchaca, *Memoirs*, p. 26.

34. "Personal Reminiscences of Moses Austin Bryan," in Moses Austin Bryan Papers, 1824–1847, 1926, box no. 2N254, BTHC. The report that centralists were pressing Tejanos into service may have been the reason some Bexareños fled to Gonzales. See n. 53.

35. George O. Coalson, "Texas Mexicans in the Texas Revolution," p. 226; Antonio Menchaca, "Memoirs," p. 80, BTHC. Students of Texas Mexicans have largely overlooked this unpublished manuscript; it is entirely different material from that included in the 1937 Yanaguana Society edition. Sadly, the first sixty-seven pages are missing, but what remains provides numerous details of the battle of San Jacinto and its aftermath that are found nowhere else. The Barker Center inventory describes the document as "Incomplete Mss. Dictated by Menchaca to Charles M. Barnes, when Menchaca was 76 years old. Describing the Battle of San Jacinto."

36. Richmond [Va.] *Inquirer*, July 1, 1836. Stephen F. Austin was one of the few American immigrants who had known Juan Seguín from boyhood. I am grateful to Gary Zaboly for bringing this source to my attention.

37. Henry S. Foote, *Texas and the Texans*, p. II: 310.

38. Juan López file, Republic Pension Applications, Comptroller's records, TSL.

39. Sam Houston to E. D. White, Oct. 31, 1837, in James Grizzard Collection, TSL; Sam Houston to Erasmo Seguín, July 6, 1842, in Houston, Writings of Sam Houston, p. IV: 125; Edward Burleson to Thomas J. Rusk, May 5, 1836, in Army Papers, Adjutant General Records, TSL.

40. Vicente Filisola to Juan Seguín [English translation], May 2, 1836, in de la Teja, ed., *A Revolution Remembered*, pp. 136–137; Thomas J. Rusk to Juan N. Seguín, May 30, 1836, in Jenkins, *Papers*, pp. VI: 423–424.

41. Huson, *Dimmitt's Commandancy*, p. 7. For the Mexican version, see Filisola, *History of the War in Texas*, pp. II: 60, 61, 63, 64, 65, 85.

42. John Henry Brown, *History of Texas, from 1685 to 1892*, pp. I: 303–304; Huson, *Dimmitt's Commandancy*, p. 7.

43. Huson, *Dimmitt's Commandancy*, p. 7. For more on the Guardias Victorianas, see Lack, *Texas Revolutionary Experience*, p. 164.

44. Stephen F. Austin to Committee of Safety, Oct. 13, 1835, in "General Austin's Order Book for the Campaign of 1835," p. 8; Huson, *Dimmitt's Commandancy*, p. 19.

45. Huson, *Dimmitt's Commandancy*, p. 81.

46. For an expanded discussion of the Lipantitán Expedition, see chap. 3 in Hardin, *Texian Illiad*.

47. Huson, *Dimmitt's Commandancy*, pp. 124–133; Lack, *Texas Revolutionary Experience*, pp. 190–191; John J. Linn to Stephen F. Austin, Nov. 11, 1835, in Jenkins, *Papers*, p. II: 379.

48. Lack, *Texas Revolutionary Experience*, p. 192; for an erudite explanation of the motives behind the Goliad Declaration of Independence, see Huson, *Dimmitt's Commandancy*, pp. 203–217; O'Connor, "Roll of Colonel Fannin's Command," in O'Connor, *The Presidio* (1966), pp. 147–156.

49. Downs, "History of Mexicans in Texas," p. 243; Hardin, "A Vatir y Perseguir," p. 166; Lack, *Texas Revolutionary Experience*, p. 164.

50. Harbert Davenport, revised by Craig H. Roell, "Goliad Campaign of 1836," pp. 38–48.

51. O'Connor, *The Presidio* (1966), p. 151; José Urrea, *Diario de las operaciones militares de la división que al mando del General José Urrea hizo en la Campaña de Tejas*, p. 14.

52. William Barret Travis to Jesse Grimes, Mar. 3, 1836, in Jenkins, *Papers*, pp. IV: 504–505; "Examination of Andrew Barsena and Ansolma Bergara," in Chabot, ed., *Texas Letters*, pp. 146–147.

53. Lewis M. Henry Washington, "Fannin and His Command," in *Georgia Citizen* (Macon), Apr. 23, 1853; see also Robert S. Davis, Jr., "Goliad and the Georgia Battalion: Georgia Participation in the Texas Revolution, 1835–1836," p. 38.

54. *Morning Courier and New York Enquirer*, July 28, 1836. See also Urrea, *Diario*, pp. 25–26. I am grateful to Gary Zaboly for bringing this source to my attention.

55. Isaac D. Hamilton vertical file, BTHC; Craig H. Roell, "Plácidio Benavides" entry in *The Handbook of Victoria County*, pp. 4–6.

56. Craig H. Roell, "Plácidio Benavides" entry in *The Handbook of Victoria County*, pp. 4–6. See also Lester Hamilton, *Goliad Survivor: Isacc D. Hamilton*.

57. Frank Goodwyn, "Francisca Álvarez (The Angel of Goliad)" entry in *The Handbook of Texas*, p. I: 38; Isaac D. Hamilton vertical file, BTHC; *Handbook of Victoria County*, pp. 4–6.

58. Isaac D. Hamilton vertical file, BTHC.

59. Menchaca, *Memoirs*, p. 23.

60. Ibid.; de la Teja, ed., *A Revolution Remembered*, p. 81.

61. Walter Lord, for example, relied heavily on Menchaca's *Memoirs*. See Lord, *A Time to Stand*, pp. 83, 98, 229; Menchaca, *Memoirs*, p. 23. As Esparza recalled: "Among the surnames of those I remember to have left during the time of the

armistice were Menchaca, Flores, Rodriguez, Ramirez, Arocha, Silvero. They are now all dead. Among the women who went out were some of their relatives": quoted in "Alamo's Only Survivor, Enrique Esparza, Who Claims to Have Been There during the Siege, Tells the Story of the Fall," San Antonio *Daily Express*, May 12, continued on May 19, 1907 p. 14.

62. "José Antonio Menchaca" entry in *Handbook of Texas*, p II: 172.

63. Samuel C. A. Rogers, "Reminiscences, 1810–1892," Archives and Manuscript Collection, Box no. 2R166, BTHC.

64. For violence on various frontiers see W. Eugene Hollon, *Frontier Violence: Another Look*, p. 36.

65. J. Frank Dobie, "James Bowie," in *Heroes of Texas: Featuring Oil Portraits from the Summerfield G. Roberts Collection*, pp. 33–53.

66. John Keegan, *The Face of Battle*, pp. 46–54. In the chapter titled "Killing No Murder," Keegan offers a brilliant analysis of the apparent contradiction between the "rules of war" which seek to humanize the battlefield, and combat which is by its nature inherently inhumane.

67. Arnoldo De León, *The Tejano Community, 1836–1900*, pp. 2–5; for other aspects of class divisions in Tejano society see Tijerina, *Tejanos and Texas*, p.10.

68. As Downs relates: "Some [Tejanos] fought on each side while the majority tried to stay clear of the combat": "History of Mexicans in Texans," p. 35. Dr. Weber echoes these sentiments in his seminal study: "Most Tejanos probably responded like any residents of a war-torn land. They looked first to their families' welfare, fought on neither side, cooperated with the group in charge at the moment, and hoped for an end to the nightmare": *Mexican Frontier*, p. 254.

69. For Tejano views regarding emmigrants from the United States and slavery see "The Making of a Tejano," in de la Teja, ed., *A Revolution Remembered*, 1–70; Juan Seguín to Pedro de Ampudia [English translation], May 3, 1836, in ibid., 138–139; also helpful is the chapter "Society and Culture in Transition," in Weber, *Mexican Frontier*, 207-241.

70. William B. Travis to Henry Smith, Jan. 29, 1836, in Jenkins, *Papers*, p. IV: 185.

71. E. R. Lindley, comp., *Biographical Directory of the Texas Conventions and Congresses, 1832–1845*, p. 170.

5. BETWEEN TWO WORLDS

1. Events in the years preceding the Texas Revolution had already demonstrated the Tejano dilemma of being caught between Anglo Americans and Mexican officials. Response at San Antonio de Béxar to the 1832 San Felipe consultation, for example, clearly illustrated Tejano efforts to promote regional interests while remaining loyal to Mexican procedures and administrators. See Weber, ed., *Troubles in Texas*.

2. Deposition of Francisco Esparza, Aug. 26, 1839, Court of Claims Voucher File no. 2558, General Land Office, Austin (hereafter GLO); "Children of the

Alamo," *Houston Chronicle*, Nov. 9, 1901; "Another Child of the Alamo," *San Antonio Light*, Nov. 10, 1901; "The Story of Enrique Esparza," *San Antonio Express*, Nov. 22, 1902; "Story of the Massacre of Heroes of the Alamo," *San Antonio Express*, Nov. 22, 1902, Mar. 7, 1904; "Alamo's Only Survivor," *San Antonio Express*, May 19, 1907; "Alamo's Fall Is Told by Witness in a Land Suit," *San Antonio Express*, Dec. 9, 1908; Rodríguez, *Rodríguez Memoirs*, pp. 15–16; "Senor Navarro Tells the Story of His Grandfather," in Howard R. Driggs and Sarah S. King, eds., *Rise of the Lone Star: A Story of Texas Told by Its Pioneers*, pp. 268–269, 272–273; Lack, *Texas Revolutionary Experience*, p. 165; R. M. Potter, "The Texas Revolution: Distinguished Mexicans Who Took Part in the Revolution of Texas, with Glances at Its Early Events," p. 18. Potter is available at BTHC and the Library of Congress.

3. Henry Smith to Edward Burleson, Dec. 9, 1835, in Binkley, ed., *Official Correspondence*, p. I: 177; Amos Pollard to Smith, Jan. 16, 1836, in ibid., p. I: 300; William Barret Travis to President of Convention, Mar. 3, 1836, in the *San Felipe de Austin* (later Houston) *Telegraph and Texas Register*, Mar. 12, 1836; Gregorio Gómez to brothers in arms and inhabitants, Oct. 17, 1835, in *San Felipe de Austin* (later Houston) *Telegraph and Texas Register*, Nov. 14, 1835 (quotation); José María Tornel, *Tejas y los Estados-Unidos de America, en sus relaciones con la Repub. Mexicana*, pp. 47, 57, 90; Carlos Sánchez Navarro, *La guerra de Tejas: Memorias de un soldado*, p. 117; Carmen Perry, ed. and trans., *With Santa Anna in Texas: A Personal Narrative of the Revolution by José Enrique de la Pena*, p. 4; Filisola, *Memorias*, pp. I: 238–239; *Mosquito Mexicano* (Mexico City), Sept. 27, 1842; Antonio Menchaca, "The Memoirs of Captain Menchaca" (typescript), ed. James P. Newcomb, p. 30, CAH. Travis's letter is also in Kennedy, *Texas*, p. II: 186; Gammel, comp., *The Laws of Texas*, pp. I: 845–846. Tornel's accusations are translated in Carlos E. Castañeda, *The Mexican Side of the Texas Revolution [1836] by the Chief Mexican Participants*, pp. 328, 338, 370.

4. *Columbia* (later Houston) *Telegraph and Texas Register*, Nov. 9, 1836; Andrew Forest Muir, ed., Texas in 1837: *An Anonymous, Contemporary Narrative*, p. 107. Mexico's president called for the reconquest of Texas shortly after Santa Anna's defeat at San Jacinto. His statement was printed in the *Houston Telegraph and Texas Register*, Apr. 18, 1838. A report that Mexican authorities sought Tejano support for a reconquest effort is found in *Houston Telegraph and Texas Register*, Jan. 6, 1841. This report was based on the testimony of Juan Seguín. See also Juan Seguín to the President of the Republic, Dec. 26, 1840, in de la Teja, ed., *A Revolution Remembered*, pp. 176–178.

5. Arista's proclamation was dated Jan. 9, 1842, and was published in the *Houston Telegraph and Texas Register*, Mar. 9, 1842. See also Juan N. Seguín, *Personal Memoirs of John N. Seguín from the Year 1834 to the Retreat of General Woll from the City of San Antonio in 1842*, p. 23. Seguín's memoirs are edited and reprinted in de la Teja, ed., *A Revolution Remembered*, pp. 73–102. For a treatment of the 1842 Mexican occupations of San Antonio, see Joseph Milton Nance, *Attack and Counter-Attack: The Texas-Mexican Frontier*, 1842, pp. 9–54, 297–408.

6. *Houston Telegraph and Texas Register*, Mar. 30, June 15, 1842; M. C. Hamilton (by order of President Sam Houston) to Alexander Somervell, Oct. 13, 1842,

in Williams and Barker, *The Writings of Sam Houston*, pp. III: 177–178; Thomas J. Green, *Journal of the Texian Expedition against Mier; Subsequent Imprisonment of the Author; His Sufferings, and Final Escape from the Castle of Perote. With Reflections upon the Present Political and Probable Future Relations of Texas, Mexico, and the United States*, p. 36; Joseph D. Mccutchan, *Mier Expedition Diary: A Texan Prisoner's Account*, pp. 14–15.

7. *Houston Telegraph and Texas Register*, Oct. 19, 1842 (quotation); Jean Marie Odin to John Timon, June 20, 1842, University of Notre Dame Archives, South Bend, Indiana (hereafter ND); Odin to Stephen Rousselon, Dec. 10, 1842, Catholic Archives of Texas, Austin (hereafter CAT). On General Woll's view of Anglo-American attitudes toward Tejanos, see Joseph Milton Nance, ed. and trans., "Brigadier General Adrian Woll's Report of His Expedition into Texas in 1842," pp. 546–548. For continuing accusations of Tejano disloyalty, see *Houston Telegraph and Texas Register*, Oct. 26, 1842.

8. Reports of Tejano participation in military forces are in W. D. Miller to Houston, Mar. 9, 1842, and Nance, *Attack and Counter-Attack*, p. 30; *Houston Telegraph and Texas Register*, Mar. 30, Apr. 27 1842; W. A. Miskel to Dr. [Francis] Moore, Dec. 14, 1842, in *Houston Telegraph and Texas Register*, Dec. 21, 1842; Seguín, *Memoirs*, pp. 24, 27–29; Green, *Journal of the Texian Expedition against Mier*, pp. 31, 35–36; Frederick C. Chabot, *The Perote Prisoners: Being the Diary of James L. Truehart, Printed for the First Time Together with an Historical Introduction*, pp. 94–96; Anderson Hutchinson, "Diary," pp. 294–295; Rodríguez, *Rodríguez Memoirs*, pp. 17–18; Nance, ed., "Woll's Report," pp. 529, 533–535, 538, 542–544. Assistance offered to the Mexican wounded is described in Harvey Alexander Adams, "Diary of Harvey Alexander Adams, in Two Parts: Rhode Island to Texas and Expedition against the Southwest in 1842 and 1843," typescript, p. II: 7, BTHC. Assistance to Texan captives is recorded in Chabot, *Perote Prisoners*, pp. 96–100; San Antonio prisoners to the American officers and citizens, Sept. 11, 1842, in Rena Maverick Green, ed., *Samuel Maverick, Texan: 1803–1870. A Collection of Letters, Journals, and Memoirs*, pp. 173–174; Samuel A. Maverick to Mary A. Maverick, Oct. 6, 1842, in Green, ed., *Samuel Maverick*, p. 197; A. Neill to Anson Jones, Jan. 29, 1843, in Winkler, ed., "The Bexar and Dawson Prisoners," p. 314.

9. Nance, ed., "Woll's Report," p. 529; Chabot, *Perote Prisoners*, pp. 93–96, 99; Hutchinson, "Diary," pp. 294–295; Antonio Menchaca, "Memoirs," Archives and Manuscripts Collection, BTHC, pp. 35–37. Some witnesses stated that three Tejano commissioners were sent to treat with Woll; these witnesses were apparently referring to the San Antonio representatives Woll mentions in his official report: Chabot, *Perote Prisoners*, p. 93; Rodríguez, *Rodríguez Memoirs*, p. 18; Hutchinson, "Diary," p. 294; William E. Jones to [Mirabeau Buonaparte Lamar], Feb. 1, 1844, in Hutchinson, "Diary," p. 321; Miskel to Moore, Dec. 14, 1842, in *Houston Telegraph and Texas Register*, Dec. 21, 1842.

10. *Houston Telegraph and Texas Register*, Aug. 24, 1842 (first quotation); Francis S. Latham, *Travels in the Republic of Texas, 1842*, p. 38 (second quotation); *Houston Telegraph and Texas Register*, May 19, 1838, Mar. 15, 1843; Rodríguez, *Rodríguez Memoirs*, pp. 9–10, 16–17; Herman Ehrenberg, *With Milam and Fannin: Adven-*

tures of a German Boy in Texas' Revolution, pp. 101–102; "Stirring Events Are Remembered by Texas Jurist," *San Antonio Express*, Sept. 8, 1912; "Aged Citizen Describes Alamo Fight and Fire," San Antonio Express, July 1, 1906; Charles Merritt Barnes, "Builders' Spades Turn Up Soil Baked by Alamo Funeral Pyres," *San Antonio Express*, Mar. 26, 1911; idem, "Men Still Living Who Saw the Fall of the Alamo," *San Antonio Express*, Aug. 27, 1911. The 1850 census confirms that San Antonio Tejanos returned to Mexico during times of conflict. One Tejano household recorded on this census had five minor children, three born in Texas and two in Mexico. The latter two were born in 1837 and 1842, apparently when the family was waiting in Mexico for peace so they could return to Texas: V. K. Carpenter, comp., *The State of Texas Federal Population Schedules Seventh Census of the United States, 1850*, p. I: 141, entry 509. Other entries on the 1850 San Antonio census tract (Carpenter, comp., *The State of Texas*, pp. I: 111–189) that indicate families who moved back and forth from Texas to Mexico include 42, 152, 201, 252, 260, 317, 334, 376, and 438.

11. The dilemma of San Antonio Tejanos is especially vivid in the experience of Juan N. Seguín, *Memoirs*, pp. 21–29.

12. *Journals of the Senate, of the Republic of Texas; First Session of the Third Congress, 1838*, p. 10 (quotation). For a Navarro contemporary's views regarding why he accepted the appointment as commissioner of the Santa Fé expedition, see Potter, *The Texas Revolution*, p. 21. Some observers claim Navarro prepared a strong pro-Texas speech to deliver at New Mexico, but it appears that he merely translated the document in question: Anonymous, "To the Inhabitants of Santa Fe and Other Towns of New Mexico East of the Rio Grande," typescript, Daughters of the Republic of Texas Library, San Antonio (hereafter DRT); "Senor Navarro Tells a Story," in Driggs and King, eds., *Rise of the Lone Star*, p. 289; Reuben M. Potter to Lamar, June 5, 1841, in Charles Adams Gulick, Jr., and Katherine Elliott, eds., *The Papers of Mirabeau Buonaparte Lamar*, pp. III: 532–533.

13. Francisco Ruiz to the Congress of the Republic of Texas, Nov. 26, 1836, Memorials and Petitions, Texas State Archives, TSL; Gammel, comp., *Laws of Texas*, pp. I: 1111–1336.

14. *Houston Telegraph and Texas Register*, May 19, 1838; Thomas Lloyd Miller, "Mexican-Texans at the Alamo," pp. 33–44. In the view of at least one historian, Anglo Americans did not experience as much difficulty in obtaining their claims: Amelia Williams, "A Critical Study of the Siege of the Alamo and of the Personnel of Its Defenders," p. 257.

15. *Austin City Gazette*, Feb. 5, 1840, in de la Teja, ed., *A Revolution Remembered*, p. 174. Also in Harriet Smither, ed., *Journals of the Fourth Congress of the Republic of Texas, 1839– 1840*, pp. I: 103–104. An act providing for translation of Texas laws into Spanish had been passed on Jan. 23, 1839: *Houston Telegraph and Texas Register*, Feb. 6, 1839; Gammel, comp., *Laws of Texas*, pp. II: 76–77. Seguín wrote a letter to Joseph Waples, Texas's chief clerk and acting secretary of state, on June 21, 1840, asking for a progress report on the promised translations. Waples responded that they still were not available: Joseph Waples to Seguín, July 1, 1840, in de la Teja, ed., *A Revolution Remembered*, p. 175. Seguín's funding proposal for

a Bexar County jail is found in Smither, ed., *Journals of the Fourth Congress*, p. I: 132. No such law was passed during that congressional session, nor in the session that followed: Gammel, comp., *Laws of Texas*, pp. II: 175–672.

16. *Houston Telegraph and Texas Register*, Jan. 26, 1839; William F. Weeks, comp., *Debates of the Texas Convention*, p. 209. No legislation passed during Navarro's term in the Third Congress of the Republic of Texas reflects his 1839 intervention on behalf of Tejano landowners: Gammel, comp., *Laws of Texas*, pp. II: 3– 167.

17. Smither, ed., *Journals of the Fourth Congress*, pp. I: 139, 206 (quotation). The pertinent legislation is in Gammel, comp., *Laws of Texas*, pp. II: 235–236, 369.

18. Weeks, comp., *Debates of the Texas Convention*, pp. 235, 158, 473–474. For accounts of Texan volunteers' cruelty to San Antonio Tejanos, see *Houston Morning Star*, May 28, June 9, 1842; *Houston Telegraph and Texas Register*, June 15, Sept. 7, 1842; Adams, "Diary," pp. II: 15, 20, 26; Odin to Jean-Baptiste Etienne, June 17, 1842, CAT; Odin to Anthony Blanc, July 4, 1842, CAT.

19. *Columbia* (later Houston) *Telegraph and Texas Register*, Sept. 20, Oct. 25, 1836; John A. Wharton to Seguin, Sept. 17, 1836, in de la Teja, ed., *A Revolution Remembered*, pp. 144–145; Seguín to President Sam Houston, Dec. 6, 1836, in de la Teja, ed., *A Revolution Remembered*, p. 147; Felix Huston to Houston, Nov. 14, 1836, CAT; Houston to Seguin, Jan. 16, 1837, in de la Teja, ed., *A Revolution Remembered*, pp. 152–153 (also in Williams and Barker, eds., *Writings of Sam Houston*, pp. II: 33–34); Seguín, *Memoirs*, pp. 15–16; John J. Linn, *Reminiscences of Fifty Years in Texas*, pp. 294–296. There is some discrepancy in these accounts concerning the date of Huston's order. John J. Linn postulated that General Huston's order may have been an attempt to induce local Tejanos to sell their land at reduced prices: Linn, *Reminiscences*, pp. 295–296. Apparently, Seguín was aware of this or similar plots: *Memoirs*, p. 18.

20. Election results from these years are summarized in Downs, "History of Mexicans in Texas," pp. 255–257. For original documentation of election results and city council minutes, see "Minutes of the City Council of the City of San Antonio from 1837 to 1849, Journal A," typescript, BTHC.

21. A list of San Antonio mayors is given in William Corner, ed. and comp., *San Antonio de Bexar: A Guide and History*, p. 66. Antonio Menchaca was also mayor for a brief period from 1838 to 1839. He was not elected, however, but served out the term of William H. Dangerfield.

22. David Montejano, *Anglos and Mexicans in the Making of Texas, 1836–1986*, pp. 34 (quotations), 35; Jane Dysart, "Mexican Women in San Antonio, 1830– 1860: The Assimilation Process," pp. 370–371.

23. Dysart, "Mexican Women in San Antonio," p. 370; John Duff Brown, "Reminiscences of Jno. Duff Brown," p. 299; William F. Gray, *From Virginia to Texas, 1835: Diary of Col. Wm. F. Gray, Giving Details of His Journey to Texas and Return in 1835–1836 and Second Journey to Texas in 1837*, p. 165; Frederick Charles Chabot, *With the Makers of San Antonio. Genealogies of the Early Latin, Anglo-American, and German Families with Occasional Biographies, Each Group Being Pref-*

aced with a Brief Historical Sketch and Illustrations, pp. 152–153; James Ernest Crisp, "Anglo-Texan Attitudes toward the Mexican, 1821–1845," pp. 351, 398.

24. Mary Maverick to Agatha S. Adams, Aug. 25, 1838, in Green, ed., *Samuel Maverick, Texan*, p. 77; Rena Maverick Green, ed., *Memoirs of Mary A. Maverick*, pp. 53–56.

25. Wesley Norton, "Religious Newspapers in Antebellum Texas," pp. 147–149, 152.

26. Martin Ruter to Secretary of the Missionary Society of the Methodist Episcopal Church, 1838, in C. C. Cody, "Rev. Martin Ruter, A.M., D.D.," p. 25; Lawrence L. Brown, *The Episcopal Church in Texas, 1838–1874: From Its Foundation to the Division of the Diocese*, pp. 24–25; Z. N. Morrell, *Flowers and Fruits from the Wilderness; or, Thirty-six Years in Texas and Two Winters in Honduras*, p. 117.

27. A. B. Lawrence, "Introduction," pp. xviii–xix; see also ibid., 245.

28. Patrick Foley, "From Linares to Galveston: The Early Development of the Catholic Hierarchy in Texas," paper read at the first Biennial Conference of the Texas Catholic Historical Society, St. Edward's University, Austin, Oct. 27, 1989.

29. Odin to Timon, July 14, 1840, CAT; Odin to Blanc, Aug. 24, 1840, CAT; Odin to Joseph Rosati, Aug. 27, 1840, CAT; Odin to Etienne, Aug. 28, 1840, CAT; Odin to James Cardinal Fransoni, Dec. 15, 1840, CAT; Odin to Etienne, Apr. 11, 1841, CAT; Jean Marie Odin, "Daily Journal," photocopy, p. 6, CAT. For a treatment of this incident and the apparent silence of San Antonio's Tejanos after the native priests' removal, see Matovina, *Tejano Religion*, pp. 42–43.

30. John Timon, "Narrative of the Barrens," p. 39, Vincentian Archives, St. Mary's of the Barrens, Perryville, Missouri; Odin to Propagation of the Faith, Mar. 28, 1852, CAT.

31. Odin to Etienne, Feb. 7, 1842, CAT; Odin, "Daily Journal," p. 34, CAT; Odin to John Baptist Purcell, June 25, 1861, ND (first quotation); Miguel Joaquín Calvo, personal file, Archivo Matritense C.M., Madrid (second quotation). The quotation from Calvo's personal file is my translation. Odin's 1842 letter is cited in the *United States Catholic Magazine and Monthly Review* 3 (Oct., 1844): 727–730. Earlier, Odin had stated that priests in Texas would "have to speak English, Spanish, and a little German": Odin to Blanc, Dec. 12, 1852, CAT. He also provided Spanish classes for recently arrived seminarians, religious, and priests, at times teaching these classes himself. See, e.g., Odin to Blanc, Jan. 6, 1853, Apr. 23, 1856, CAT; Odin to Propagation of the Faith, Jan. 9, July 1, 1853; Odin to Rousselon, Jan. 21, 1853, all in CAT.

32. Papal recognition had been given to the Guadalupan image in 1754, when Benedict XIV proclaimed her the patroness of New Spain and declared Dec. 12 her feast day.

33. Odin to Etienne, Feb. 7, 1842. In a society that kept women subordinate to men, the relative prominence of Tejanas in the planning of these celebrations is striking. See Weber, *The Mexican Frontier*, pp. 215–216. For an analysis of women's leadership role in Latin American Catholicism, see Ana María Díaz-Stevens, "The Saving Grace: The Matriarchal Core of Latino Popular Religion."

34. Odin to Etienne, Feb. 7, 1842, CAT; Green, ed., *Memoirs of Mary A. Mav-*

erick, pp. 53–54. For a fuller treatment of these celebrations, see Timothy M. Matovina, "Our Lady of Guadalupe Celebrations in San Antonio, Texas, 1840–41." As has been mentioned, Mary Maverick was the wife of Samuel Maverick, who was mayor of San Antonio from 1839 to 1840.

35. For the participation of visitors to San Antonio in *fandangos*, along with contemporary descriptions of these festive Tejano dances, see Ehrenberg, *With Milam and Fannin*, pp. 102–105; Muir, ed., *Texas in 1837*, pp. 104–106; J. W. Benedict, "Diary of a Campaign against the Comanches," p. 305; George Wilkens Kendall, *Narrative of the Texan Santa Fé Expedition, Comprising a Description of a Tour through Texas, and across the Great Southwestern Prairies, the Camanche and Cayuga Hunting-Grounds, with an Account of the Sufferings from Want of Food, Losses from Hostile Indians, and Final Capture of the Texans, and Their March, as Prisoners, to the City of Mexico. with Illustrations and a Map*, p I: 46; Green, *Journal of the Texian Expedition against Mier*, pp. 41–42; Auguste Fretelliere, "Adventures of a Castrovillian," p. 93; Samuel E. Chamberlain, *My Confession*, pp. 44–45; Ferdinand Roemer, *Texas: With Particular Reference to German Immigration and the Physical Appearance of the Country*, pp. 121–123, 131.

36. "Minutes of the City Council of the City of San Antonio from 1837 to 1849," May 13, 1841, BTHC; Seguín and others to Lamar, May 15, 1841, in Gulick and Elliott, eds., *Papers of Lamar*, p. III: 521; Green, ed., *Memoirs of Mary A. Maverick*, pp. 55–56; *Houston Telegraph and Texas Register*, June 9, 1841; *Columbia* (later Houston) *Telegraph and Texas Register*, Mar. 28, Apr. 4, 1837 (quotation); Seguín to General Albert Sidney Johnston, Mar. 13, 1837, in de la Teja, ed., *A Revolution Remembered*, pp. 161–162. Seguín's speech is also in de la Teja, ed., *A Revolution Remembered*, p. 156.

37. Nance, ed., "Woll's Report," p. 542; Green, ed., *Memoirs of Mary A. Maverick*, p. 53; W. Eugene Hollon and Ruth Lapham Butler, eds., *William Bollaert's Texas*, p. 230 (quotation).

38. "Esparza, the Boy of the Alamo, Remembers," in Driggs and King, eds., *Rise of the Lone Star*, pp. 214–215.

39. Tijerina, *Tejanos and Texas*, p. 113.

6. THE CÓRDOVA REVOLT

1. Joseph Milton Nance, *After San Jacinto: The Texas-Mexican Frontier, 1836– 1841*, pp. 113–141, provides the most complete account. John R. Wunder and Rebecca J. Herring, "Law, History, Turner, and the Cordova Rebellion," pp. 51–67, have emphasized the contest for land from the frontier perspective.

2. Weber, *The Mexican Frontier*, pp. 141, 162–163, 166–167, 176–178.

3. James Michael McReynolds, "Family Life in a Borderland Community: Nacogdoches, Texas, 1779–1861," pp. 229–234, 256–261; Gray, *From Virginia to Texas*, pp. 92 (quotation), 94, 96.

4. Binkley, *The Texas Revolution*, pp. 16–21; Eugene C. Barker, *Mexico and Texas, 1825–1835*, pp. 2–23, 32–61, 87–95.

5. Paul D. Lack, "East Texas Mexicans and the Texas Revolution," pp. 141–145.

6. "Antonio Menchaca to the Governor of the State," Aug. 23, 1835, BA.

7. "Vicente Córdova to the Militia Co. of Nacogdoches," Aug. 31, 1835, Robert Bruce Blake Research Collection, Special Collections, Ralph W. Steen Library, Stephen F. Austin University, Nacogdoches, (hereafter Blake), p. XLIII: 251.

8. Lack, "East Texas Mexicans," pp. 145–146.

9. "Vicente Córdova to the citizen alcalde of this village," Oct. 20, Nov. 10, 1835, NAT, pp. 84: 57, 69; John M. Dor to Sam Houston, Nov. 29, 1835, in Jenkins, ed., *Papers*, p. III: 22.

10. Lack, "East Texas Mexicans," pp. 147–149.

11. D. A. Hoffman, "Notice Given in the Town of Nacogdoches," Apr. 9, 1836, A. J. Houston Papers, TSL (hereafter AJH).

12. R. A. Irion to Sam Houston, Apr. 17, 1836; Henry Raguet to Samuel Houston, Apr. 17, 1836; Vicente Córdova to Dr. Irion, Apr. 14, 1836 (quotation), all in AJH.

13. Vicente Córdova to R. A. Irion, Apr. 14, 1836, AJH.

14. R. A. Irion to V. Córdova, Apr. 14, 1836, AJH.

15. R. A. Irion to Sam Houston, Apr. 17, 1836, AJH; Sam Houston to Henry Raguet, July 4, 1836, Nacogdoches Committee of Vigilance and Safety Records, NAT.

16. Sterling C. Robertson to T. J. Rusk, June 30, 1836, AJH (quotations); Records of the Office of Alcalde, NAT; Blake, pp. XV: 12, 111.

17. [Nacogdoches petition] To the Senate and House of Representatives, Sept., 1836, Memorials and Petitions, TSL.

18. See cases numbered 3, 10/2, 11, and 13/2 in the Execution Docket for the District Court of Nacogdoches County, Book A, Special Collections, Ralph W. Steen Library, Stephen F. Austin University, Nacogdoches, Texas (hereafter SFA); [conveyance], May 25, 1837, Thomas J. Rusk Papers, BTHC.

19. Tijerina, *Tejanos and Texas*, pp. 319–325.

20. U.S. Senate, Executive Documents, XIV, 32nd Congress, 2nd sess. (hereafter Senate Doc 14), pp. 37–41; P. L. Chouteau to Wm. Armstrong, Mar. 1, 1837 (quotation), and J. Bonnell to the authorities of Nacogdoches, Mar. 7, 1837, AJH.

21. T. J. Rusk to Sam Houston, Mar. 11, 1837, AJH; George P. Garrison, ed., *Diplomatic Correspondence of the Republic of Texas*, pp. II: 260–261.

22. Henry Millard to Sam Houston, Mar. 23, 1837, AJH (first quotation); E. W. Winkler, ed., *Secret Journals of the Senate, Republic of Texas, 1836–1845*, p. 75 (second quotation).

23. William Goyens [to Sam Houston], Mar. 22, 1837, AJH; Houston *Telegraph and Texas Register*, Apr. 18, 1838; "petition of 115 Nacogdoches citizens" [n.d., tabled by Congress on Apr. 28, 1838]; "James Reily *et al* petition to Congress" [n.d., received May 15, 1838] (quotations), both in Memorials and Petitions, TSL.

24. Vicente Córdova et al to Mr. Roze, Feb. 26, 1838, AJH.

25. Thos. J. Rusk to Sam Houston, Aug. 14, 1838, AJH.

26. Sam Houston, Proclamation, Aug. 8, 1838, AJH; Sam Houston to Andrew

Jackson, Aug. 11, 1838, Williams and Barker, eds., *The Writings of Sam Houston*, p. II: 271. To officials in the U.S. government Houston also placed the Córdova rebellion in the context of a wicked Mexican "abolition policy": Sam Houston to S. B. Marcy, Aug 25, 1838, AJH.

27. Houston *Telegraph and Texas Register*, Mar. 27, 1839.

28. This proclamation exists in several printed formats in both English and Spanish, all with minor errors or inelegant translation. This version was graciously done by Jesús F. de la Teja from a copy of the original document, which is in the Córdova Rebellion Papers, 1838, Nacogdoches County Court Records, Civil Cases [box 26, folder 15], SFA. The signatures on the proclamation are Vicente Córdova, Nathaniel Norris, Juan Arriola, J. Vicente Micheli, José Ma. Arocha, Juan Santos Coy, Anastacio de la Serda, Crecencio Morales, Joshua M. Robertson, Juan José Rodrigues, José de la Baume, Antonio Calderón, Julio Lazarín, James Quinnelty, Anto. Flores, Guadalupe Cárdenas, Napoleon Dewaltz, and William Donovan. Among the Anglo participants, the Norris family had long been involved in conflict with elements that successfully seized power during the late stages of Mexican Texas rule and the Texas Revolution.

29. Quoted in [Harriet Matilda Jamison Durst], "Early Days in Texas," Durst Family Collection, SFA.

30. R. A. Irion to Pickney Henderson, Mar. 20, 1838, Department of State Letterbook in the Executive Record Books, microfilm, TSL; Ashbel Smith to Daniel Seymour, May 19, 1838, letter press, Ashbel Smith Papers, BTHC.

31. Private instructions . . . by Vicente Filisola, Pedro Julian Miracle memorandum book, both in Senate Doc 14, pp. 13, 14–15 (quotations), 16–17; Vicente Córdova to Manuel Flores, July 19, 1838, Valentine O. King Collection, TSL. Texas officials in 1838 described the Miracle diary as "written in pencil and so much defaced that the translators, Mr. Newlands and Major Zavalla, had considerable difficulty in deciphering it": R. A. Irion to the President of the Republic of Texas, Nov. 14, 1838, Department of State Letterbook in the Executive Record Books, microfilm, TSL. This indicates that the document was genuine, but it is no longer extant. For another translation, made by D. A. G. Wright on Aug. 20, 1838, differing somewhat in wording and in selection of excerpts, see Malcolm D. McLean, ed., *Papers Concerning Robertson's Colony in Texas*, pp. XVI: 544–556.

32. R. A. Irion to M. Hunt, Mar. [illegible date] 1838, Department of State Letterbook in the Executive Record Books, microfilm, TSL; V. R. Palmer to Sam Houston, June 18, 1838 (first quotation); Sam Houston to Jeff Wright, June 23, 1838 (remaining quotations), both in AJH; Houston *Telegraph and Texas Register*, Mar. 27, 1839.

33. Houston *Telegraph and Texas Register*, Sept. 29, 1838.

34. Ibid., Mar. 27, 1839.

35. Ibid., Sept. 29, 1838, Mar. 27, 1839 (quotation).

36. Sam Houston to José María Madrano, Aug. 8, 1838; Sam Houston Proclamation [and Proclama], Aug. 8, 1838, both in AJH.

37. Sam Houston to Big Mush, Aug. 10, 1838; Mirabeau B. Lamar Papers, Texas State Library, Archives Division (hereafter MBL).

38. Sam Houston to T. J. Rusk, Aug. 10., 1838; Sam Houston to R. B. Maney, Aug. 11, 1838, both in AJH; [Thomas J. Rusk] to the Third Brigade of Texas Militia, Aug. 10, 1838, Rusk Papers, BTHC.

39. The transcript of the trial is printed in Blake; see p. LIII: 315, for this grand jury indictment. P. A. Sublett to Sam Houston, Aug. 9, 1838, AJH.

40. Dianna Everett, *The Texas Cherokees: A People between Two Fires, 1819–1840*, chap. 4, and pp. 116–117; Thomas J. Rusk to Sam Houston, Aug. 11, 12, 13 [3 letters], 1838, AJH.

41. Sam Houston to Col. Bowles, Aug. 14, 1838; Thomas J. Rusk to Col. Bowles, Aug. 15, 1838, Rusk Papers, BTHC. D. S. Kaufman to Sam Houston, Aug. 14, 1838; T. J. Rusk to Sam Houston, Aug. 15, 1838, both in AJH.

42. Sam Houston to Thomas J. Rusk, Aug. 10 [16?], 15, 1838; Tho. J. Rusk to Sam Houston, Aug. 14, 1838; Sam Houston to G. W. Hockley, Aug. 14, 1838, all in AJH. Thos. J. Rusk to Sam Houston, Aug. 14, 1838, Rusk Papers, BTHC.

43. Thos. J. Rusk to Sam Houston, Aug. 16, 1838, Rusk Papers, BTHC; J. M. Henrie to M. B. Lamar, Aug. 17, 1838, in Gulick and Elliott, eds., *Papers of Lamar*, p. II: 205; Tho. J. Rusk to Sam Houston, Aug. 19, 1838, AJH. Actually, the Kickapoo did view the Texas government as their enemy and acted in concert during this rebellion and subsequently: John Gesick, "Kickapoo Migrations to Mexico," paper presented at the Texas State Historical Association meeting, Houston, Mar. 4, 1993.

44. Sam Houston, Proclamation, Aug. 19, 1838; Tho. J. Rusk to Sam Houston, Aug. 22, 24, 1838; Sam Houston to J. B. Marcy, Aug. 27, 1838, all in AJH. J. W. Burton to M. B. Lamar, Aug. 25, 1838; Tho. J. Rusk to Colonel Bowles, Aug., 28, 1838, both in MBL.

45. L. H. Mabbitt to T. J. Rusk, Oct. 1, 1838; Thos. J. Rusk to Sam Houston Oct. 4, 1838, both in AJH. Elisha Clapp to T. J. Rusk, Oct. 5, 1838, Rusk Papers, BTHC. Fort Houston was two miles west of present-day Palestine in Anderson County.

46. J. W. Burton to Sam Houston, Oct. 16, 1838, AJH. D. H. Campbell to M. B. Lamar, Oct. 22, 1838, MBL. Petition of Nathaniel Killough, Mar. 2, 1839, Nacogdoches County Courthouse Records, box 1, folder 7, SFA. Tho. J. Rusk to [?], Oct. 14, 1838, Rusk Papers, BTHC (quotation).

47. Thos. J. Rusk to Col. Bowles, Oct. 20, 1838; H. McLeod to M. B. Lamar, Oct. 22, 1838 (quotations), both in MBL. Houston *Telegraph and Texas Register*, Nov. 3, 1838.

48. Valentín Canalizo to Manuel Flores, Feb. 27, 1839, Valentín Canalizo to [chiefs], Feb. 27, 1839, Sen Doc 14, pp. 31–32, 35; Valentín Canalizo to Vicente Córdova, Mar. 1, 1839, AJH.

49. Valentín Canalizo to Vicente Córdova, Feb. 27, [1839], Sen Doc 14, pp. 33–34; Houston *Telegraph and Texas Register*, Apr. 10, 17, 1839.

50. Houston *Telegraph and Texas Register*, Apr. 10, 17, 24, May 1, 1839; Ewd. Burleson to M. B. Lamar, Apr. 4, [1839], in Gulick and Elliott, eds., *Papers of Lamar*, p. II: 50; Edward Burleson to A. Sidney Johnston, May 22, 1839, in Smither, ed., *Journals of the Fourth Congress*, p. III: 113.

51. Sam Houston to Thomas J. Rusk, Aug. 10, 1838; Sam Houston, General Orders, Aug. 11, 16, 1838, AJH.

52. Sam Houston to T. J. Rusk, Aug. 22, 23, 1838; Sam Houston to H. W. Augustine, Aug. 23, 1838, AJH.

53. John Applegate to Sam Houston, Aug. 15, 1838; Thomas J. Rusk, Orden General, Aug. 22, 1838; Thomas J. Rusk to Sam Houston, Aug. 25, 1838; Tho. J. Rusk to John M. Dor, Aug. 27, 1838; John S. Roberts to Sam Houston, Sept. 7, 1838, all in AJH.

54. Bernard Bee to David G. Burnet, Sept. 6, 1838, MBL; Sam Houston, Proclamation, Sept. 27, 1838, AJH.

55. Houston *Telegraph and Texas Register*, Mar. 27, 1839; Sam Houston to Adolphus Sterne, Aug. 18, 1838, AJH.

56. H. McLeod to M. B. Lamar, Aug. 26, 1838, MBL; Houston *Telegraph and Texas Register*, Sept. 29, 1838.

57. All quotations from testimony are taken from the account carried by the San Augustine Red Lander, reprinted in Houston *Telegraph and Texas Register*, Mar. 27, 1839. Quotations and summaries of procedures from the trial records are available in Blake, pp. XLIII: 271–339. This version has been corroborated and supplemented by original documents in the Nacogdoches County Courthouse Records, folder 8, Criminal Cases, 1838, SFA.

58. E. W. Cullen to M. B. Lamar, Feb. 10, 1839, MBL; "Proclamation by Mirabeau B. Lamar to the Sheriff of San Augustine County," Feb. 18, 1839, Blake, p. XLIII: 344.

59. Downs, "History of Mexicans in Texas," pp. 260–262; McReynolds, "Nacogdoches," pp. 38–40, 123–128, 266–267; Rebecca Finley vs. Vicente Córdova, Sept. 17, 1840, Executive Docket for the District Court of Nacogdoches County, Book A, SFA; Civil Cases, List of Taxable Property, 1838 and 1839, box 30, Nacogdoches County Courthouse Records, SFA

60. M. B. Lamar to Col Bowles, May 26, 1838, in Gulick and Elliott, eds., *Papers of Lamar*, pp. II: 590–591; Sam Houston, Speech in the Texas House of Representatives, Dec. 3, 1839, in Williams and Barker, eds., *Writings*, pp. II: 318–321; Houston *National Intelligencer*, Mar. 1, 1839; *Richmond Telescope*, June 1, 1839; Houston *Telegraph and Texas Register*, June 19, 1839; Everett, *Texas Cherokees*, pp. 99–116.

61. Nance, *After San Jacinto*, pp. 249–299, 317, 361.

62. Bernard Bee to M. B. Lamar, Sept. 6, 1838, MBL.

7. FINDING THEIR WAY

1. The first authors to consider the plight of the Mexicans were Barker, *Mexico and Texas*, and Lowrie, *Culture Conflict*. The 1970s produced an outpouring of works that focused on the antagonism aimed at Mexicans, in particular, Seymour V. Connor, *Texas: A History*; Crisp, "Anglo-Texan Attitudes; Tijerina, *Tejanos and Texas*; Arnoldo de León, *Apuntes Tejanos: An Index of Items Related to Mexican Americans in 19th Century Texas Extracted from the San Antonio Express (1869–*

1900) and San Antonio Herald (1855-1878). By the 1980s, a great deal of work was being done in the field: Arnoldo de León, *They Called Them Greasers: Anglo Attitudes toward Mexicans in Texas, 1821-1900*; Montejano, *Anglos and Mexicans*; Gilberto M. Hinojosa, *A Borderlands Town in Transition: Laredo*; Abel G. Rubio, *Stolen Heritage: A Mexican-American's Rediscovery of His Family's Lost Land Grant*; Manuel Barrera, *Then the Gringos Came — The Story of Martín de León and the Texas Revolution.* Looking across the border from Mexico were Vito Alessio Robles, *Coahuila y Texas en la época colonial*, and Josefina Zoraida Vásquez and Lorenzo Meyer, *México frente a Estados Unidos (Un ensayo histórico, 1776-1988).*

2. General histories of Texas written by Anglo-American authors have been the most prevalent in dismissing the Mexican Texans as insignificant, beginning with Henderson Yoakum, *History of Texas from Its First Settlement in 1685 to Its Annexation to the United States in 1846*; Victor M. Rose, *Some Historical Facts in Regard to the Settlement of Victoria, Texas*; Fehrenbach, *Lone Star*; Rupert N. Richardson, Ernest Wallace, and Adrian N. Anderson, *Texas: The Lone Star State.*

3. The best descriptions of the activities of the Tejanos of Victoria County and the Goliad and Refugio area are Hobart Huson, *Refugio, a Comprehensive History of Refugio County from Aboriginal Times to 1953*; William H. Oberste, *Texas Irish Empresarios and Their Colonies*; Downs, "History of Mexicans."

4. The presidio contingent numbered only 69. See 1782 Census of the Cavalry Company of the Royal Presidio of La Bahía del Espíritu Santo, Nov., 1782, BA. In 1790, the number of soldiers had increased to 94 and the town population had reached 641, excluding Indians at the mission. See Census Report Taken by the Cavalry Lieutenant Don Manuel de Espadas . . . , Dec. 31, 1790, La Bahía, BA.

5. Texas Surveyors Association, *One League to Each Wind: Accounts of Early Surveying in Texas*, p. 8.

6. Land records, Martín de León colony, GLO, box 131, folders 1-19; Jean Louis Berlandier, *Journey to Mexico during the Years 1826 to 1834*, pp. I: 382n, 383.

7. Fehrenbach, *Lone Star*, pp. 140-142; Andreas Reichstein, *Rise of the Lone Star: The Making of Texas*, p. 37; Barker, *The Life of Stephen F. Austin* (1985), p. 81.

8. Reichstein, *Rise of the Lone Star*, 32, 37-29; Cecil Alan Hutchinson, "General José Antonio Mexía and His Texas Interests," p. 125.

9. Kelly et al., "Tadeo Ortiz de Ayala and the Colonization of Texas, 1822-1833"; Lucas Alamán, *Historia de Méjico*, p. V: 808; Hutchinson, "General José Antonio Mexía," p. 125.

10. The contract between Power and Hewetson and Governor José María Viesca was signed on June 11, 1828, but denunciations by neighboring impresario Martín de León held up the settlement for two years.

11. Oberste, *Texas Irish Empresarios*, p. 64.

12. "Libro formado por el capitán de milicias y primer Alcalde Constitucional de la Bahía del Espíritu Santo en que constan las Actas que Semanalmente celebra este ayuntamiento, Comensado desde el 22 de Marzo del presente año," vol. XL, Sección Historia, AGN-H. Various complaints by the La Bahía Ayuntamiento during 1829, 1830, and 1831 were ignored by the officials in Saltillo. When Powers and Hewetson were unable to complete their contracts with Irish colonists, they

had to turn to local ranchers to fulfill their required quota. Only in this way were the local ranchers finally provided protection from land expropriation.

13. Oberste, *Texas Irish Empresarios*, pp. 42–43; Mary Virginia Henderson, "Minor Empresario Contracts for the Colonization of Texas, 1825–1834"; Kelly et al., "Ortiz de Ayala," p. 315.

14. Oberste, *Texas Irish Empresarios*, p. 64.

15. Ibid., p. 141.

16. Ibid., p. 143.

17. Kelly et al., "Ortiz de Ayala," p. 315.

18. Henderson, "Minor Empresario Contracts," p. 11.

19. Oberste, *Texas Irish Empresarios*, p. 80, claims that Power and Hewetson encouraged the locals to apply for titles, since Power could thereby more easily acquire title to his 5 league and 5 *labor* grant as soon as the first hundred families were settled. Henderson, "Minor Empresario Contracts," p. 11, suggests that the first land commisioner, Juan Guajardo, the future brother-in-law of James Hewetson, did not respect the grants of the Goliad residents, that Land Commissioner Manuel del Moral resigned under pressure, and that Land Commissioner Jesús Vidaurri was objected to by the Ayuntamiento of Goliad. In spite of the problems, many La Bahía residents, as evidenced by the Appendix in Oberste, *Texas Irish Empresarios*, after p. 310, did receive title to their lands.

20. Appendix: List of Titles issued by José Jesús Vidaurri in Powers and Hewetson Colony, in Oberste, *Texas Irish Empresarios*, after p. 310.

21. See BA, Martín de León, for litigation complaints and accusations against Thomas Powell, Briche, Green de Witt, and others. For favorable treatment of Victoria's Anglo Americans, see Linn, *Reminiscences*.

22. Contract of Martín de León for second grant, 1829, Rafael Manchola to Governor, GLO; Roy Grimes, *300 Years in Victoria County*, pp. 64–65.

23. Ricki S. Janicek, "The Development of Early Mexican Land Policy: Coahuila and Texas, 1810–1825," p. 11.

24. *Colección de las leyes y decretos expedidos por el Congreso General de los Estados-Unidos Mejicanos, en los años de 1829 y 1830*, p. 12.

25. *Ordenanzas municipales para el gobierno y manejo interior del ayuntamiento de la Villa de Goliad*, arts. 6, 8, p. 12; Weber, *The Mexican Frontier*, pp. 17–18.

26. "Libro formado por el capitán de milicias y primer Alcalde Constitucional de la Bahía del Espíritu Santo en que constan las Actas que Semanalmente celebra este ayuntamiento, Comensado desde el 22 de Marzo del presente año," vol. XL, Sección Historia, AGN-H. Hobart Huson suggests that the de León family "dominated Goliad" and controlled its *ayuntamiento* through Aldrete and Manchola during the colonial period: *Refugio*, p. 120.

27. "Libro formado por el capitán de milicias y primer Alcalde Constitucional de la Bahía del Espíritu Santo en que constan las Actas que Semanalmente celebra este ayuntamiento, Comensado desde el 22 de Marzo del presente año," vol. XL, Sección Historia, AGN-H.

28. Alamán, *Historia de Méjico*, pp. V:807–808; Weber, *The Mexican Frontier*, pp. 24–26; Nettie Lee Benson, "Texas As Viewed from Mexico, 1820–1834," pp. 244–246.

29. De León colony papers, GLO.

30. "Libro formado por el capitán de milicias y primer Alcalde Constitucional de la Bahía del Espíritu Santo en que constan las Actas que Semanalmente celebra este ayuntamiento, Comensado desde el 22 de Marzo del presente año," vol. XL, Sección Historia, AGN-H.

31. Huson, *Refugio*, p. 118.

32. Austin to Saucedo, May 8, 1826, and Austin to Governor, Oct. 11, 1827, in Barker, ed., *The Austin Papers* (1926), pp. II: 338, 1112, n. 136.

33. Barker, *Life of Austin* (1926), p. II: 326; Texas Surveyors Association, *One League to Each Wind*, p. 30.

34. Barker, *Life of Austin* (1926), p. II: 326.

35. Grimes, *300 Years*, pp. 76−77.

36. Linn, *Reminisences*, p. 259; Grimes, *300 Years*, pp. 88, 135; J. W. Petty, Jr., ed., *Victor Rose's History of Victoria*, pp. 190−191.

37. Grimes, *300 Years*, pp. 129, 135; Huson, *Refugio*, p. 213; Castañeda, *Our Catholic Heritage*, p. VI: 284.

38. O'Connor, *The Presidio*, pp. 250−254; Melissa Rendón, descendant of Carlos de la Garza, interview by author, July 2, 1991, Victoria College, Victoria, Tex.; Mrs. Thomas O'Connor, "Reminiscences of Mrs. Annie Fagan Teal," pp. 321−323.

39. Huson, *Refugio*, p. 301; Harbert Davenport, "Men of Goliad," pp. 11−12.

40. Huson, *Refugio*, p. 310; O'Connor, *Presidio*, pp. 125−128.

41. Lack, *Texas Revolutionary Experience*, p. 164.

42. Huson, *Refugio*, p. 385; O'Connor, "Reminiscences," pp. 322−323.

43. Grimes, *300 Years*, p. 88.

44. Linn, *Reminiscences*, p. 248; Grimes, *300 Years*, p. 86.

45. Huson, *Refugio*, p. 398.

46. Philip Dimmitt to Thomas Rusk, from Corpus Christi, June, 1836, Rusk Papers, BTHC.

47. Fernando de León, Petition to the Legislature, Dec., 1849, Records of the Legislature, Archives Division, TSL.

48. Henry Teal and H. Carnes to Gen. Rusk, June 2, 1830; Tho. J. Rusk to Col. James Smith, June 17, 1836; P. Dimmitt, June 22, 1836, in Rusk Papers, Correspondence, BTHC. Thomas J. Rusk to Alexander Somerville, June 19, 1836, in Jenkins, ed., Papers, p. VII: 203.

49. Philip Dimmitt to T. Rusk, June, 1836, Rusk Papers, BTHC.

50. Huson, *Refugio*, pp. 160−161; Carlos de la Garza claims, Secretary of State Records, TSL.

51. O'Connor, *Presidio*, p. 251.

52. Victoria County tax records, 1850, 1867, 1872, Archives, Victoria College/ University of Houston–Victoria, Victoria, Tex.

53. Fernando de León, Land Records, Victoria County Clerk's Office, Victoria, Tex. (hereafter VCCO).

54. Will of Patricia de la Garza de León, County Court Records, VCCO.

55. Marriage and baptismal records, St. Mary's Catholic Church of Victoria, CAT.

BIBLIOGRAPHY

ARCHIVES

Archivo de la Secretaría de Gobierno, Saltillo, Coahuila. Transcripts. Barker Texas
    History Center (SA)
Archivo del Convento de Guadalupe
Archivo General de Indias, Audiencia de Guadalajara (AGI)
Archivo General de la Nacíon, Mexico, Sección Historia (AGN-H)
Archivo General de la Nación, Mexico, Provincias Internas (AGN-PI)
Archivo Matritense C.M., Madrid
Barker Texas History Center, University of Texas at Austin, Archives and Manu-
    script Collection (BTHC)
Jean Louis Berlandier Papers, Thomas Gilcrease Institute of American History
    and Art, Tulsa, Oklahoma
Bexar Archives, Barker Texas History Center, University of Texas at Austin (BA)
Bexar Archives Translations, Bexar County Courthouse, San Antonio, Texas (BAT)
Bexar County Archives, Bexar County Courthouse, San Antonio, Texas (BCA)
Robert Bruce Blake Research Collection, Special Collections, Ralph W. Steen
    Library, Stephen F. Austin University, Nacogdoches, Texas (Blake)
Catholic Archives of Texas, Austin (CAT)
Daughters of the Republic of Texas Library, San Antonio, Texas (DRT)
General Land Office, Austin, Texas (GLO)
A. J. Houston Papers, Texas State Library, Archives Division, Austin (AJH)
Mirabeau B. Lamar Papers, Texas State Library, Archives Division, Austin (MBL)
Nacogdoches Archives, Texas State Library, Archives Division (NA)
Nacogdoches Archives Transcripts, Barker Texas History Center, University of
    Texas at Austin (NAT)
Special Collections, Ralph W. Steen Library, Stephen F. Austin University,
    Nacogdoches, Texas (SFA)
Texas State Library, Archives Division (TSL)
University of Notre Dame Archives, South Bend, Indiana (ND)

Victoria College/University of Houston–Victoria, Archives, Victoria, Texas
Victoria County Clerk's Office, Victoria, Texas, Land Records (VCCO)
Vincentian Archives, St. Mary's of the Barrens, Perryville, Missouri

SECONDARY SOURCES

Ahlborn, Richard E. "European Dress in Texas, 1830: As Rendered by Lino Sánchez y Tapia." *American Scene* 13: 4 (1972): 1–18

Alamán, Lucas. *Historia de México desde los primeros movimientos que prepararon su independencia en el año de 1808 hasta la época presente*. 5 vols. 1850; reprint, Mexico City: Fondo de la Cultura Económica, 1985.

Alessio Robles, Vito. *Coahuila y Texas desde la consumación de la independencia hasta el tratado de paz de Guadalupe Hidalgo*. 2 vols. Mexico City: N.p., 1945.

———. *Coahuila y Texas en la época colonial*. 1938; reprint, Mexico City: Porrúa, 1978.

Almaráz, Félix D., Jr. *Governor Antonio Martínez and Mexican Independence in Texas: An Orderly Transition*. San Antonio: Bexar County Historical Commission, 1979.

———. *Tragic Cavalier: Governor Manuel Salcedo of Texas, 1808–1813*. Austin: University of Texas Press, 1971.

Almonte, Juan N. *Nota estadística sobre Tejas*. Mexico City: Ignacio Cumplido, 1835.

———. "Statistical Information of Texas." In Vicente Filisola, *Memoirs for the History of the War in Texas*, trans. Wallace Woolsey. 2 vols. 1848; reprint, Austin: Eakin Press, 1986, 1987.

Anna, Timothy E. *The Fall of the Royal Government in Mexico City*. Lincoln: University of Nebraska Press, 1978.

———. "The Independence of Mexico and Central America." In *The Independence of Latin America*, ed. Leslie Bethell. Cambridge: Cambridge University Press, 1987.

Austin, Mattie Alice. "The Municipal Government of San Fernando de Béxar, 1730–1800." *Quarterly of the Texas State Historical Association* 8: 4 (Apr., 1905): 277–352.

Bancroft, Hubert Howe. *The History of North Mexican States and Texas*. 2 vols. San Francisco: A. L. Bancroft, 1884–1886.

Barcarisse, Charles A. "Baron de Bastrop." *Southwestern Historical Quarterly* 58: 3 (Jan., 1955): 319–330.

———. "The Barón de Bastrop: The Life and Times of Philip Hendrick Nering Bogel, 1759–1827." PhD dissertation, University of Texas at Austin, 1955.

———. "The Union of Coahuila and Texas." *Southwestern Historical Quarterly* 61: 3 (Jan., 1958): 341–349.

Barker, Eugene C., ed. *The Austin Papers*. 3 vols. Austin: University of Texas Press, 1926.

———. *The Austin Papers*. 2 vols. Annual Report of the American Historical Association of 1919. Washington, D.C.: U.S. Government Printing Office, 1924.

————. *The Austin Papers.* 2 vols. Annual Report of the American Historical Association of 1922. Washington, D.C.: U.S. Government Printing Office, 1928.

————. "The Government of Austin's Colony 1821–1831." *Southwestern Historical Quarterly* 21: 3 (Jan., 1918): 223–252.

————. *The Life of Stephen F. Austin, Founder of Texas, 1793–1836.* 1925; reprint, Austin: University of Texas Press, 1985.

————. *Mexico and Texas, 1825–1835.* Dallas: P. L. Turner, 1928.

————. "Native Latin American Contribution to the Colonization and Independence of Texas." *Southwestern Historical Quarterly* 46: 4 (Apr., 1943): 317–335.

Barr, Alwyn. *Texans in Revolt: The Battle for San Antonio, 1835.* Austin: University of Texas Press, 1990.

Barrera, Manuel. *Then the Gringos Came — The Story of Martín de León and the Texas Revolution.* Laredo, Tex.: Barrera Publications, 1992.

Benavides, Adán, Jr., ed. and comp. *The Bexar Archives (1717–1836): A Name Guide.* Austin: University of Texas Press for the University of Texas at San Antonio Institute of Texan Cultures, 1989.

Benedict, J. W. "Diary of a Campaign against the Comanches." *Southwestern Historical Quarterly* 32: 4 (Apr., 1929): 300–310.

Benson, Nettie Lee. "The Plan of Casa Mata." *Hispanic American Historical Review* 25: 1 (Feb., 1945): 45–56.

————. *The Provincial Deputation in Mexico: Harbinger of Provincial Autonomy, Independence, and Federalism.* Austin: University of Texas Press, 1992.

————. "Texas As Viewed from Mexico, 1820–1834." *Southwestern Historical Quarterly* 90: 3 (Jan., 1987): 219–291.

————. "Texas' Failure to Send a Deputy to the Spanish Cortes, 1810–1812." *Southwestern Historical Quarterly* 64: 1 (July, 1960): 14–35.

Berlandier, Jean Louis. *Journey to Mexico during the Years 1826 to 1834.* 2 vols. Trans. Sheila M. Ohlendorf, Josette M. Bielow, Mary M. Standifer. Austin: Texas State Historical Association and Center for Studies in Texas History, 1980.

Binkley, William C., ed. *Official Correspondence of the Texan Revolution, 1835–1836.* 2 vols. New York: D. Appleton–Century, 1936.

————. *The Texas Revolution.* Baton Rouge: Louisiana State University Press, 1952.

Birge, M. "The Casas Revolution." M.A. thesis, University of Texas at Austin, 1911.

Bolton, Herbert Eugene. *Texas in the Middle of the Eighteenth Century.* 1915; reprint, Austin: University of Texas Press, 1970.

Brading, D. A. *Haciendas and Ranchos in the Mexican Bajío: León, 1680–1860.* Cambridge: Cambridge University Press, 1978.

Broussard, Ray F. "San Antonio during the Texas Republic: A City in Transition." *Southwestern Studies* 5 (1967): 3–40.

Brown, John Duff. "Reminiscences of Jno. Duff Brown." *Quarterly of the Texas State Historical Association* 12: 4 (Apr., 1909): 296–311.

Brown, John Henry. *History of Texas, from 1685 to 1892.* 2 vols. Saint Louis: L. Daniell, 1892–1893.

Brown, Lawrence L. *The Episcopal Church in Texas, 1838–1874: From Its Foundation to the Division of the Diocese.* Austin, Tex.: Church Historical Society, 1963.

Carpenter, V. K., comp. *The State of Texas Federal Population Schedules Seventh Census of the United States, 1850.* Huntsville, Ark.: Century Enterprises, 1969.

Castañeda, Carlos E. *Our Catholic Heritage in Texas, 1519–1936.* 7 vols. 1936–1958; reprint, New York: Arno Press, 1976.

———, trans. *The Mexican Side of the Texas Revolution [1836] by the Chief Mexican Participants.* Dallas: P. L. Turner, 1928.

Castillo Crimm, Ana Carolina. "Success in Adversity: The Mexican Americans of Victoria County, Texas, 1800–1880." PhD dissertation, University of Texas at Austin, 1994.

Chabot, Frederick C. *The Perote Prisoners: Being the Diary of James L. Truehart, Printed for the First Time Together with an Historical Introduction.* San Antonio: Naylor, 1934.

———. *With the Makers of San Antonio. Genealogies of the Early Latin, Anglo-American, and German Families with Occasional Biographies, Each Group Being Prefaced with a Brief Historical Sketch and Illustrations.* San Antonio: Artes Gráficas, 1937.

———, ed. *Texas in 1811: The Las Casas and Sambrano Revolutions.* San Antonio: Yanaguana Society, 1941.

———, ed. *Texas Letters.* San Antonio: Yanaguana Society, 1940.

Chartrand, Rene. "Leather Jacket Soldiers: The 'Cuera' Cavalry of the American South-West." *Military Illustrated, Past & Present* 53 (Oct., 1992): 24–29, and 54 (Nov., 1992): 36–42.

Chipman, Donald. *Spanish Texas, 1519–1821.* Austin: University of Texas Press, 1992.

Christiansen, Paige W. "Hugo O'Conor: Spanish-Indian Relations on the Frontiers of New Spain, 1771–1776." PhD dissertation, University of California, Berkeley, 1960.

Clark, Doris. "Spanish Reaction to French Intrusion into Texas from Louisiana, 1754–1771." M.A. thesis, University of Texas at Austin, 1942.

Cleaves, W. S. "Lorenzo de Zavala in Texas." *Southwestern Historical Quarterly* 36: 1 (July, 1932): 29–40.

Coalson, George O. "Texas Mexicans in the Texas Revolution." In Ronald Lora, ed., *The American West: Essays in Honor of W. Eugene Hollon.* Toledo: University of Ohio, 1980.

Cody, C. C. "Rev. Martin Ruter, A.M., D.D." *Texas Methodist Historical Quarterly* 1: (July, 1909): 7–38.

Colección de las leyes y decretos expedidos por el Congreso General de los Estados-Unidos Mejicanos, en los años de 1829 y 1830. Mexico City: Imprenta de Galván, 1831.

Connor, Seymour V. *Texas: A History.* New York: Thomas Y. Crowell, 1971.

Contreras, Roberto. "José Bernardo Gutiérrez de Lara: The Forgotten Man." M.A. thesis, Pan American University, 1975.

Corner, William, ed. and comp. *San Antonio de Bexar: A Guide and History.* 1890; reprint, San Antonio: Graphic Arts, 1977.

Costeloe, Michael P. *La primera república federal de México (1824–1835): Un estudio de los partidos políticos en el México independiente.* Mexico City: Fondo de Cultura Económica, 1975.

Crisp, James Ernest. "Anglo-Texan Attitudes toward the Mexican, 1821–1845." PhD dissertation, Yale University, 1976.

Crook, Carland Elaine. "San Antonio, Texas, 1846–1861." M.A. thesis, Rice University, 1964.

Cruz, Gilbert R. *Let There Be Towns: Spanish Municipal Origins in the American Southwest, 1610–1810.* College Station: Texas A&M University Press, 1988.

Dabney, Lancaster E. "Louis Aury: The First Governor of Texas under the Mexican Republic." *Southwestern Historical Quarterly* 42: 2 (Oct., 1938): 108–116.

Dary, David. *Cowboy Culture: A Saga of Five Centuries.* New York: Avon Books, 1981.

Davenport, Harbert. "Captain Jesus Cuellar, Texas Cavalry, Otherwise 'Comanche.'" *Southwestern Historical Quarterly* 30: 1 (July, 1926): 56–62.

———. "Goliad Campaign of 1836." In *The Handbook of Victoria County*, pp. 38–48. Revised by Craig H. Roell. Austin: Texas State Historical Association, 1990.

———. "Men of Goliad." *Southwestern Historical Quarterly* 43: 1 (July, 1939): 1–41.

Davis, John L. *San Antonio: A Historical Portait.* Austin, Tex.: Encino, 1978.

Davis, Robert S., Jr. "Goliad and the Georgia Battalion: Georgia Participation in the Texas Revolution, 1835–1836." *Journal of Southwest Georgia History* 4 (Fall, 1986).

Dawson, Joseph Martin. *José Antonio Navarro: Co-Creator of Texas.* Waco, Tex.: Baylor University Press, 1969.

Day, James M., comp. and ed. *The Texas Almanac, 1857–1873: A Compendium of Texas History.* Waco, Tex.: Texian Press, 1967.

de la Teja, Jesús F. "Indians, Soldiers, and Canary Islanders: The Making of a Texas Frontier Community." *Locus* 3: 1 (Fall, 1990): 81–96.

———. *San Antonio de Béxar: A Community on New Spain's Northern Frontier.* Albuquerque: University of New Mexico Press, 1995.

de la Teja, Jesús F., and John Wheat. "Béxar: Profile of a Tejano Community, 1820–1832." *Southwestern Historical Quarterly* 89: 1 (July, 1985): 7–34.

———, ed. *A Revolution Remembered: The Memoirs and Selected Correspondence of Juan N. Seguín.* Austin, Tex.: State House Press, 1991

de León, Arnoldo. *Apuntes Tejanos: An Index of Items Related to Mexican Americans in 19th Century Texas Extracted from the San Antonio Express (1869–1900) and San Antonio Herald (1855–1878).* Austin: Texas State Historical Association, 1978.

———. *The Tejano Community, 1836–1900.* Albuquerque: University of New Mexico Press, 1982.

———. "The Tejano Experience in Six Texas Regions." *West Texas Historical Association Year Book* 65 (1989): 36–49.

———. "Tejano History Scholarship: A Review of the Literature." *West Texas Historical Association Year Book* 59 (1985): 116–133.

———. "Tejanos and the Texas War for Independence: Historiography's Judgment." *New Mexico Historical Review* 61 (Apr., 1986): 137–146.

———. "Texas Mexicans: Twentieth-Century Interpretation." In Walter Buenger and Robert Calvert, eds., *Texas through Time: Evolving Interpretations*. College Station: Texas A&M University Press, 1991.

———. *They Called Them Greasers: Attitudes toward Mexicans in Texas, 1821–1900*. Austin: University of Texas Press, 1983.

Díaz-Stevens, Ana María. "The Saving Grace: The Matriarchal Core of Latino Popular Religion." *Latino Studies Journal* 4 (Sept., 1993): 60–78.

Dixon, Helen. "The Middle Years of the Administration of Juan María Barón de Ripperdá, Governor of Texas, 1773–1775." M.A. thesis, University of Texas at Austin, 1934.

Downs, Fane. "Governor Antonio Martínez and the Defense of Texas from Foreign Invasion, 1817–1822." *Texas Military History* 7: 1 (Spring, 1968): 27–43.

———. "The History of Mexicans in Texas, 1820–1845." PhD dissertation, Texas Tech University, 1970.

Driggs, Howard R., and Sarah S. King, eds. *Rise of the Lone Star: A Story of Texas Told by Its Pioneers*. New York: Frederick A. Stokes, 1936.

Dunn, Fabius. "The Administration of Don Antonio Cordero, Governor of Texas, 1805–1808." PhD dissertation, University of Texas at Austin, 1962.

Dysart, Jane. "Mexican Women in San Antonio, 1830–1860: The Assimilation Process." *Western Historical Quarterly* 7: 4 (Oct., 1976): 365–375.

Ehrenberg, Herman. *With Milam and Fannin: Adventures of a German Boy in Texas' Revolution*. Ed. Henry Smith, trans. Charlotte Churchill. Dallas: Tardy, 1935.

Estep, Raymond. "The Life of Lorenzo de Zavala." PhD dissertation, University of Texas, 1942.

———. "Lorenzo de Zavala and the Texas Revolution." *Southwestern Historical Quarterly* 57: 3 (Jan., 1954): 322–335.

Everett, Dianna. *The Texas Cherokees: A People between Two Fires, 1819–1840*. Norman: University of Oklahoma Press, 1990.

Faulk, Odie B. *The Last Years of Spanish Texas, 1778–1821*. The Hague: Mouton, 1964.

———. "The Penetration of Foreigners and Foreign Ideas into Spanish East Texas, 1793–1810." *East Texas Historical Journal* 2: 2 (Oct., 1964): 87–98.

———. "Texas during the Administration of Governor Domingo Cabello y Robles, 1778–1786." PhD dissertation, Texas Tech University, 1960.

Faye, Stanley. "Commodore Aury." *Louisiana Historical Quarterly* 24: 3 (July, 1941): 611–697.

Fehrenbach, T. R. *Lone Star: A History of Texas and the Texans*. New York: Macmillan, 1968.

Filisola, Vicente. *Memoirs for the History of the War in Texas*. Trans. Wallace Woolsey. 2 vols. Austin, Tex.: Eakin Press, 1986, 1987.

———. *Memorias para la historia de la guerra de Tejas*. Mexico City: Ignacio Cumplido, 1849.

Foley, Patrick. "Beyond the Missions: The Immigrant Church and the Hispanics in Nineteenth Century Texas." In *Hipanicism and Catholicism: Great Forces in Motion*. San Antonio: Mexican American Cultural Center Press, 1992.

Foote, Henry S. *Texas and the Texans.* 2 vols. Philadelphia: Thomas Cowperthwait, 1841.

Fretelliere, Auguste. "Adventures of a Castrovillian." In Julia Nott Waugh, *Castroville and Henry Castro, Empresario,* pp. 80–97. San Antonio: Standard, 1934.

Friend, Llerena B. *Sam Houston: The Great Designer.* Austin: University of Texas Press, 1969.

Gaddy, Jerry J., comp. and ed. *Texas in Revolt: Contemporary Newspaper Account of the Texas Revolution.* Fort Collins, Colo.: Old Army Press, 1973.

Gammel, H. P. N. *The Laws of Texas, 1822–1897.* 10 vols. Austin, Tex.: Gammel Book Company, 1898.

García, Mario T. *Desert Immigrants: The Mexicans of El Paso, 1880–1920.* New Haven, Conn.: Yale University Press, 1981.

Garrett, [Julia] Kathryn. "The First Newspaper of Texas: Gaceta de Texas." *Southwestern Historical Quarterly* 40: 3 (Jan., 1937): 200–215.

———. "Gaceta de Texas: Translation of the First Number." *Southwestern Historical Quarterly* 42: 1 (July, 1938): 21–27.

———. *Green Flag over Texas. A Story of the Last Years of Spain in Texas.* New York: Cordova Press, 1939.

Garrison, George P. *Texas: A Contest of Civilizations.* Boston: Houghton Mifflin, 1903.

———, ed. *Diplomatic Correspondence of the Republic of Texas.* 3 vols. Washington: Government Printing Office, 1908–1911.

"General Austin's Order Book for the Campaign of 1835." *Quarterly of the Texas State Historical Association* 11: 1 (July, 1907): 1–55.

González, Gilbert G., and Raúl Fernández. "Chicano History: Transcending Cultural Models." *Pacific Historical Review* 63: 4 (Nov., 1994): 469–497.

Gray, William F. *From Virginia to Texas, 1835: Diary of Col. Wm. F. Gray, Giving Details of His Journey to Texas and Return in 1835–1836 and Second Journey to Texas in 1837.* 1909; reprint, Houston: Fletcher, 1965.

Green, Rena Maverick, ed. *Memoirs of Mary A. Maverick.* San Antonio: Alamo, 1921.

———, ed. *Samuel Maverick, Texan: 1803–1870. A Collection of Letters, Journals, and Memoirs.* San Antonio: Privately printed, 1952.

Green, Thomas J. *Journal of the Texian Expedition against Mier; Subsequent Imprisonment of the Author; His Sufferings, and Final Escape from the Castle of Perote. With Reflections upon the Present Political and Probable Future Relations of Texas, Mexico, and the United States.* New York: Harper & Brothers, 1845.

Grimes, Roy. *300 Years in Victoria County.* Austin, Tex.: Nortex Press, 1985.

Griswold Del Castillo, Richard. "Quantitative History in the American Southwest: A Survey and Critique." *Western Historical Quarterly* 15 (Oct., 1984): 407–426.

Gronet, Richard W. "The United States and the Invasion of Texas, 1810–1814." *The Americas* 25 (Jan., 1969): 281–306.

Gulick, Charles Adams, Jr., and Katherine Elliott, eds. *The Papers of Mirabeau Buonaparte Lamar.* 6 vols. 1921–1927; reprint, Austin: Von Boeckmann–Jones, 1973.

Gutiérrez, David D. "Significant to Whom?: Mexican Americans and the History of the American West." *Western Historical Quarterly* 24: 4 (Nov., 1993): 519–539.

Haggard, J. Villasana. "The Counter-Revolution of Bexar, 1811." *Southwestern Historical Quarterly* 43: 2 (Oct., 1939):222–235.

———. "The Neutral Ground between Louisiana and Texas, 1806–1821." PhD dissertation, University of Texas at Austin, 1942.

Hamilton, Lester. *Goliad Survivor: Isacc D. Hamilton.* San Antonio: Naylor, 1971.

Hammett, Arthur B. *The Empresario Don Martín De León.* Waco, Tex.: Texian Press, 1973.

Hamnett, Brian R. *Roots of Insurgency: Mexican Regions, 1750–1824.* Cambridge: Cambridge University Press, 1986.

The Handbook of Texas. 3 vols. Austin: Texas State Historical Association, 1952, 1976.

The Handbook of Victoria County. Austin: Texas State Historical Association, 1990.

Hardin, Stephen L. "A Vatir y Perseguir: Tejano Deployment in the War of Texas Independence, 1835–1836." In Lisa T. Davis, ed., *The E. C. Barksdale Student Lectures, 1985–1986.* Arlington: University of Texas at Arlington, 1986.

———. "Long Rifle and Brown Bess: Weapons and Tactics of the Texas Revolution, 1835–1836." M.A. thesis, Southwest Texas State University, 1985.

———. *Texian Iliad: A Military History of the Texas Revolution.* Austin: University of Texas Press, 1994.

———, ed. "The Félix Núñez Account and the Siege of the Alamo: A Critical Appraisal." *Southwestern Historical Quarterly* 94: 1 (July, 1990): 65–84.

Harris, Helen Willits. "Almonte's Inspection of Texas in 1834." *Southwestern Historical Quarterly* 41: 3 (Jan., 1938): 195–211.

Harrison, James Christopher. "The Failure in East Texas: The Occupation and Abandonment of Nacogdoches." PhD dissertation, University of Nebraska, 1980.

Hatcher, Mattie Austin, trans. "Joaquin de Arredondo's Report of the Battle of the Medina, August 18, 1813." *Quarterly of the Texas State Historical Association* 11: 3 (Jan., 1908): 220–236.

———. "Municipal Government of San Fernando de Béxar, 1730–1800." *Quarterly of the Texas State Historical Association* 8: 4 (Apr., 1905): 277–352.

———. *The Opening of Texas to Foreign Settlement, 1801–1821.* 1927; reprint. Philadelphia: Porcupine Press, 1976.

Helm, Mary S. *Scraps of Early Texas History.* Ed. Lorraine Jeter. 1884; reprint, Austin, Tex.: Eakin Press, 1987.

Henderson, Harry McCorry. "The Magee-Gutiérrez Expedition." *Southwestern Historical Quarterly* 55: 1 (July, 1951): 43–61.

Henderson, Mary Virginia. "Minor Empresario Contracts for the Colonization of Texas, 1825–1834." *Southwestern Historical Quarterly* 31: 4 (Apr., 1928): 295–324.

Heros of Texas: Featuring Oil Portraits from the Summerfield G. Roberts Collection, Waco, Tex.: Texian Press, 1964.

Hinojosa, Gilberto M. *A Borderlands Town in Transition: Laredo, 1755–1870*. College Station: Texas A&M University Press, 1983.

———. "The Enduring Hispanic Faith Communities: Spanish and Texas Church Historiography." *Journal of Texas Catholic History and Culture* 1: 1 (Mar., 1990): 20–41.

Hoffman, Fritz Leo. "The First Three Years of the Administration of Juan María Barón de Ripperdá, Governor of Texas, 1770–1773." M.A. thesis, University of Texas at Austin, 1930.

Holley, Mary Austin. *Texas*. 1836; reprint, Austin: Texas State Historical Association, 1985.

Hollon, W. Eugene. *Frontier Violence: Another Look*. New York: Oxford University Press, 1974.

Hollon, W. Eugene, and Ruth Lapham Butler, eds. *William Bollaert's Texas*. Norman: University of Oklahoma Press, 1956.

Howrene, Alleine, "Causes and Origin of the Decree of April 6, 1830." *Southwestern Historical Quarterly* 16: 4 (Apr., 1913): 378–422.

Huson, Hobart. *Refugio, a Comprehensive History of Refugio County from Aboriginal Times to 1953*. 2 vols. Woodsboro, Tex.: Rooke Foundation, 1953.

Hutchinson, Anderson. "Diary." In "The Bexar and Dawson Prisoners," ed. E. W. Winkler, pp. 294–295. *Quarterly of the Texas State Historical Association* 13: 4 (Apr., 1910): 292–324.

Jackson, Jack. *Los Mesteños: Spanish Ranching in Texas, 1721–1821*. College Station: Texas A&M University Press, 1986.

Janicek, Ricki S. "The Development of Early Mexican Land Policy: Coahuila and Texas, 1810–1825." PhD dissertation, Tulane University, 1985.

Jarrett, Rie. *Gutiérrez de Lara, Mexican-Texan: The Story of a Creole Hero*. Austin, Tex.: Creole Texana, 1949.

Jenkins, John Holmes, ed. *The Papers of the Texas Revolution, 1835–1836*. 10 vols. Austin, Tex.: Presidential Press, 1973.

Jiménez, Judith M. "Joaquín Arredondo, Loyalist Officer in New Spain, 1810–1821." PhD dissertation, University of Michigan, 1933.

John, Elizabeth A. H. "Nuturing the Peace: Spanish and Comanche Cooperation in the Early Nineteenth Century." *New Mexico Historical Review* 59: 4 (Oct., 1984): 345–370.

———. *Storms Brewed in Other Men's Worlds: The Confrontation of Indians, Spanish, and French in the Southwest, 1540–1795*. College Station: Texas A&M University Press, 1975.

Jones, Oakah L. *Los Paisanos: Spanish Settlers on the Northern Frontier of New Spain*. Norman: University of Oklahoma Press, 1979.

Jordan, Terry G. "A Century and a Half of Ethnic Change in Texas, 1836–1986." *Southwestern Historical Quarterly* 89: 4 (Apr., 1986): 385–422.

Journals of the Senate, of the Republic of Texas; First Session of the Third Congress, 1838. Houston: National Intelligencer Office, 1839.

Juárez, José Roberto. "La Iglesia Católica y el Chicano en Sud Texas, 1836–1911." *Aztlán* 4: 2 (Fall, 1973): 217–255.

Keegan, John. *The Faces of Battle*. New York: Viking Press, 1976.

Kendall, George Wilkens. *Narrative of the Texan Santa Fé Expedition, Comprising a Description of a Tour through Texas, and across the Great Southwestern Prairies, the Camanche and Cayuga Hunting-Grounds, with an Account of the Sufferings from Want of Food, Losses from Hostile Indians, and Final Capture of the Texans, and Their March, as Prisoners, to the City of Mexico. With Illustrations and a Map*. 2 vols. 1844; reprint, Ann Arbor, Mich.: University Microfilms, 1966.

Kennedy, William. *Texas: The Rise, Progress, and Prospects of the Republic of Texas*. Facsimile. Fort Worth, Tex.: Molyneaux Craftsmen, 1925.

Kimball, John P., comp. *Laws and Decrees of the State of Texas and Coahuila*. Houston: Secretary of State, 1839.

King, Nyal C. "Captain Antonio Gil Y'Barbo: Founder of Modern Nacogdoches, 1729–1809." M.A. thesis, Stephen F. Austin State University, 1949.

Lack, Paul D. "East Texas Mexicans and the Texas Revolution." *Locus* 3 (Spring, 1991).

———. "In the Long Shadow of Eugene C. Barker: The Revolution and the Republic." In *Texas through Time: Evolving Interpretations*, ed. Walter Buenger and Robert Calvert. College Station: Texas A&M University Press, 1991.

———. *The Texas Revolutionary Experience: A Political and Social History, 1835–1836*. College Station: Texas A&M University Press, 1992.

Ladd, Doris. *The Mexican Nobility at Independence*. Austin: University of Texas Press, 1976.

Laquest, Katherine W. "A Social History of the Spaniards in Nacogdoches." M.A. thesis, Baylor University, 1941.

Latham, Francis S. *Travels in the Republic of Texas, 1842*. Ed. Gerald S. Pierce. Austin, Tex.: Encino, 1971.

Lawrence, A. B. "Introduction." In *Texas in 1840, or the Emigrant's Guide to the New Republic; Being the Result of Observation, Enquiry and Travel in That Beautiful Country. By an Emigrant, Late of the United States*. New York: William W. Allen, 1840.

Leal, Carmela, comp. and ed. "Translations of Statistical and Census Reports of Texas, 1782–1836, and Sources Relating to the Black in Texas, 1603–1803." Microfilm. San Antonio: University of Texas Institute of Texan Cultures, 1979.

Linati, Claudio. *Trajes civiles, militares y religiosos de Mexico*. 1828; reprint, Mexico City: Miguel Ángel Porrúa, 1979.

Linn, John J. *Reminiscences of Fifty Years in Texas*. 1883; reprint, Austin, Tex.: State House Press, 1986.

Lockhart, James, and Stuart B. Schwartz. *Early Latin America: A History of Colonial Spanish America and Brazil*. Cambridge: Cambridge University Press, 1983.

Long, Jeff. *Duel of Eagles: The Mexican and U.S. Fight for the Alamo*. New York: William Morrow, 1990.

Lord, Walter. *A Time to Stand*. New York: Harper & Brothers, 1961.

Lowrie, Samuel Harman. *Culture Conflict in Texas, 1821–1835*. 1931; reprint, New York: AMS Press, 1967.

McCaleb, Walter F. "The First Period of the Gutierrez-Magee Expedition." *Quarterly of the Texas State Historical Association* 4: 3 (Jan., 1901): 218–229.

McCutchan, Joseph D. *Mier Expedition Diary: A Texan Prisoner's Account*. Ed. Joseph Milton Nance, with a foreword by Jane A. Kenamore. Austin: University of Texas Press, 1978.

McDonald, David R., and Timothy M. Matovina. *Defending Mexican Valor in Texas: José Antonio Navarro's Historical Writings, 1853–1857*. Austin, Tex.: State House Press, 1995.

McElahannon, Joseph C. "Imperial Mexico and Texas, 1821–1823." *Southwestern Historical Quarterly* 53: 2 (Oct., 1949): 117–150.

McGrath, Sister Paul of the Cross. "Political Nativism in Texas, 1825–1960." PhD dissertation, Catholic University of America, 1930.

MacLachlan, Colin M., and Jaime E. Rodríguez O. *The Forging of the Cosmic Race: A Reinterpretation of Colonial Mexico*. Berkeley & Los Angeles: University of California Press, 1980.

McLean, Malcolm D., ed. *Papers Concerning Robertson's Colony in Texas*. 18 vols. Arlington: University of Texas at Arlington Press, 1990.

McMurtrie, Douglas C. "The First Texas Newspaper." *Southwestern Historical Quarterly* 36: 1 (July, 1932): 41–46.

McReynolds, James Michael. "Family Life in a Borderland Community: Nacogdoches, Texas, 1779–1861." PhD dissertation, Texas Tech University, 1978.

Matovina, Timothy M. *The Alamo Remembered: Tejano Accounts and Perspectives*. Austin: University of Texas Press, 1995.

———. "Lay Initiatives in Worship on the Texas *Frontera*, 1836–1860." *U.S. Catholic Historian* 12: 4 (Fall, 1994): 107–120.

———. "Our Lady of Guadalupe Celebrations in San Antonio, Texas, 1840–1841." *Journal of Hispanic/Latino Theology* 1: 1 (Nov., 1993): 77–96.

———. *Tejano Religion and Ethnicity: San Antonio, 1821–1860*. Austin: University of Texas Press, 1995.

Menchaca, Antonio. *Memoirs*. San Antonio: Yanaguana Society, 1937.

Miller, Howard. "Stephen F. Austin and the Anglo-Texan Response to the Religious Establishment in Mexico, 1821–1836." *Southwestern Historical Quarterly* 91: 3 (Jan., 1988): 283–316.

Miller, Thomas Lloyd. "Mexican-Texans at the Alamo." *Journal of Mexican American History* 2 (Fall, 1971): 33–44.

———. "Mexican Texans in the Texas Revolution." *Journal of Mexican American History* 3: (1973): 105–130.

Milligan, James Clark. "José Bernardo Gutiérrez de Lara, Mexican Frontiersman, 1811–1841." PhD dissertation, Texas Tech University, 1975.

Montejano, David. *Anglos and Mexicans in the Making of Texas, 1836–1986*. Austin: University of Texas Press, 1987.

Moore, James Talmadge. *Through Fire and Flood: The Catholic Church in Frontier Texas, 1860–1900*. College Station: Texas A&M University Press, 1992.

Moorhead, Max L. *The Presidio: Bastion of the Spanish Borderlands*. Norman: University of Oklahoma Press, 1975.

Morey, Elizabeth May. "Attitude of the Citizens of San Fernando toward Independence Movements in New Spain, 1811–1813." M.A. thesis, University of Texas at Austin, 1930.

Morfí, Fray Juan Agustín. *History of Texas, 1673–1779*. 2 vols. Trans. and ed. Carlos E. Castañeda. Albuquerque, N.M.: Quivira Society, 1935.

Morton, Ohland. *Terán and Texas: A Chapter in Texas-Mexican Relations*. Austin: Texas State Historical Association, 1948.

Muir, Andrew Forest, ed. *Texas in 1837: An Anonymous, Contemporary Narrative*. Austin: University of Texas Press, 1988.

Myers, Sandra L. *The Ranch in Spanish Texas, 1691–1800*. University of Texas at El Paso Social Science Series, no. 2. El Paso: Texas Western Press, 1969.

Nance, Joseph Milton. *After San Jacinto: The Texas-Mexican Frontier, 1836–1841*. Austin: University of Texas Press, 1963.

———. *Attack and Counter-Attack: The Texas-Mexican Frontier, 1842*. Austin: University of Texas Press, 1964.

———, ed and trans. "Brigadier General Adrian Woll's Report of His Expedition into Texas in 1842." *Southwestern Historical Quarterly* 58: 4 (Apr., 1955): 523–552.

Norton, Wesley. "Religious Newspapers in Antebellum Texas." *Southwestern Historical Quarterly* 79: 2 (Oct., 1975): 145–165.

Oberste, William H. *Texas Irish Empresarios and Their Colonies*. Austin: Von Boeckmann–Jones Co., 1953.

O'Connor, Kathryn Stoner. *The Presidio La Bahía del Espíritu Santo de Zúñiga, 1721–1846*. 2nd ed. Victoria, Tex.: Armstrong, 1984.

O'Connor, Mrs. Thomas, contrib. "Reminiscences of Mrs. Annie Fagan Teal." *Southwestern Historical Quarterly* 34: 4 (Apr., 1931): 317–328.

Ordenanzas municipales para el gobierno y manejo interior del ayuntamiento de la Villa de Goliad. Leona Vicario, Coah.: Imprenta del Gobierno del Estado a cargo del C. José Manuel Bangs, 1829.

Perry, Carmen, ed. and trans. *With Santa Anna in Texas: A Personal Narrative of the Revolution by José Enrique de la Peña*. College Station: Texas A&M University Press, 1975.

Petty, J. W., Jr., ed. *Victor Rose's History of Victoria*. 1883; reprint, Victoria, Tex.: Book Mart, 1961.

Pitts, John Bost, III. "Speculation in Headright Land Grants in San Antonio from 1837–1842." M.A. thesis, Trinity University, 1986.

Potter, R. M. "The Texas Revolution: Distinguished Mexicans Who Took Part in the Revolution of Texas, with Glances at Its Early Events." *Magazine of American History* (Oct., 1878).

Poyo, Gerald E., and Gilberto M. Hinojosa, eds. *Tejano Origins in Eighteenth-Century San Antonio*. Austin: University of Texas Press for the Institute of Texan Cultures at San Antonio, 1991.

———. "Spanish Texas and Borderlands Historiography in Transition: Implications for United States History." *Journal of American History* 75: 2 (Sept., 1988): 393–416.

Rather, Ethel Zivley. "DeWitt's Colony." *Quarterly of the Texas State Historical Association* 8: 2 (Oct., 1904): 95–192.

Reichstein, Andreas. *Rise of the Lone Star: The Making of Texas*. College Station: Texas A&M University Press, 1989.

Remy, Caroline. "Hispanic-Mexican San Antonio: 1836–1861." *Southwestern Historical Quarterly* 71: 4 (Apr., 1968): 564–582.

Rendón Lozano, Rubén. *Viva Tejas: The Story of the Tejanos, the Mexican-Born Patriots of the Texas Revolution*. San Antonio: Alamo Press, 1985.

Richardson, Rupert N., Ernest Wallace, and Adrian N. Anderson. *Texas: The Lone Star State*. 3rd ed. Englewood Cliffs, N.J.: Prentice-Hall, 1970.

Rippy, J. Fred. "Border Troubles Along the Rio Grande, 1848–1860." *Southwestern Historical Quarterly* 23: 2 (Oct., 1919): 91–111.

Rodríguez, José María. *Rodríguez Memoirs of Early Texas*. 1913; reprint, San Antonio: Standard, 1961.

Roemer, Ferdinand. *Texas: With Particular Reference to German Immigration and the Physical Appearance of the Country*. Trans. Oswald Mueller. 1935; reprint, Waco, Tex.: Texian Press, 1967.

Rose, Victor M. *Some Historical Facts in Regard to the Settlement of Victoria, Texas*. Laredo, Tex.: Daily Times Print, 1883.

Rubio, Abel G. *Stolen Heritage: A Mexican-American's Rediscovery of His Family's Lost Land Grant*. Ed. Thomas Kreneck. Austin, Tex.: Eakin Press, 1986.

Sánchez, José María. "A Trip to Texas in 1828." Trans. Carlos E. Castañeda. *Southwestern Historical Quarterly* 29: 4 (Apr., 1926): 249–288.

Sánchez Navarro, Carlos. *La guerra de Tejas: Memorias de un soldado*. Mexico City: Editorial Polis, 1938.

Sandoval, Moisés. *On the Move: A History of the Hispanic Church in the United States*. Maryknoll, N.Y.: Orbis, 1990.

Santos, Richard G. *José Francisco Ruiz*. Bexar County, Tex.: James W. Knight, County Clerk, 1966.

Saragoza, Alex M. "Recent Chicano Historiography: An Interpretative Essay." *Aztlán* 19: 1 (Spring, 1988–1990): 1–76.

Schoelwer, Susan Prendergast, with Tom E. Glaser. *Alamo Images: Changing Perceptions of a Texas Experience*. Dallas: DeGolyer Library and Southern Methodist University Press, 1985.

Seguín, Juan N. *Personal Memoirs of John N. Seguín from the Year 1834 to the Retreat of General Woll from the City of San Antonio in 1842*. San Antonio: Ledger Book and Job Office, 1858.

Siegel, Stanley. *A Political History of the Texas Republic, 1836–1845*. Austin: University of Texas Press, 1956.

Smither, Harriet, ed. *Journals of the Fourth Congress of the Republic of Texas, 1839–1840*. 3 vols. Austin: Von Boeckmann–Jones, 1929.

Smithwick, Noah. *The Evolution of a State: Or, Recollections of Old Texas Days*. Comp. Nanna Smithwick Donaldson. 1900; reprint, Austin: University of Texas Press, 1983.

Spears, Louis. "Galveston Island, 1816–1821: Focal Point for the Contest for Texas." M.A. thesis, University of Texas at El Paso, 1973.

Stagner, Stephen. "Epics, Science, and the Lost Frontier: Texas Historical Writing, 1836–1936." *Western Historical Quarterly* 12: 2 (Apr., 1981): 165–181.

Steen, Ralph W. "Analysis of the Work of the General Council, 1835–1836." *Southwestern Historical Quarterly* 41: 4 (Apr., 1938): 330–348.

Stuck, Walter Goodloe. *José Francisco Ruiz, Texas Patriot*. San Antonio: Witte Museum, 1943.

"Tadeo Ortiz de Ayala and the Colonization of Texas, 1822–1833." Trans. Edith Louise Kelly and Mattie Austin Hatcher. *Southwestern Historical Quarterly* 32: 4 (Apr., 1929): 311–316.

Taylor, Virginia H., trans. and ed. *The Letters of Antonio Martínez, Last Governor of Texas, 1817–1822*. Austin: Texas State Library, 1957.

Texas Surveyors Association. *One League to Each Wind: Accounts of Early Surveying in Texas*. Ed. Sue Watkins. Austin: Von Boeckmann–Jones, 1973.

Thonhoff, Robert H. *Forgotten Battlefield of the First Texas Revolution: The Battle of the Medina, August 18, 1813*. Austin, Tex.: Eakin Press, 1985.

———. *The Texas Connection with the American Revolution*. Burnet, Tex.: Eakin Press, 1981.

Tijerina, Andrés Anthony. *Tejanos and Texas under the Mexican Flag*. College Station: Texas A&M University Press, 1994.

Timmons, Wilbert H. *Tadeo Ortiz, Mexican Colonizer and Reformer*. El Paso: Privately printed, 1974.

Tjarks, Alicia V. "Comparative Demographic Analysis of Texas, 1777–1793." *Southwestern Historical Quarterly* 77: 3 (Jan., 1974): 291–338.

Tornel, José María. *Tejas y los Estados-Unidos de América, en sus relaciones con la República Mexicana*. Mexico City: Ignacio Cumplido, 1837.

Tutino, John. *From Insurrection to Revolution in Mexico: Social Bases of Agrarian Violence, 1750–1940*. Princeton, N.J.: Princeton University Press, 1988.

Urrea, José. *Diario de las operaciones militares de la división que al mando del General José Urrea hizo en la Campaña de Tejas*. Victoria de Durango: N.p., 1838.

Vásquez, Josefina Zoraida, and Lorenzo Meyer. *México frente a Estados Unidos (Un ensayo histórico, 1776–1988)*. 1982; reprint, Mexico City: Fondo de Cultura Económica, 1989.

Vigness, David. *The Revolutionary Decades: The Saga of Texas, 1810–1836*. Austin, Tex.: Steck-Vaughn, 1965.

Villarello Vélez, Ildefonso. *Historia de Coahuila*. Saltillo, Coah.: Escuela Normal de Coahuila, 1969.

Villoro, Luis. *El proceso ideológico de la revolución de independencia*. 2d ed. Mexico City: Universidad Nacional Autónoma de México, 1967.

Warren, Harris Gaylord. "José Álvarez de Toledo's Initiation as a Filibuster, 1811–1813." *Hispanic American Historical Review* 20 (Feb., 1940): 56–82.

———. "The Origin of General Mina's Invasion of Mexico." *Southwestern Historical Quarterly* 42: 1 (July, 1938): 1–20.

———. *The Sword Was Their Passport: A History of American Filibustering in the Mexican Revolution*. Baton Rouge: Louisiana State University Press, 1943.

Weber, David J. *The Mexican Frontier, 1821–1846: The American Southwest under Mexico*. Albuquerque: University of New Mexico Press, 1982.

———. *Myth and the History of the Hispanic Southwest*. Albuquerque: University of New Mexico Press, 1988.

———. *The Spanish Frontier in North America*. New Haven, Conn.: Yale University Press, 1992.

————, ed. *Northern Mexico on the Eve of the American Invasion*. New York: Arno Press, 1976.

Weber, David J., ed., and Conchita Hassell Winn, trans., *Troubles in Texas, 1832: A Tejano Viewpoint from San Antonio with a Translation and Facsimile*. Dallas: DeGolyer Library, Southern Methodist University, 1983.

Weddle, Robert S., and Robert H. Thonhoff. *Drama and Conflict: The Texas Saga of 1776*. Austin, Tex.: Madrona Press, 1976.

Weeks, William F., comp. *Debates of the Texas Convention*. Houston: J. W. Cruger, 1846.

West, Elizabeth Howard, ed. and trans. "Diary of José Bernardo Gutiérrez de Lara, 1811–1812." *American Historical Review* 34: 1 (Oct., 1928): 55–77; 34: 2 (Jan., 1929): 281–294.

Wilkinson, J. B. *Laredo and the Rio Grande Frontier*. Austin, Tex.: Jenkins Publishing Co., 1975.

Williams, Amelia. "A Critical Study of the Siege of the Alamo and of the Personnel of Its Defenders." Pts. 1–5. *Southwestern Historical Quarterly* 36: 4 (Apr., 1933); 37: 4 (Apr., 1934).

Williams, Amelia W., and Eugene C. Barker. *The Writings of Sam Houston*. 8 vols. Austin: University of Texas Press, 1938–1943.

Wilson, Maurine T., and Jack Jackson. *Philip Nolan and Texas: Expeditions to the Unknown Land, 1791–1801*. Waco, Tex.: Texian Press, 1987.

Winkler, E. W., ed. *Secret Journals of the Senate, Republic of Texas, 1836–1845*. Austin, Tex.: Austin Printing Co., 1911.

Wortham, Louis J. *A History of Texas from Wilderness to Commonwealth*. 5 vols. Fort Worth, Tex.: Wortham-Molyneaux, 1924.

Wright, Robert E. "Local Church Emergence and Mission Decline: The Historiography of the Catholic Church in the Southwest during the Spanish and Mexican Periods." *U.S. Catholic Historian* 9 (Winter/Spring, 1990): 27–48.

Wunder, John R., and Rebecca J. Herring. "Law, History, Turner, and the Cordova Rebellion." *Red River Valley Historical Review* 5 (Summer, 1982): 51–67.

Yoakum, Henderson. *History of Texas from Its First Settlement in 1685 to Its Annexation to the United States in 1846*. 2 vols. 1855; reprint, Austin, Tex.: Steck Co., 1935.

Zavala, Adina de. *History and Legends of the Alamo and Other Missions in and around San Antonio*. San Antonio: Privately printed, 1917.

INDEX